# PRACTICAL OPERATING BUDGETING

# PRACTICAL OPERATING BUDGETING

**LAWRENCE M. MATTHEWS**
*Certified Management Consultant*

## McGraw-Hill Book Company

*New York · St. Louis · San Francisco · Auckland · Bogotá · Düsseldorf ·*
*Johannesburg · London · Madrid · Mexico · Montreal · New Delhi ·*
*Panama · Paris · São Paulo · Singapore · Sydney · Tokyo · Toronto*

Library of Congress Cataloging in Publication Data

Matthews, Lawrence M
  Practical operating budgeting.

  1. Budget in business.  I. Title.
HF5550.M4884      658.1′5        76-56116
ISBN 0-07-040950-1

1234567890KPKP786543210987

The editors for this book were W. Hodson Mogan and Joan
Zseleczky, the designer was Elliot Epstein, and the
production supervisor was Teresa Leaden. It was set in
Caledonia by University Graphics, Inc.

Printed and bound by The Kingsport Press.

*To Ann*

# CONTENTS

# PREFACE

This book is written for managers who are involved with an operating budget. Thus, it is intended for the department head, the foreman, and the chairman of the board. It is not aimed solely at budgeting people, though certainly it deals with many of the problems they face daily. Particular emphasis is placed on operating managers' understanding and use of their budgets. Budgets are too widely used and too potentially productive to allow operating managers, at whatever level, to be unsure about them. The operating budget is their tool for their operation. Therefore, they need to understand how their budget fits into the enterprise's plans, how it is best developed, and how it is best used.

In thirty years of management consulting, I have had the good fortune and opportunity to design and install operating budgets in a wide range of industries. I have also conducted over 150 seminars on budgeting in the past few years, both here and abroad. Speaking to and dealing with some 4200 people from 2800 different companies has been a revelation. I have been startled by the commonalty of problems, both psychological and technical, and by the lag that exists in the actual application of proven budgeting techniques.

These experiences have made me realize that we in management have far to go before we will be getting full use of this vital management tool. They also have led me to believe that there is a need for a book aimed at specifying common budgeting problems and offering constructive suggestions based on actual experiences. Therefore, I owe a great deal to the men and women who attended the seminars and who so helpfully discussed their problems and their experiences with what worked, as well as with what failed, in the area of budgets.

This book deals with *operating budgets* in manufacturing and service companies, whether profit or nonprofit. Budgeting is an integral part of many management concerns such as long-range planning, cash flow, capital investment, and project management. These are great and important subjects in themselves but are beyond the intended scope of this book. Instead, we are concerned here with the practical development and use of the operating budget by the various levels of management in an organization.

Emphasis is placed on those budgeting matters where I believe the greatest first need exists, where the mistakes are most often made. There are many subtleties, refinements, and sophistications discussed and written of the budgeting area. But I am convinced that, before becoming involved in all these, most organizations have a great many basic things to do first. For example, while there is an increasing preoccupation with long-range planning, there is an obvious neglect of day-to-day budgeting problems. The results are poor budgets and a minimal return from what should be a valuable management tool. The emphasis in this book is on today's practical needs. It is written for the thousands of managers and budgeting persons who are seeking not greater sophistication but practical approaches and suggestions for their day-to-day budgeting problems.

Not everything offered will be applicable to your situation. However, we all have so many budgeting problems in common that much of what is discussed should be of practical help. If this book stresses the mistakes being made, it is not for the sake of simply being negative. The more aware we are of the mistakes of others in the practice of budgeting, the likelier we are to become aware of our own budgeting deficiencies.

Budgeting, like all management, comes down to "the art of the possible." We operate in a cold, practical world. Often, we cannot do all the things or immediately take all the improving action we would like. Sometimes the people under us are not yet capable enough. Sometimes the people over us are not yet receptive enough. But it is the smart management that at least identifies existing limitations and works gradually to correct them. In budgeting we should be doing a better job each successive year. To do this we have to be introspective. We have to review periodically what we are doing. We must decide what most needs improvement and can be improved now. This book may help you by specifying what others so often do poorly and by discussing practical steps that others have taken to improve their budgets.

One final note should be made on style. Personal pronouns are used liberally and wherever I thought they would be effective or considered them necessary. Sentences have been kept reasonably short and polysyllabic words have been avoided wherever possible. Idioms are used.

The word *data* is used as a group term in the singular instead of the Latin plural noun it is. All this is for a reason. Management people have too little time available for reading. Therefore, what is offered them should be stated as familiarly, simply, and clearly as possible and that is the attempt made here. Hopefully then, not only will this book be valuable; it will also be easily read.

*Lawrence M. Matthews*

# 1

# BASIC UNDERSTANDINGS
# IN BUDGETING

At the start, it is wise to establish certain basic understandings about budgeting. Not to do so is to assume that we all have the same fundamental concepts. We must define what we mean by the *operating budget* and consider its use by various types of enterprises. We must fit the operating budget into its place in the overall management process and examine its limitations. Finally, we can identify some of the ways the budget is both misused and underused. Having done all this, we can go on to examine what we want from an operating budget and what kinds are available to us.

## BUDGETING VIS-A-VIS PLANNING

A well-managed enterprise usually has a long-range plan. The people responsible for the enterprise's continuation and success have deliberately taken the time and effort to project where they want the enterprise to be next year, the year after that, and through at least a half decade ahead. Being realistic, they do not expect to attain all goals; they know they will win some and lose others. But having done this planning, they are in a position to make better short-range plans and decisions. Some of these also will turn out poorly, but at least they will not conflict with the long-range plan. In contrast, some companies that fail to make long-range plans find their short-range plans conflicting, contradictory, and as a result, short-lived and wasteful of the available resources.

The essence of a long-range plan lies in a product program, a market forecast, a capital investment program, and projected balance sheet and profit and loss statements for the years included in the plan. It is a prediction of income and costs, and thus it can be called a budget.

Because the goals established in the long-range plan are the standards against which subsequent realities are compared, its function, in truth, is budgeting.

However, the management term "budget" is usually applied to a shorter period of time. The normal period is a year, thus the term "budget year" within which there are "budget months." Therefore, the term "budget" as used here is the most current year of the long-range plan.

Many an enterprise has a yearly budget, but not a quantified long-range plan. This is particularly true of smaller and medium-sized companies. In effect, they live from year to year. However, it is a good bet that in the years ahead, the use of long-range planning will spread to these smaller companies. As with most management techniques, the smarter managements in these smaller enterprises will use it first, and their success will force action upon less alert competitors.

## DEFINITION OF AN OPERATING BUDGET

The *operating budget* can be defined as a realistic statement of income and cost objectives for a year. It is a *plan* against which the ensuing actual performance is compared so as to achieve *control* by detecting and correcting off-standard performance. The broad term "budget," with its concept of a plan used to control, is applied to many areas, such as inventory, capital investment, and cash flow. But we are concerned here specifically with the kind of budget that is used by an operation as a whole for a specified period of one year. The other types of budgets are subsidiary to it.

An operating budget encompasses, for the one-year period, all the prime operating aspects of the function(s) for which the enterprise exists. For example, a manufacturing company exists to design, manufacture, and sell a product or products. Therefore, its operating budget for a year will include sales, operating costs, research and development costs, and by deduction, profit. Operating costs include not only manufacturing and engineering but also selling and administrative costs. Therefore, included are all the costs required for performing the company's function.

Similarly, since a service company is in the business of selling a service, its operating budget will include revenue and operating costs and, by deduction, profit. Again, operating costs include all the costs required to perform its function.

The operating budget of a nonprofit organization will include revenue and all operating costs. Frequently, this kind of budgeting situation is equated with budgeting in government because of its "nonprofit" aspects. I think this is a mistake. The principles that apply in budgeting in a profit-making enterprise should be equally applicable to a nonprofit enterprise.

If the operating budget is a statement of objectives, it can also be considered a forecast or an estimate. In budgeting we are predicting what will happen. We can expect to be reasonably close, and the better we do the job, the closer we will be. However, we cannot believe our budget will be absolutely correct, and this understanding has important implications in the area of budget maintenance and follow-up, particularly at the departmental level. Practical points on this aspect of budgeting will be discussed in Chapters 12 and 13.

## "BEAT THE BUDGET"

First we must come to a basic understanding in budgeting that is obvious, yet in practice, often unaccepted: it is that effective operating budgeting presumes that the managers being budgeted will try to do better than their budget standard. Thus, the marketing manager will try to sell more than was forecast. The production manager, or the administrative manager, will try to spend less than his or her budget allows.

When stated so bluntly, this sounds obvious and yet naive. Immediately there flashes into our minds the images of certain marketing managers we all know who are always wildly optimistic in their sales forecasts. So wild are they that we dare not plan our budgets or establish our master production schedules on their forecasts. Or we think of the departmental managers who not only spend over budget but also are always pressuring for higher allowances. Then some of us may know of companies in which the budgets are so poor or ineffective that everyone is more than happy if he or she simply lives within the budget. The various levels of management have no stimulus or incentive to improve the operation.

However, in my basic principle, I am talking about effective budgeting and good managers who help establish realistic budgets and then attempt to make realistic income and cost improvements during the budget year. A smart management that is doing an effective budgeting job expects and works to achieve a continually improving operating performance. Such a management seeks improved product designs or services, better operating methods, costs, and performances. These are continuing goals in the management process. Effective budgets are just one of the devices used to plan for these goals and to measure how well they are being achieved.

This principle of doing better than standard applies at the individual level. Think of the foremen and department heads you know and work with. Which ones do you have the most respect for? Are they not the ones who have ideas for improving their operation or who are receptive to others' ideas on the subject? Are they not the ones who show sufficient interest and energy to be curious and open-minded, so as to see different and better ways to do things? Aren't they the ones who are upwardly mobile? You instinctively classify your fellow managers into "time-servers" and managers.

And of course, it isn't all this black and white. There are managers at many levels who are doing an adequate job. The problem is to encourage them toward a better performance. Budgets that are properly developed and installed are one means to this end.

## BUDGETING LIMITATIONS IN CERTAIN COST AREAS

Another important point to make is that budgeting should be considered as only the beginning of adequate control in certain areas of large cost—particularly direct labor and raw material. In these areas, most enterprises need additional cost controls, beyond what is available through the operating budget alone.

The operating budget is usually expressed in monthly terms. A monthly *performance-to-budget report* shows actual expenditures against budget allowances by cost account. But in certain large cost areas such as direct labor and raw material we need closer control than can ever be provided by a monthly report. In the case of direct labor, for example, we want to know what was spent against standard by day, and even by job in many cases. The same is true with raw material and its scrap cost. For raw material and scrap cost, in some cases, we want to know that cost for each job, or at least for a shorter time interval than a month.

In some companies, however, the operating budget is the only control tool that exists over these two important costs. In these cases the budget has to do. Certainly, it is better than no control at all. But management should recognize that the budget is a gross measurement in terms of time. The degree of control is not as good as it should and could be via other means such as labor standards and material usage and scrap control reports.

This observation does not diminish budgeting's importance as a cost control tool. The operating budget is, today, the best and most practical tool that we have available to achieve control over many other areas of cost. These areas add up to a lot of money. Typical, but by no means all-inclusive, of the expense areas that are most practically controlled by budgets are power, operating supplies, indirect labor, and perishable tooling. These are only a few items that first come to mind. You can probably think of others in your own situation. We also have other means to control such costs, particularly if individually they amount to a great deal of money. But, for most of us, the most practical and economical way to control them is by effective budgets.

## BUDGETING IN A SERVICE COMPANY

A manufacturing company changes the form of the raw material it uses. It adds value to that material in the course of making its products. A service company provides a needed service. That is its prime function. Any value a service company adds to the material it uses is incidental. (Nonprofit enterprises are usually service organizations. However, at this point we are considering profit-making service companies such as transportation companies, steel service centers, restaurant chains, retail stores, laundries, wholesaling houses, jobbers, mail order houses, etc.)

The same budgeting principles and understandings that apply to the manufacturing company apply to the service company. However, there are certain difficulties that in practice apply to budgeting in a service company. They are:

1. Top managements and owners in many service enterprises commonly do not understand or appreciate the potentials of effective budgeting. All too frequently their attitude is that "our business is different." As a result they utilize, at best, a very rudimentary form of fixed budget. A surprisingly large percentage do not avail themselves of the cost control benefits of flexible operating budgets.

2. The state of the art of operating budgeting is not nearly as advanced in most service industries as it is in manufacturing. Service company management cannot avail itself of an established body of practice such as there is in manufacturing. As a result, there often has to be a lot more originality and development work in the application of budgeting in a service company.

3. Many service industries have unique characteristics that increase the "intangibles" involved. As a result, some of their operating conditions can be difficult to quantify. For example, some have to budget for creative work, or for difficult-to-predict manpower deployment, or for the estimated income expected from many costly sales presentations. Or activity measures may be a problem to both identify and quantify. This does not mean that a full application of operating budgets is not possible; it just becomes more difficult.

4. Because of all the above, budgets can be more expensive to develop and apply in a service company or industry.

5. Finally, in certain service industries, management has limited opportunity to adjust expenses to falling revenue. Where practicable cost flexibility is limited, management must identify the areas of cost flexibility they do have and apply their wit and ingenuity accordingly. (In contrast, other service industries have the opportunity to adjust their costs as income drops, seasonally or cyclically, to the same degree as do most manufacturing industries.)

The most important difficulty, of course, is the first one. Effective budgeting is impossible without top management's appreciation of what the tool can do for the enterprise and without their initiative and support behind the effort. The second and third difficulties do not present insurmountable problems. They are problems of technique that, with a little ingenuity, can usually be overcome.

Concerning the fourth difficulty, the question of whether budgets or better budgeting would produce a desired return on the money spent for budgeting has to be answered individually by each management for the particular situation. The most pertinent observation that can be made is that the experience of most practitioners has been that properly done, budgets usually save many times their cost of installation or improvement. It is difficult to conclude that this is not true for those service companies that have either no budgets or poor ones.

## BUDGETING IN A NONPROFIT ORGANIZATION

Earlier, the point was made that the principles of effective budgeting apply to nonprofit as well as to profit-making organizations. (Nonprofit organizations include colleges and universities, hospitals, religious organizations, historical centers, and museums, to name a few.) It was also observed that often budgeting in a nonprofit organization is equated with government budgeting, and that this is wrong. These points should be supported in greater detail.

The management of every one of these nonprofit organizations could use more money. They all have functions or services they would like to expand or new programs they would like to initiate. They could do these things with increased income or reduced expenses. But they have limited sources of revenue—fees, grants, appropriations, etc. Because of this constraint, it is essential that their managements utilize monetary resources as effectively as possible. In other words, they must maximize their income and minimize their expenses. This is the basic understanding of effective budgeting, namely, doing better than budget in terms of both revenue and expenses.

A few specific ideas come readily to mind. If you like museums and have been to a variety of them, you have seen a great range in the reproductions that are made available for public purchase. A few have excellent reproductions of the paintings, prints, and *objets d'art* they have in their collection. Many of them, however, have too little to offer and what they do have is poorly displayed. Did you ever see a "buy-of-the-month" highlighted in a museum shop? I suggest that most museums would be wise to solicit the volunteer services of a few local successful retailers. The effort could still be tasteful and dignified, but the revenues would be increased. Management would "beat" their revenue budget.

A very few universities and colleges have highly successful management seminar programs, conducted by their extension schools and continuing education departments. It has taken these schools some years to develop the programs and mailing lists and to build an image, but now when local businesses receive brochures, they read them, and if interested in the subject, the businesses send their people. From past experience they know the seminars will be worthwhile. As a result, the school is providing a service to the local business community, and the school earns additional revenue. That money provides funds for other things that university management would like to do. (In contrast, many universities and colleges have a very minor effort in this area and lose money on what they do.)

Another example is one metropolitan hospital which, because of its location, has a transient nursing staff equalling 40 percent of its total nursing expense. In other words, management can increase or reduce the nursing staff within that 40 percent by hiring or not hiring the transients as activity rises or falls. (Hospital activity does vary over the course of the year. For example, December is a relatively low-activity month. Everyone who can stays out of the hospital during that time.) Yet every month this hospital has the same nursing expense. Management is not taking advantage of its ability to adjust its costs to variations in activity. Thus, it is not minimizing its expenses. In contrast, in some hospitals flexible budgeting is standard operating procedure.

It all comes down to a matter of understanding, of attitude, or of management orientation. The management of a nonprofit enterprise should have the same attitude toward using an effective operating budget, including its flexible aspects, that the management of a profit-making enterprise should have.


## BUDGETS AND COMPANY SIZE

Frequently, you hear managers make such statements as "We have no budget," or "We're too small for budgets," or "Budgets are OK for big companies, but not for us." Sometimes, when you dig a little deeper, you find that they really are using a rudimentary form of fixed budget. Sometimes, on the other hand, you find that they are absolutely correct: they have no budget in any form.

This kind of management skepticism is nonsense. For example, at the most basic level imaginable, if you only run a "mom-and-pop" hardware store, you should, at the minimum, sit yourself down one Sunday afternoon a year with a pad and pencil and project what volume you expect to do in the coming year, what minimum income you need to keep body and soul together, and, by deduction, within what limits you have to hold your expenses. If you don't do this, you will not know enough to try to make things happen. Things will just happen to you, perhaps some of them not so pleasant.

It is not likely, I admit, that most small retailers do this. They order and sell, they take out living expenses, they pay their bills when they have to, and if at the end of the year they have more money in the bank than they did at the start of the year, they have had a "good year." However, for good management, they should also do the minimal, primitive budgeting described above.

If this is what a hardware store owner should do, then certainly it should also be done by the owner of a manufacturing or service enterprise with, say, $500,000 of yearly sales volume. No company, manufacturing or service, is too small to do some kind of budgeting.

Finally, it is certainly foggy thinking on the part of an owner or manager of a small business to say, "We're too small for budgets," when he or she is actually doing a rudimentary form of fixed budgeting. When this occurs, the owner does not understand this management tool or know how to use it. However, in such a case there is a real possibility that a little more attention and work might obtain a much greater yield from the underdeveloped budget the business already has.

To sum it all up, the management of *any* enterprise should recognize that, no matter how small they are, they should have an operating budget in some form.

## BUDGETING IN GOVERNMENT

It must be very difficult, I have always thought, to be a manager in government. The greatest difficulty lies in the basic difference in management orientation between profit-making operations and government operations at the federal, state, or local level. In a profit-making enterprise, the primary orientation has to be to spend less than the revenues received. And this thinking filters down through all levels of management. The need can be recognized and enforced. It had better be, to a sufficient degree, or there will be no profit. In that case, there eventually will be a new management—or no business.

In contrast, in government management, the basic orientation has historically been to perform a function as best as can be done within the budget limits imposed. In real-life practice in government, there is not the attitude, the "thrust," to do better than budget, such as necessarily exists in profit-making enterprises. In fact, many a government manager has learned by bitter experience that he or she had better commit all allocated funds by the end of the budget year or the next year's budget may be cut.

As the result of all these difficulties, a lot of good people are not attracted to government in the first place, or if they enter it, they can become frustrated and leave. In either case, we all lose—the government that needs good management, as does any enterprise, and the taxpayers whose funds are used less effectively.

All this is said not to be negative, but to spell out the differences that exist in practice between budgeting in government and budgeting in private industry. Some of the basic budget principles and understandings that we in private industry accept as truisms are not available to managers in government. This makes operating budgeting and thus management in government a great deal more difficult. However, there are some hopeful signs developing. For example, the United States Government Printing Office has revenue increments as well as cost increments in its operation. They now throw a monthly profit and loss statement and are proud to be operating at a profit. Under these conditions government management can apply the same budgeting principles that we use in private industry.

There is also increasing interest and acceptance of the concept of program budgeting at the state level of government. Under program budgeting, you identify costs in terms of the services provided and you quantify those services. Doing this you can relate cost of government programs to the benefits expected from them. Then you can begin to think in terms of performance standards. Admittedly, it is impossible in some governmental areas to quantify benefits, or you can do this only partially, namely, in a count of numbers of incidents but not in terms of quality. However, there are many areas of governmental operations where activity and results can be measured. When they are so measured and effectively budgeted, the results are more likely to be better planning of and control over the use of the money spent, and this is better management.

However, this is not a book on government budgeting. Therefore, only some of the practical points discussed are applicable to government situations. Others may be usable in theory but not in practice.

## CATEGORIES OF COMPANIES AND BUDGETS

Companies and budgets can be considered as falling into three categories:

1. Companies with no budgets. These are usually small companies or those at the lower end of the "medium-size" company grouping. Many of them are quite profitable and successful. But no matter how profitable they are, these companies still have excellent potential for cost improvement. This is true because without budgets they have not yet established standards in many areas of cost within their organization. And without standards, they do not have control.

Cost standards are an absolute prerequisite for cost control. As human beings, we inevitably need standards to achieve control—in business or private life. *Control* means to exercise a directing or restraining influence and to do this we need a gauge or bench mark of what should be, against which we can compare what actually happened. It is that comparison that tells us whether corrective action is, or is not, needed. Consider how you evaluate a newly purchased car. One of the first things you do is calculate how many miles per gallon you are getting with the new car. Then you almost instinctively compare that with the mileage per gallon you had on your previous car. In other words, you are using the old car as the standard for the new one.

Anything we do as human beings and over which we want to achieve at least some measure of control, including business management, demands a standard, no matter how vague or ill-defined. The company without budgets has not established standards over many of its costs. Without standards, it has no control, and the odds are superb that its costs are greater than necessary, despite its possibly excellent profits. The conclusion, therefore, for the managements of this minority of companies, which have no budgets, is that they should have budgets.

Fortunately, such companies are a very small minority of the total business world. That estimate is based upon asking seminar attendees, "How many of you have no budgets?" Overall, fewer than 5 percent will say they have none in their company. Therefore, we are talking about a management technique that has found widespread acceptance at this time. (This was not true in the nineteen-forties.) Fortunately, budgeting is a management technique that does not still suffer from the "applications lag" as do so many of the techniques we read about in the professional journals. Most of our managements have accepted budgets as a tool that they need and use.

2. Companies with well-maintained, effective budgets. These budgets have had continual top management attention and support, and they become more effective with each successive year.

This situation might be called "A-OK." Unfortunately, companies in this category are also in the minority. Or at least that is my considered judgment. I suggest that instead, the great majority of companies fall into the third and last category.

3. Companies with ineffective budgets. Their budgets are not as dynamic and effective a tool as they could and should be. In fact, it might truthfully be said that the budgets could well be revitalized. This is the category that contains, I believe, the great majority of companies.

Over the years, I have come to identify this category of company with what might be called the "seven signs of budget weakness." Before listing these symptoms, I will make two preliminary points: (a) In my experience, I've never seen one of these signs alone. There are always two or more on site at the same time. (b) These signs are the ones that stand out in my mind. You might well be able to add others.

## "SEVEN SIGNS OF BUDGET WEAKNESS"

1. *Foremen and superintendents who ignore their budgets*

This is the situation where the department heads or foremen are rarely, if ever, called in by their boss for a review of their budget performance, good or bad. There can be many reasons why they are not called in. For example, both the boss and the department head may be convinced that the budget cost standards are so poor that they are unusable. In any case, you find the individual foreman, as well as the boss, paying little or no attention to the budget.

*A case in point.* I undertook a consulting assignment for a multiplant electronics company. It was a production planning and control job, and whenever you do work in this area you inevitably spend a lot of time on the production floors and with the foremen. Often I would be reviewing some production problem with a foreman who, always pressed for time, would sit opening some intracompany mail. Also, very often I'd see the foreman pull out a colored computer printout sheet, glance at it, then drop it into the bottom right-hand drawer of the desk.

This happened so often that on one occasion I asked, "What is that sheet?" The reply was "Oh, that's our weekly budget sheet." Consider that—budget reports both computerized and issued weekly! Obviously a lot of money was being spent. I went on and asked, "Doesn't anyone review it with you, praise you for good variances, question bad variances?" The reply was, "Naw, nobody pays attention to that sheet."

This was a harsh lesson in futility. A lot of work was being done and a lot of money was being spent, but the resulting product was unused. When I pointed this out to top management, I was asked to identify the causes. As you would expect, the budget standards turned out in many cases to be quite unrealistic: some too high, others too low. The operating people realized this, and they even pointed it out—for a while. When no one did anything to correct the budget standards, the managers simply began to ignore their budgets. Fortunately, a budget correction and revitalization program was started.

2. *Nonparticipation of all management levels in the budget development*

You might sum up this next situation in the phrase "budgeting by fiat." Down from the rarified heights of mahogany row wherein dwell top management comes the budget. The person at the first line of management, the foreman or department head, has never seen it before. He (or she) has had no part in its development and very little, or even nothing, to say about the goals it is setting. And, of course, neither has his boss, the superintendent, nor perhaps has *his* boss, the production manager or plant manager.

Usually such budgets contain serious errors. They not only have been installed in a psychologically poor way, but are very frequently technically wrong. They contain errors and absurdities which have never been communicated back to the people topside who established the budgets.

When budgets have been installed by fiat, there is usually a great deal of verbal and memorandum pressure early in the game, but soon it all dies down. Perhaps a few heads might roll, but usually very few. After all, you can't fire everyone. As the variances develop, they are allowed for by Accounting, for profit-planning and product-costing needs, and the company ends up with budgets that are weak, and thus not nearly as effective as they should be.

3. *Continued large variances, plus or minus, that remain uncorrected*

*Variance* is the difference between the budget allowance and the actual expenditure. A *favorable* cost variance, also called a *black* or *plus* variance, is generated when the budget allowance exceeds the actual money spent. An *unfavorable* cost variance, also called a *red* or *minus* variance, is generated when the actual money spent exceeds the budget allowance. With items of income or activity, these meanings are reversed. For example, if a budgeted activity is 100,000 units and actual activity is 110,000 units, you have a favorable variance of 10,000 activity units. If actual activity is only 90,000 units, you have a 10,000-unit unfavorable variance. (All companies calculate variances this way, although nomenclature does vary. I have had both a lady in Buffalo, New York, and a man in California tell me that historically their companies call favorable cost variances "red" variances.)

Under this third symptom of weakness, when you study a series of the periodic budget reports being issued, you find many large variances, favorable or unfavorable, showing up month after month. This is an obvious sign of poor budgeting. It indicates one or more of the following conditions: a. unrealistic or poor budget standards, b. blatantly poor budget maintenance, c. poor management follow-up on performance to budget, or d. bad management policy, such as "the budget shall remain as initially established for the budget year."

4. *Budget people who do not get out into the operation*

This may at first seem like a rather odd sign of budget weakness, but I have come to find it extremely indicative. When you encounter a situation where the personnel involved in the budgeting effort either do not have the time or do not have the interest to get out into the operation enough, you invariably find weak budgets. The causes for such inaction by the budgeting people may be either understaffing or, worse, inertia.

Operating budgeting deals with operating matters, and operating matters are dynamic. The only way to keep current with them is to get out into the operation often. If it is a manufacturing plant, the budget people have to get out onto the plant floors. If it is a bank, they have to get out onto the bank floor and out to the branches. How often they have to get out will depend on the dynamics of the situation, but they have to keep current. If they do not, absurdities will begin to creep into the budgets. And they will not be continuing to learn more about the enterprise they are helping to budget.

The maxim that should be seared into every budget person's consciousness is: "You can't set budgets from a desk alone!"

*A case in point.* It took four months to install flexible budgets in a glass container plant. During that time, one of the client's cost accountants and I worked together and developed and installed the budgets. Both his boss, who was the controller, and I trained him in budgeting, and all three of us agreed on a program for future action. The program could not be specified precisely, but we all agreed on the nature of the refinements that would be desirable in the years to come. It was a successful start, and the president was pleased with what had been accomplished and the gains that were made.

I came back some eight years later on a different matter, namely, the streamlining of standard cost application to new container items. Naturally, the first person I looked up was the budget man with whom I had worked so closely. "How is it going?" I asked. "Fine" he replied. "When were you out in the plant last?" I continued. "Gee, I've been so busy, it's been three months" was his answer. Instinctively I knew that those budgets might not be as good as they needed to be. In fact, they were not. They had to be revitalized.

Looking back, I think we were all at fault: the budget man, the controller, the president, and I. They should not have allowed the budgets to deteriorate, and I should have sold them on the idea of periodic consulting follow-up. The latter idea historically has never been advanced effectively enough by consultants. Happily in this case, I participated in the budget revitalization program.

5. *Foremen who don't know how their allowances were determined nor what makes up the charges to their budget*

When you find foremen or department heads who do not really know how the allowances on their budget were determined, or what kinds of expense are charged to individual budgeted cost items, you can safely suspect that the budget is not the vital management tool it should be. They simply don't understand the data they are supposed to be using.

This situation can be a result of several things:

a. Inadequate initial training

b. Failure to enforce the training with a follow-up program

c. Lack of sufficient management support or use of the budget

d. Too little contact between the budgeting function and operating people

e. Failure to have foremen participate sufficiently in their budget's development

Notice that I have not included in the above listing "failure by department heads to evince active interest." Perhaps in theory, management, above the department-head level, should expect this kind of active inquiry. In practice, however, I cannot agree. Management at the department or cost-center level, namely, foremen or department heads, have so many pressures on them, so many things to handle, and often so little training that I think higher management has to take over the burden of correcting any failure in this area.

You might test your own enterprise for this symptom. Next time you are with one of your department heads, take his or her budget report, and for three or four of the items ask: "How was that budget allowance determined? What items of cost are charged to that account?" A department head who can't give you intelligible answers to those budgeting questions doesn't understand his or her budget. You, in turn, have to honestly ask yourself, "Has this person had the training needed from higher levels of management and from the budgeting function?"

6. *No improvement action because of the budget*

A great many constructive things may be going on in a company, namely, new techniques being started in a number of operating areas, new planning, or control procedures initiated. But the key question, from a budgeting standpoint, has to be, "Which were started because of what the budgeting process revealed?"

Budgets result in periodic reports. And the acid test of any report is what happens because of it. If neither the budget-development steps nor the performance-to-budget reports cause changes, then there are only two possibilities—either you have the perfect enterprise, which you and I will never live to see, or the budgets are not resulting in the needed improvement action.

The solutions to this situation can be varied and will depend basically on top management's vitality and use of the budgets. But any budget person involved in such a symptomatic situation should be concerned, because the question must inevitably arise: "What are we really getting out of this effort and expense?"

7. *No continuing measure of budget results*

Good budgeting costs money. The larger and the more complex the organization, the greater the cost. Budgets demand an investment to design and install, and a continuing investment to maintain properly. We do not capitalize budgeting costs, but in fact, we should evaluate them in the same manner that we evaluate a capital investment.

When a well-managed company buys a new machine for the production floor, it makes a post-audit to check that the results expected of that machine are actually being realized. The same logic should be applied to the investment made in budgets. If this is not done, you may end up with too low or no return on the investment being made in the budgeting effort.

Despite all the modern techniques such as operations research, and mathematical modeling to quantify decision making, management continues to consist largely of the application of experienced judgment to large and important areas of operations. Therefore, where we can measure, where we can quantify, we should. We often can in budgeting, and thus we should. It can be done relatively simply at the time of a new installation or with a budget revitalization program, as we will see later.

Where a management does not measure the results of its budgets, you have to question the interest and the faith they have in this widely used management tool.

Lord Kelvin summed it all up very well: "When you can measure what you are speaking about, and express it in numbers, you know something about it; but when you cannot measure it, when you cannot express it in numbers, your knowledge is of a meagre and unsatisfactory kind."

As said earlier, these signs of budget weakness are the ones that I have identified through my experience in client companies. You may or may not consider them common. However, after listing them, and speaking about them at budget seminars, I ask each group, "Are any of these familiar to you? Do you have any of them? If so, will you please raise your hand?" At every session without exception, a majority of attendees raise their hands! I can only conclude that my own experience has been representative. The majority of companies have budgets that could well be improved and revitalized.

This discussion has been critical and negative, but for a purpose. We management people are so busy and often so harried that when some-thing is done that goes well, we automatically go on to the next thing. We haven't the time to be introspective, to analyze why it worked so well. We may copy it, repeat it, but we usually don't study *why* it worked. We don't have the time to learn from what goes right. But when we make a mistake, we are forced to analyze and study the situation in order to correct it. As a result, we tend to learn more from our mistakes.

The initial task for you, or any manager, is to determine if you have a problem in budgeting. And that is the purpose of listing, early on, the seven signs of budget weakness. This listing may help you be intro-spective about your own budgets, to give them a mental audit. In your case perhaps, while you have some of these symptoms, they may not be serious enough to warrant corrective action. On the other hand, they may be, now or in the foreseeable future. Identifying weaknesses and taking corrective action where possible can result in more effective budgets in your company.

## BUDGETING PSYCHOLOGY AND STANS' LAW

When new budgets are installed or weak budgets revitalized properly, the savings that result are always much greater than the cost of doing the budgeting. That at least has been my experience and the experience of others I meet at budget seminars. When I question those who tell me they have lived through a budget installation or revitalization program, the great majority of them say that the results far outweighed the costs. Only a very small minority say the effort wasn't productive or at best, wasn't more than self-supporting. A few say that in their company it is still too soon to tell. A few, however, go on to say that while budgets saved a lot of money, to quote one respondent, "Boy! Did we have morale problems!"

The fact that budgets often cause significant morale problems is an experience acknowledged by many operating and budgeting managers. In fact, in some cases, the morale problems become so critical that the budgets just do not work. They cause so many difficulties and end up requiring so much management time and effort that their cost out-weighs any benefits they might achieve.

This problem of management morale, particularly at the department-head or foreman level, reflects Stans' Law of Budgeting, which states: "Effective budgeting is the uniform distribution of dissatisfaction." This is an acute, if partial, observation because, let's face it, a budget is a constraint, and all of us would much rather have carte blanche and blank checks. However, you and I understand the need for budgets. We have the training and experience to know that the constraint of budgets imposed on us by ourselves or by higher levels of management is necessary. We know that the organization needs budgets if it is to plan and control its operation.

However, consider a not untypical foreman in, say, a manufacturing plant. He (or she) may be at best a high school graduate. (The number of foremen with college degrees may be increasing, but it is as yet a tiny fraction of the whole.) However, he certainly knows the process and operations involved in the department. He has shown interest, ability, and some signs of leadership. He may have been a group leader and done well at the job. But his business management training has been minimal, or more likely nonexistent. Then, suddenly he is made a foreman. He is now part of management, the first line of management. Can we honestly expect him to consider his budget as anything but a constraint? Can we honestly expect him to understand and accept the need for budgets, and to see how they combine to form the financial operating plan for the company? That is asking too much! He needs training and education not only at the start, but continuingly.

In fact, in too many cases department heads assume that the budget is a bludgeon that will be used against them. This assumption may be the result of past personal experiences with budgets. The interpretations of these experiences may be wrong, but the feeling is still there. When such an attitude exists, it is a problem for management. Somehow the department heads must be shown, by exposition and by training, that while the budget is a constraint, it is necessary to the management process. Also they must be persuaded that as they learn more about the practical facts of management, they will, themselves, derive benefits from budgeting, namely, participation and recognition.

At any rate, too many budgets have been installed or revitalized *without* great morale problems to conclude blandly that such problems must be expected and accepted. In fact, morale problems can be minimal. And when you examine those cases where budgets have been implemented with few morale problems, I suggest that two characteristics will stand out:

1. Management people at the lower levels, particularly at the first line, were thoroughly indoctrinated as to the company's need for budgets. Such indoctrination included a complete exposition of how their departmental budgets fit into the entire program, how their results affected the whole picture, and how improvements which they could

achieve would reflect not only on them but on the enterprise as a whole. Also, such exposure and education was supplemented by effective follow-up sessions that were an ongoing feature of the budget program.

2. Departmental managers were directly involved in the development of their own budgets. This may have required persuasion, even cajoling on the part of the budgeting people, and their not always welcomed intrusion into the overcrowded hours of the department heads, but when the project was all done, those department heads had to admit to themselves that they were "part of the act." They had had every opportunity to voice their judgments, advance their ideas, and ask for the allowances they thought they needed. They may have received less or more than they asked for, but in either case, they were given fair and intelligent reasons for the differences. Where they had no particular ideas concerning their budget allowances, there was a thorough explanation made to them on the budget that was to be applied, and how the allowances were determined. Finally, now that the budgets have been installed, the managers continue to have an open line of communication through which they can ask questions that arise and advance ideas that they develop. In fact, the budgeting people come to them and solicit questions and ideas.

Obviously, where these two characteristics are found, the senior management and the budgeting people involved are psychologically acute. They accept and understand the doubts, fears, and lack of knowledge of their fellow managers. The burden is particularly heavy on the budgeting people. They have to be both students of human nature and "practical psychologists." They normally not only have the job of education and training to worry about, but they also bear the brunt of any active opposition and the confrontations that sometimes arise. The abler the budget people, the fewer these crises. When the budget personnel are very good, confrontations do not arise. Disputes are avoided entirely, not by neglect but by positive action that foresees and overcomes the conditions leading up to future conflict. Such positive action requires awareness and sensitivity.

One final point may be helpful on this matter. It concerns a rationale that I have very frequently used to show department heads how their budget can be helpful to them. By means of clear and complete exposition in nontechnical terms, a department head can be persuaded that management needs budgets. He (or she) can understand the overall plan, and his (or her) part in that plan. However, being human, he not infrequently asks himself, "What's in it for me?" If you suspect he has that question, or even if you do not suspect it, you should tell him how the budget will enable his boss to be more objective in his evaluation of the department heads under his direction. Many a foreman or department head has the active suspicion that his boss doesn't really understand and appreciate how good a job he is doing. Some of them are emotionally convinced that the boss plays favorites. (Unfortunately, they are not always wrong.) However, it is true that the budgets, if properly done, will give a quantified objective picture of performance. If a department head does a good and ever-improving job of running his department, it will show up on his budget reports. The boss is, therefore, more likely to recognize the good performance.

Interestingly enough, the boss himself often has the correlative problem. One chairman I worked for used to say that his most difficult job was determining year-end bonuses. His decision making was rife with subjective judgments and he never felt the least bit sure that he was being fair. For him, performance to budget became one of the few quantifiable measures available. It still didn't make the decision making automatic, but it helped him to be a little bit more objective.

# FIXED VERSUS
# FLEXIBLE BUDGETS

What should a budget do for us? What kinds of budgets are available to us? Which kinds of budgets do the things we need done?

In seeking practical answers to these important questions you should be warned that the inquiry follows a tight chain of logic. In this chain if you accept one conclusion, you are perforce trapped into accepting the next. So read and think with a critical mind and don't accept any statement or conclusion unless it really makes sense to you.

## WHAT SHOULD A BUDGET DO FOR US?

There is no management unanimity on the question: What should a budget do for us? An article in *Business Week*[1] offered evidence of this lack of agreement. Commenting on the annual meeting of the then-called Budget Executives Institute, the reporter developed "a disquieting feeling that few of those assembled ever would agree on just what a budget is." In my consulting work and from my discussions with so many people in management, there is little evidence to believe that there has been any substantial change in the situation. In fact, you will frequently find, as did the reporter at this professional meeting, that there are two different schools of thought as to what a budget should do for an enterprise.

The first group looks at budgeting as solely a *profit-planning* mechanism. In other words, under their budgeting procedure they forecast expected sales revenue, project expected operating costs, and then, by deduction, calculate planned pretax profit. They also break these three factors down into monthly increments. Then as the year unfolds, they

[1]"Business Budgets—To Each His Own," *Business Week,* May 30, 1964, pp. 76–78.

compare year-to-date forecast sales to year-to-date actual sales, year-to-date budgeted costs to year-to-date actual costs, and by deduction, year-to-date planned pretax profit to year-to-date actual pretax profit. And that is it, *period.*

The second group looks at budgeting as solely a technique of *operating cost control.* In fact, some such companies even include the phrase *cost control* in the formal name of their budgeting effort. (For example, one man told me that in his company the budgeting effort is called "The Cost Control Department.") Under this approach, management establishes budget allowances for each cost account at the cost center or department level. Then by comparing actual costs against budget allowances, they seek to achieve control over those operating costs. And again, that is it, *period.*

I suggest that each of these views is 50 percent of the picture. It seems to me that a budget, properly used, should be *both* a mechanism for profit planning and a technique of operating cost control. If a company goes to all the work of laying down a profit plan by forecasting sales income and expected operating costs, they have only half the use of the tool if they do not use these budget cost allowances for controlling costs. In fact, they usually have built up their estimates of expected total operating costs by a cost center or department accumulation. Thus, they already have the breakdown.

In like manner, consider the company that has established budgeted cost allowances at the department level for cost control purposes. They also have only half the use of the tool if they do not combine the total projected operating costs, compare them with a forecast of sales income, and lay down a profit plan.

The conclusion is that a company's budget should provide two concurrent uses: a mechanism for profit planning, and a technique for controlling operating costs. Do you agree? This all seems rather obvious as stated. But think carefully and critically before you agree. Because if you do agree that a budget should provide *both* uses, then you are trapped into accepting a later conclusion, as we shall see in the following discussion of fixed and flexible budgets.

## FIXED BUDGETING

If we agree that a budget should serve both our profit-planning and cost control needs, let us next consider what kinds of budgets are available for us to use. To do this, let us develop a very simple "model" of the budgeting process as it so often occurs.

Assume that another budget and fiscal year starts January 1, 19__.

Along about the previous August, perhaps earlier or later, the word comes down to prepare the next year's budget. At the department level perhaps, certainly at the plant level, an operating cost budget is prepared, ideally with budgeting staff assistance. If it is a big enough enterprise, this budget goes up to Division, and from Division it goes to Corporate. At any one of these operating levels, there may be some backtracking, under which the budget is returned to "sharpen the pencil" and to set the cost standards tighter or the sales goals higher, but hopefully by 1/1/19__, a budget will have been laid down, by month, for the coming year.

Remember your point in time. It is 1/1/19__ and an operating budget has been established for each month of the coming year. Consider now just one of those months, for just one department, and we will detail in very simple terms a part of that department's budget.

Assume that for March we have forecast an activity of 100,000 units. This is a measure of physical operating activity. In a service enterprise, it equates very closely to income. In manufacturing, the measure has a high correlation to sales, assuming no inventory change. In a manufacturing department such a measure will be in terms of standard hours produced, tons, machine-hours, dozens, or whatever measure is applicable and meaningful. In a branch bank it might be customer transactions. In a hospital it might be patient-days. In any case, it is a measurement of the level of operating activity. Now to keep the model simple, let us consider only two well-known items of cost for which we have established budget allowances, namely, direct labor and operating supplies. The latter item is the cost of the miscellaneous supplies needed in running the operation. In a machine shop, for example, it would include such items as wiping rags, gloves, floor-sweeping compound, cooling fluids, and perhaps perishable tooling. At the forecast activity of 100,000 units, we have budgeted $40,000 for direct labor and $2000 for operating supplies.

Thus, our budget for March, as of 1/1/19__, is shown in Table 2–1.

**Table 2–1**

|                     | March, 19__ Budget |
| ------------------- | ------------------ |
| Activity            | 100,000            |
| Expenses            |                    |
| Direct labor        | $40,000            |
| Operating supplies  | $ 2,000            |

Now there are very few things certain in management life, but probably one certainty is that March will not turn out to have an activity of 100,000. It would be most unusual, and sheer chance, if March happened to be precisely a 100,000 month, as originally forecast. We may try with our predictions to be within ±5 percent for the total year, but as practical people, we expect variations from budgeted activity in each actual month. Therefore, let us model this situation under two conditions: first, one of higher-than-budgeted activity, and then, one of lower-than-budgeted activity.

We now go forward in time. It is 4/10/19__, the data for March has all been collected, and we can see what actually happened. Assume that March enjoyed an actual activity of 120,000 and that $42,000 was spent for direct labor and $2100 for operating supplies. Given these facts we can draw up a monthly *performance-to-budget* report for March, complete with variances, as shown in Table 2–2.

Activity is the opposite of cost. It relates to the "income" type of account. Therefore, when the actual amount exceeds the budget, the activity variance is favorable. However, for both cost items in the model, the actual money spent exceeded the budget allowance. Therefore, both cost items have an unfavorable or minus variance, and this is shown by putting the variances in parentheses.

Let us now test this against the two things we said we want from our budget. First, consider profit planning. By 4/10/19__ we should have the year-to-date income figures, and we should be able to compare year-to-date forecast income with actual income. We can compare year-to-date budgeted costs with actual costs, and by deduction, calculate and then compare year-to-date planned profit and actual profit. Splendid!

But look at the nonsense we have for operating cost control for this specific month. In the model developed above, we have an operating manager who handled a 20 percent greater-than-budgeted activity and held these two well-known costs to only a 5 percent increase. Yet this

**Table 2–2**

|  | March, 19__ | | |
|  | Budget | Actual | Variance |
|---|---|---|---|
| Activity | 100,000 | 120,000 | 20,000 |
| Expenses |  |  |  |
|    Direct labor | $40,000 | $42,000 | $(2,000) |
|    Operating supplies | $ 2,000 | $ 2,100 | $ (100) |

procedure shows an unfavorable variance. If the manager had spent only one-half of 1 percent over budget, he or she would still be assigned an unfavorable variance. In management and budgeting, there is very little misunderstanding about the term *unfavorable variance.* It has a definite connotation of censure. Thus, this manager is being censured when praise might be more indicated.

Next, let us change the conditions to a lower-than-budgeted activity. Assume that March turned out to be a month with an activity of only 80,000, and that $38,000 was actually spent for direct labor and $1900 for operating supplies. Now the report would look like this:

**Table 2–3**

|  | March, 19__ | | |
|  | Budget | Actual | Variance |
|---|---|---|---|
| Activity | 100,000 | 80,000 | (20,000) |
| Expenses |  |  |  |
|    Direct labor | $40,000 | $38,000 | $2,000 |
|    Operating supplies | $ 2,000 | $ 1,900 | $ 100 |

Again, what nonsense! Here is an operating manager who suffered a 20 percent decline in activity and only reduced these two well-known costs 5 percent; yet this budgeting procedure specifies *favorable* variances. If this manager had spent only one-half of 1 percent less than budget when activity was 20 percent below what had been projected, he or she still would have achieved favorable variances. Favorable variances imply praise, but if you were the owner, you would have some serious questions to ask under these circumstances. In this case, the procedure praises, when censure might be indicated.

With this kind of budget to use for cost control, the poor devil to be pitied is the operating manager who is trying to direct and control the managers of a group of cost centers or departments under him. He (or she) receives this kind of misleading data, and he is too smart to censure the manager whose activity is over budget, or to praise the one whose activity is less than budget. But he doesn't know what to do. In the first instance of greater-than-forecast activity, should the unfavorable variances really be favorable? Or are they, in truth, unfavorable variances? But, if so, by how much? In the second instance of less-than-forecast activity, are the favorable variances really unfavorable? If so, by how much? Are they large enough to warrant attention or action? He has no answers to questions like these. He has no standards to measure against and thus, he has no control. He is in the dark.

The above model is an example of what is commonly called *fixed budgeting*. This kind of budgeting may roughly meet the needs of profit planning, but it is almost completely inadequate as a cost control technique. In fact, as we have seen, it can lead us 180 degrees astray in our control action.

In addition, fixed budgeting, from the standpoint of cost control, violates logic. Under good logic, the only correct comparison is the comparison of two things to a like base. With fixed budgets we are comparing budgeted costs at budgeted activity with actual costs at actual activity—two things with two different bases. This is not good logic.

Obviously, the operating manager who has only fixed budgets has two basic problems:

1. A poor performance may be undetected and thus uncorrected, and a good performance may go unrecognized.

2. If the comparison of budgeted versus actual costs is recognized as being wrong, and mental corrections are made, the manager still has no way of determining the degree of good or bad performance.

Some companies defend their use of fixed budgets as a cost control technique by maintaining that their operation is so stable, and the variations in activity are so slight, that activity changes have little effect on either budgeted or actual costs. It may be so, but I have always found this difficult to believe. Sales volume may be relatively stable, but are the operations always equally stable? Speaking in manufacturing terms, there are so many things that happen in a manufacturing organization— model changeovers, unbalances in the workflow, equipment break-downs—that while sales may be stable, operating activity may not be stable. In my experience, the very great majority of operations vary from month to month. If they do, fixed budgets are not the budgets to use as a cost control technique.

Are fixed budgets prevalent? Do many companies have only fixed budgets? I know of no recent survey that answers such questions. I do have some indications, however. At seminars, in the course of building up the above model of fixed budgeting, I always ask, "How many of you do it this way?" A positive response invariably comes from over 50 percent of the attendees. In fact, I would estimate that close to 60 percent agree that they follow fixed budgeting procedures. If this is a reasonable indication, the conclusion is startling. Less than half of the companies get more than one-half the possible use from their budgets!

## THE DANGERS OF RATIOS IN BUDGETING

Enterprises with fixed budgets still have the need for cost control, and their managements recognize that need. As a result, they attempt by a number of different means to utilize their fixed budgeting data for cost control. None of these means really works. At best, they have only partial applicability. At worst, they can be dangerously misleading.

Some companies with fixed budgets attempt to achieve cost control with a palliative, by adding a ratio or percentage column to their monthly performance-to-budget reports. They may, for example, divide each cost by the activity measure and express the dollars and cents that the cost equals per activity unit. However, this is rational only for a pure variable cost, i.e., one which varies directly with activity and has no fixed increment. For all other types of cost, the process is not only arithmetically unsound but also illogical, as we shall see in the next chapter, on cost analysis.

This particular use of ratios is frequently found in budgeting. Also, it is often strongly defended by its users. However, when you review with them the various types of cost, and the fact that it is rational *only* with pure variable costs, the defense retreats. The reason for continued use of the ratio approach is, of course, that with fixed budgets, the user has nothing else. This palliative can provide a logical control for the pure variable costs, but such costs, while large, are relatively few in number. Unfortunately, the approach is also used with equal certitude for other types of costs, and for these it is both arithmetically wrong and illogical. Again, this matter will be discussed in detail when we are into the subject of cost analysis.

This procedure has an interesting parallel in many cases of financial reporting that you see. Many companies, in presenting their profit and loss statements for management's use, express each item of cost, the cost subtotals, and profit as a percentage of sales income. This procedure might be helpful for total cost of sales and for profit but you have to question its value when expressed for individual items of cost. For example, what is the significance of the fact that depreciation costs expressed as a percentage of sales dropped one percentage point from the previous month when depreciation costs actually stayed the same but sales were higher?

029947

Other companies attempt to use their fixed budgets for cost control purposes by dividing the absolute amount of a given cost's variance by its budgeted allowance to calculate the percent variance. The size of the percentage then tends to get prime attention. Thus, if $40,000 is budgeted and $42,000 is actually spent, the unfavorable variance of $2000 is divided by the $40,000 and a "−5%" is recorded alongside.

This procedure obviously is fraught with danger, on two counts:

First, the "−5%" is a percent of what? It was calculated by first subtracting the actual cost at actual activity from the budgeted allowance at budgeted activity and then dividing that difference by the budgeted allowance at budgeted activity. What does that tell you? You are comparing an actual cost against a standard established for projected activity. (This is equivalent to subtracting apples from oranges and dividing the difference by oranges.) Certainly, operating management cannot use a percentage so calculated. It is a meaningless figure.

Second, a 2 percent unfavorable variance on a $50,000 per month cost is four times as important as a 10 percent unfavorable variance in a $2500 per month cost. This example highlights one of the dangers inherent in using percentages.

The prime danger is the first one. Whether you express the variance in absolute dollars or as a percent of budget, it is a meaningless figure under fixed budgeting. You cannot develop a meaningful variance between actual cost and budget allowance when that budget allowance is calculated at budgeted, not actual, activity. And this is the way it is done with fixed budgeting.

Admittedly, ratios or percentages are very easy to calculate. In fact, they are so easy to use that we often fail to remember their limitations and the dangers inherent in their incorrect use. Typical of these dangers are:

1. They cannot replace the original data. They can only serve to focus attention on specific aspects of that data.

For example, consider the operating result under the profit plan of two divisions for a given month, as shown in Table 2-4.

The pretax profit percentages that are calculated tell you that both divisions enjoyed the same percent of pretax profit. In terms of percent of profit to sales, the two divisions are right on plan. The percentages calculated highlight these two facts. But that is all they say. In this case, percentages don't tell you, for example:

Despite a 10 percent drop-off in sales, Division A maintained its profit margin. Good!

In the face of a 10 percent greater sales volume, operating costs of

**Table 2-4**

|  | Budget | % | Actual | % |
|---|---|---|---|---|
| **Division A** | | | | |
| Sales | 100,000 | 100 | 90,000 | 100 |
| Operating costs | 90,000 | 90 | 81,000 | 90 |
| Pretax profit | 10,000 | 10 | 9,000 | 10 |
| **Division B** | | | | |
| Sales | 200,000 | 100 | 220,000 | 100 |
| Operating costs | 180,000 | 90 | 198,000 | 90 |
| Pretax profit | 20,000 | 10 | 22,000 | 10 |

Division B also increased to the extent that there was no improvement in percent profit to sales. Bad: what happened?

You have to go to the original data to see other very important facts.

2. Percentages can usually be used only in the context for which they were calculated. Reading additional meanings into them can be completely wrong.

For example (again in the context of a profit plan), two months of sales statistics for three divisions of the corporation, shown in Table 2-5, tell us the following:

**Table 2-5**

| Division | Budget ($000) | Actual ($000) | % of Budget |
|---|---|---|---|
| **Month 1** | | | |
| X | 110 | 115 | 105 |
| Y | 200 | 220 | 110 |
| Z | 150 | 160 | 107 |
| Total | 460 | 495 | 108 |
| **Month 2** | | | |
| X | 150 | 120 | 80 |
| Y | 250 | 230 | 92 |
| Z | 200 | 170 | 85 |
| Total | 600 | 520 | 87 |

In this case the percentages as calculated might be read as indicating a sharp drop-off in sales, particularly when management might be accustomed to seeing rising sales. When you look at the data on which the percentages were calculated, however, each division actually had an *increase* in sales. Such a use of the percentages in this case, namely as a comparison between months, is reading in additional and wrong meanings. Obviously these percentages can be used only in the context for which they were calculated, namely as a measure of performance to the sales budget for the individual month, not as a comparison between months.

3. Percentages often tend to disguise important aspects of the original data. A 10 percent increase in one cost may or may not be twice as important as a 5 percent increase in another cost. If the 5 percent increase is in a cost amounting to $50,000 per month and the 10 percent increase is in a cost amounting to $12,500 per month, then obviously the 5 percent increase is twice as important as the 10 percent increase, not vice versa.

4. Percentages usually can be used only for comparison purposes. And unless they are equal in value, or derived from the same base, we cannot do a thing with them arithmetically. We cannot add them, subtract them, multiply or divide them. Therefore, when we use percentages for comparison great care must be taken to be sure that they represent proportions of the same base quantity. While the percentage sign, as W. J. Reichmann quietly observed, has a comfortably persuasive air of respectability and finality, it sometimes lends itself to uses where its respectability becomes open to doubt.

## FLEXIBLE BUDGETING

What must we do if we want operating budgets to serve not only as a mechanism for profit planning but also as a technique of operating cost control? Well, obviously, we must provide a logical comparison of budget allowances with actual costs, i.e., a comparison on a like basis. (This requires that we vary, adjust, or "flex" our budget allowances to the actual activity. When that is done, we are comparing actual costs at actual activity with budgeted costs at actual activity—two things to a like base. This is *flexible budgeting*. It is primarily flexible budgeting with which we will deal in this book. It is the only type that will give us both things we want from our budget, namely, profit planning and operating cost control.

Two names commonly applied to this kind of budget are *flexible budget* and *variable budget*. Either term can be used. However, the word "variable" is used by so many, and in such a specific way, when dealing with cost analysis that it may be best to confine it to that application. Therefore, in discussing the different types of budgets, the terms "flexible budget" and "fixed budget" will be used here.

Thus, in flexible budgeting, we adjust our budget cost allowances to that level required by the actual activity of the operation. On our departmental performance-to-budget report, we show the measured actual activity of the department, and we show, for each individual cost item, both the actual money spent and the budget allowance at the actual activity indicated.

Recognize that the need for flexibility in your budget allowances arises from the fact that you cannot predict exactly, at the start of the budget year, what the activity level will be for each budget period, i.e., month or week. If your operation is so stable, so unvarying, that your actual monthly activity equals your predictions for each specific month, you do not need flexible operating budgets. But of course, in real life, this situation is very, very rare. Actual activity usually varies from that predicted and as a result, budgeted cost allowances must also vary.

By the end of the year, your revenue and activity forecast might be very closely matched by actual sales. But this is not good enough. You budget for increments of the year, most commonly, months. And it is for each individual month that you have to predict exactly, if you want to avoid the need for budget flexibility. Since you cannot predict with such exactness, you must build flexibility into your budget program. That means flexible budgets.

The more volatile the industry, the greater the need for flexible budgets. This is true because the greater the volatility the more difficult it is to predict activity by individual budget month. In turn, it is more likely that there will be greater differences between actual and budgeted activity. We may come very close by the end of the year, but we must expect greater variation in any one month.

For example, where strong seasonal patterns exist, management usually recognizes the need to adjust costs to the seasonal load. However, they frequently do not recognize the need for flexible budgets. Instead, they lay down a monthly fixed budget for each month of the profit plan year, with due regard for the seasonal pattern. Then as the months occur, they compare actual costs to budgeted costs. This perpetuates the fallacy. They are assuming that each month's actual activity will equal each month's budgeted activity. The more volatile the seasonal pattern, the less likely this will be true. When it is not true, management ends up with the old, irrational fixed budgeting comparison of actual costs at actual activity versus budgeted costs at budgeted activity.

You can build variations into the individual months of your overall profit plan, but you cannot build in flexibility. That flexibility has to be built in month by month as, and after, each month occurs. And this brings us to an important aspect of flexible budgeting. The flexible allowances are established *after* the actual activity is known. It is not until then that we can calculate the budget allowances for the actual activity. This means that except for fixed cost items, it is only after the month is over that we can give the department head their budget allowances.

This fact, not infrequently, is cited as an objection to flexible budgeting. The criticism says, in effect, that since you cannot tell department heads what they should spend before the month starts, they cannot be expected to live within the budget allowances. They may innocently spend more than the budget will eventually allow because that allowance was not provided until after the money was spent. This is a proposition worthy of notice. But where does it leave us? The only logical conclusion from it is that flexible budgeting cannot be fair and that it will not work. But too many organizations successfully use flexible budgets to make that conclusion acceptable.

The fact is that flexible budgeting does work because in the real world, a department head knows the operation day by day. If activity is dropping, the department head knows it. He or she knows how busy the department has been month-to-date and can estimate quite closely, if the month-to-date activity level continues, what activity will end up being for the month. In turn, the higher management levels, if they are good managers, will be telling the department head if they foresee any sharp changes in activity, up or down, coming within the month.

A more serious and practical difficulty with flexible budgeting is the fact that it entails more effort, time, and thus money than fixed budgeting. If you want to do flexible budgeting, you have to do a good job of cost analysis, and this takes time and money. The establishment of monthly budget allowances is also somewhat more time-consuming than with fixed budgets. This, however, usually does not incur a large additional cost. Also, when you establish and maintain flexible budgets, you almost inevitably do a more detailed study of individual cost facts in individual departments than is usually required for fixed budgets.

You want to know a lot more, and this "digging" costs time and money. However, your effort results not only in flexible allowances but in better budget standards. Thus, the experience of most managements that use them is that flexible budgets save much more than they cost. The only alternative is fixed budgeting and sharply reduced cost control in many areas of large expense.

## FLEXIBLE BUDGETS AND PROFIT PLANNING

The basic and vital difference between fixed budgets and flexible budgets can be summarized as follows:

*Fixed Budget*

| | | |
|---|---|---|
| Activity and/or sales @ budget | vs. | Activity and/or sales @ actual |
| Budgeted costs @ budgeted activity | vs. | Actual costs @ actual activity |

*Flexible Budget*

| | | |
|---|---|---|
| Activity and/or sales @ budget | vs. | Activity and/or sales @ actual |
| Budgeted costs @ actual activity | vs. | Actual costs @ actual activity |

Thus, for full use of the budgeting tool, we need flexible budgets. With these we can apply, with justice, the operating cost control that we need.

We can also do the profit planning with a flexible budget. The profit plan starts with a sales forecast which "fixes" levels of expected activity and sales revenue. With our flexible budget data we are prepared to establish budgeted costs within any reasonable range of activity. Thus, we can establish our budgeted operating costs for the activity forecast by the profit plan. Thus, we use our flexible budget data to develop our profit plan.

Some managers think of the process in terms of fixed budgets for profit planning and flexible budgets for cost control. This thinking is not exact enough. You have flexible budget data for cost control, and you use that data to develop your profit plan, which normally remains fixed as to its goals for the budget year.

We can now summarize our chain of logic and show where it finally leads us:

If we agree that we want our budgets to be *both* a mechanism for profit planning and a technique of operating cost control, then we must have *flexible budgets* to achieve a logical comparison between budgeted costs at actual activity and actual costs at actual activity. With such a comparison, we can apply operating cost control in a fair and just way.

This conclusion, in turn, leads us to our last step in the chain of logic: If we want flexible budgets, we must analyze our costs individually, and we must analyze all of them, in order to know which ones to "flex" and how much to flex them for whatever level of activity our enterprise happens to encounter.

Thus, we are led into the important subject of cost analysis and cost identification, and into the next chapter.

# COST ANALYSIS
# AND IDENTIFICATION

Operating managers usually do not get involved in cost analysis. The pressures of time and responsibilities require that such analysis be done by the budgeting or cost accounting staff. However, it behooves every operating manager to know what types of costs there are and what techniques are available to identify them properly. He or she may not have to do the analysis work, but should be able to evaluate how well it is being done. A manager who can do that is able to participate more intelligently in the development of the budget allowances.

In the discussion of fixed versus flexible budgeting, the principle was advanced that our budget should serve us for both profit planning and cost control. We then saw that only flexible budgets give us a logical and fair basis for comparing actual costs against budgeted standards in order to achieve control. This, in turn, led us to the conviction that we have to analyze and identify our costs so that we know which ones to flex and how much to flex them for whatever level of operational activity we actually experience as the budget year unfolds.

## MANAGEMENT'S NEED FOR COST ANALYSIS

All the above presents a strong case for good cost analysis. We need realistic cost analysis if we are going to do practical flexible operating budgeting. However, this need is really only the beginning. There are a multitude of other equally strong reasons for good cost analysis. The management areas involved in these other reasons are not the subject of this book, but they are so important that they are worth listing.

Before we list these reasons, let us spell out the prime objective of cost analysis for modern management. Stated very simply, it is the *separation* of the *fixed* from the *variable* costs.

If the management of an enterprise is going to make good decisions it needs the best cost data that it is practical to develop. With such data, management is better able to:

1. Make realistic estimates of product costs. In the long run, product price depends on product cost. Realistic product costs estimates can only be developed from good data on the variable and fixed costs involved. It is also the kind of data that Accounting needs for developing sensible standard costs.

2. Make sound operating decisions. Management needs to know its fixed and variable costs in order to make wise decisions on methods and operational changes, capital investment, make-or-buy, etc.

3. Make effective marketing decisions. When the marketing function is given product costs that are only an unidentified aggregate of variable plus allocated fixed costs, they have insufficient data upon which to make good decisions. Marketing needs to know product variable (direct) costs and contribution margins. It needs this data to allocate effectively its always scarce resources of sales capacity and advertising dollars, and to make sensible price changes or concessions.

4. Make profitable long-range decisions. Top management needs direct-cost data to make its long-range plans in areas such as product development and operations expansion and contraction. Which products or services do you push? Which do you restrict or even abandon? The direct-cost data needed to answer these questions most profitably requires the separate identification of the variable and the fixed costs.

The list could be extended. Important subtleties could be developed. But hopefully, the case has been made. Modern management, in all its phases and at all its levels, needs the identification of its fixed and variable costs to make more profitable decisions. Such identification can only be made by objective cost analysis, not by guessing, or by uninformed judgments.

A few basic understandings concerning cost analysis and identification should be stated at this point:

Good objective cost analysis involves time and money. This has to be accepted—you know what you get for nothing. The required investment will vary with the complexity of the situation, but as we have seen, there are multiple uses for such analysis. The same cost facts developed for operating budgeting can be made usable and can be applied to all the other areas.

However, the tools available for our use in achieving objective cost identification are limited. As a result, at the current state of the art, cost analysis and identification are still very dependent on great inputs of judgment. This fact makes it doubly important that we use to the fullest extent the limited techniques we do have. Otherwise, we are completely dependent on subjective judgment, which may be guessing. The result can be far from optimized decision making.

On the other hand, the techniques that we do have to reduce our guessing and to increase our objectivity are much too underused. As a result, in many enterprises the cost data that goes topside, where the important decisions are made, is frequently based on conjecture, not facts.

Thus, if an organization of any type is going to have good cost facts, the higher levels of management must push and support the effort. Otherwise, good cost analysis is not going to get done. Senior management must recognize the need for the best available cost facts and not be satisfied until it has them.

## PREREQUISITES FOR COST ANALYSIS

Before going deeper into the task of cost analysis and identification, it is important to recognize that we need adequate cost accounting if we want to accomplish usable cost analysis. Thus, we must have reasonably good cost reporting, and well-defined and disciplined cost-charging practices. We may not need perfection in these areas, but we should adhere to reasonably good practices.

Typical of the disciplined reporting and accounting practices required are the following:

1. Proper charging to cost centers or departments. If in your enterprise, a department head, or agent, can get away with requisitioning a supply item while using some other department's charge number, or without even making a record of the withdrawal, then you have cost problems. You also will have poor cost data to analyze. Costs must be charged to the different cost centers or departments fairly and accurately. A good example is the charges for electric power. If the power bill has to be spread among a number of departments, a few of which are heavy users of electricity, then you need a factual basis for charging

that power, such as the total horsepower rating of each department's equipment, or the use of individual lines and meters for certain major users. If you use some broad averaging basis, or other kind of incorrect basis, you can overcharge some departments, or be completely inconsistent month to month in both your budget allowances and your actual charges. Wrong actual charges result in bad cost data to analyze.

2. Correct labor reporting and piece counts. These can often be a real problem in manufacturing enterprises. Such things as incorrect job numbers, fictitious time reporting, and imaginary piece counts can give you unusable cost and activity data. The sin lies only partly with operating management. The accounting function must also be blamed. They are just not being insistent enough. In most organizations, the accounting/financial function has an equal voice with operations. The managers of both are on comparable levels. Where this kind of poor reporting exists, the accounting managers are not doing what they should. They have to expose faulty conditions and initiate corrective action. Too many companies are doing an adequate job in this area to accept the conclusion that it cannot be done.

3. Defined and consistent charging of costs to specific accounts. This requirement specifies that the receiving, purchasing, and accounting functions charge the proper cost account. If, for example, a given supply which is destined for a specific department or use is charged one time to one account and the next time to another account, then you are going to have bad data.

It is difficult to be more specific. The charging practices, cost reporting, and cost accounting procedures used must always depend upon the product or service, the process, and the organization involved. You have to evaluate your own situation, define what you need, correct what is wrong, and start collecting any additional data that may be required. Usually, in a given situation these requirements can be quite readily identified and the data needed can be defined. Sometimes, however, collecting that data and enforcing the needed reporting disciplines can be a problem.

The first requirement on the part of the accounting department is to "sell" management on what is needed. This requires a full explanation of why it is needed. In the budgeting context this should be no great problem. Management wants budgets, and budgets require analysis of the correct cost data. If Budgeting/Accounting can show that the cost data that exists is wrong or incomplete, they should be able to sell their needs and obtain management support and cooperation.

This matter of "selling" Budgeting/Accounting's needs is worth further exploration. When you analyze a given organization that is suffering from some of the cost-reporting problems listed above (poor time reporting, wild piece counts, mischarging, etc.), very often the accounting/financial function has to share some of the responsibility. Not infrequently, the people at the lower levels of that function recognize all the weaknesses. They perceive the deficiencies in the data that they are collecting and passing on, and are uneasy about the situation. But they cannot do a thing about it because they cannot get the support of the people over them.

Clearly then, the first requirement is that the accounting managers, including the top manager, namely, the controller (or in some cases, the treasurer), must recognize the existing problems and resolve to correct them. They can have some big initial problems to overcome. Some organizations are dominated by specific functions such as marketing or engineering or, less frequently, production. To get action, accounting managers have to be diplomatically persuasive, and they have to have the facts. But it is a very rare situation in which the management of the accounting/financial function cannot eventually be heard and get action. After all, they deal with a prime mover—money!

To be persuasive, they have to be confident of what they know and what they need. To be confident that they are asking for realistic, possible action, they have to know the operation. They must know enough to feel "easy" in their knowledge. Then they can be sure that what they are asking for is possible. They can prove it by example and facts.

Thus, the requirements are awareness of the need, persuasiveness, diplomacy, and facts. And isn't that, by and large, "selling?"

Another prerequisite for good cost analysis is a very mundane but important thing, namely, a good chart of accounts. The chart of accounts lists and classifies accounts according to type, i.e., income, costs, assets, liabilities, etc. Many an enterprise has a chart of accounts that is perfectly adequate for the accounting/financial function. But it does not meet the needs of operating management. It does not collect and present the cost facts in the manner or in the detail they need.

The principle involved can be simply stated: The chart of accounts must meet the needs not only of the accounting/financial function but also of the operating functions.

*A case in point.* The client was a large equipment-rebuild plant that rebuilt the heavy equipment used by about 250 operating centers. One of the plant departments was a large welding shop. When the cost of operating supplies in this weld shop was analyzed against the activity measure (in this case, standard hours produced), there was a complete lack of correlation between cost and activity. Depending on the given situation, this can be due to several things. However, in this case, the practice of charging certain individual items of cost to "operating supplies" was responsible. After an inspection, it was found that into this one account the accounting department was collecting the cost of welding rod, welding gases, and miscellaneous operating supplies. Now theoretically perhaps, all these should vary at the same rate with production. In this case, from the data available, they did not. The department needed three accounts: one for welding rod, one for welding gases, and one for miscellaneous operating supplies. Individually these are large cost items in a large weld shop. When we did achieve this account breakdown, we had usable data to analyze, with a reasonable correlation between cost and activity for each. And from a practical budgeting standpoint, the need for such a breakdown is apparent. If you were the foreman of this department you would want to know what you were spending for welding rod, for gases, and for miscellaneous operating supplies. The person responsible for running such a shop needs that kind of cost breakdown, and the chart of accounts should provide it.

To summarize, the cost accounting prerequisites for objective cost analysis are: defined and reasonably disciplined cost reporting, and a chart of accounts that meets the needs of *both* the accounting/financial function and the operating function.

Finally, we must probe and analyze each cost account separately and individually. We cannot lump cost accounts together and attempt to analyze and identify them as a group. If we do, we can be victims of a first and probably wrong assumption, i.e., that all the costs we are grouping are of the same type. Assumptions are guesses, and here we do not have to guess—if we analyze each cost account individually.

## BASIS FOR CATEGORIZING COSTS

To identify costs we have to recognize their individuality and then place them into categories. On what basis should we categorize them in order to facilitate our analysis?

One frequently encountered categorization is one which labels costs *controllable* or *noncontrollable*. The term "noncontrollable" is usually used in connection with the so-called fixed costs. A possible implication of this description is that we must accept the costs at their existing level. This, of course, is directly contrary to the attitude all managers should have, namely, that *all* costs are *controllable.* It is just a question of at what management level they are to be controlled. Psychologically speaking, this basis of categorization is unfortunate. Practically speaking, it is of little use. In all respects, the sooner this kind of nomenclature is abandoned, the better.

The categorization that is of most practical help to us describes how costs vary with activity. What kind of activity? In a manufacturing company, it will be production and sales activity. In a service company, it will be service operations and thus, revenue activity.

On this basis of categorization, we can identify three types of costs: fixed costs, pure variable costs, and mixed costs.

These will be considered individually.

## REQUIREMENTS FOR AN ACTIVITY MEASURE

The term "objective cost analysis" implies the use of facts and the quantification of those facts. We have already discussed the prerequisites for the money or cost facts. We have also seen that a practical basis for categorizing costs is how they vary with activity. That, in turn, requires us to quantify the activity measures we use.

The specific activity measure used will depend on the situation. The only principle that can be advanced is that in almost every operation one or more activity measures are available and can be used. They may not yet be identified or the quantities recorded, but the activity measures are there. And this is true whether the operation is manufacturing, service, profit, or nonprofit. For example:

> In a manufacturing company, the measures might be standard hours produced. Or they might be in terms of product produced, such as bushels, tons, gross, dozen, square feet, cubic feet, or pounds.

> In a transportation company it might be such measures as passenger-miles, ton-miles, number of flights, number of trips.

> In a fast food chain, it might be number of purchases, perhaps broken down by type.

> In a hospital the measure might be patient-days, broken down by types, such as preoperative, postoperative, postnatal, etc. Another might be the number of outpatients.

In a museum, it might be number of people entering, and in the museum shop it might be number of purchases or dollar value purchased.

The most common exception to the general availability of quantifiable activity measures is in the engineering functions. For most of us, this is a real problem. Activity measures that can be quantified are extremely difficult to develop in such areas as research and development, product engineering, manufacturing engineering, and industrial engineering. Only a very few cases are exceptional. Sometimes, if an engineering effort is large enough, it can be broken down into subcenters, and activity measures can be developed for them individually. For example, activity measures have been identified and successfully applied in such areas as drafting and drawing reproduction.

*A case in point.* In an electronic components company, the function and department called product engineering had the task of translating customer orders and specifications into company part numbers and manufacturing specifications. This usually meant some relatively simple designing to specify component make-up and enclosure or container size. Some of the orders were repeats of previous orders and merely had to be so identified. Some orders involved customer specifications that easily fit existing components and their enclosures. Other orders, however, asked for very high specs and were difficult to fit into existing product and enclosure sizes.

The department was organized into five subgroups, each of which handled separate product types. In total, it was a large and costly department, but of course, very necessary. Senior management, always conscious of keeping overhead down, was very reluctant to add additional engineers to the department. Departmental management, on the other hand, was under continuing pressure from Marketing and Production to process the orders more promptly. Obviously, all levels of management needed some objective measure of workload and output (activity).

Engineered work standards would have been very expensive to develop for this situation. Instead management estimates and a tool from job evaluation were used. The work that had to be done was first categorized by type of customer order. As stated above, they varied in their difficulty. Each category was defined in writing and agreed to by all concerned. The department manager, his assistant, the manager of the subgroup, and his lead engineer independently estimated how many of each kind of order an average engineer could do in an eight-hour working day. Then sitting together, they compared their independent estimates, and the differences were exposed. These differences were then discussed and reconciled. Thus, standard hours for each type of order, for each departmental subgroup, were developed. They were applied to the backlog and to the current activity to support or disprove departmental management's requests for additional engineers. The measurements gave senior management quantified assurance that the staff size was right for the workload. As a measure of activity in terms of standard hours produced, the data could also be used for budgeting.

On the other hand, one activity measure that is notoriously dangerous to use for calculating budget allowances is *actual labor hours* or *actual labor dollars*. In flexible budgeting, you calculate the budget allowances for pure variable and for mixed costs on the basis of the activity measure being used. If you use these particular activity measures, it does not take very long for a shrewd department head to realize that the more people hired, the greater the budget allowances for these other costs. Then his or her very human tendency can be to seek any possible justification for adding more labor. As a result, the department head increases the allowances for the other costs. A manager should not do this—but we are talking about practical budgeting.

You have to identify and test which particular activity measures are best suited for your situation. In doing this, keep in mind certain requirements needed by a practical activity measure:

1. It should be relatively unaffected by variable factors other than volume. Consider, for example, a job machine shop. Such an enterprise adds value to metal to produce a variety of items, either for the shop's own finished products or for the products of other companies. In such a manufacturing situation, *pieces produced* would be a very poor activity measure. As a measure it is affected not only by the number of pieces produced but by the configuration of those pieces. Clearly, the shop could be twice as busy turning out 500 very complicated, multioperation pieces as it would be producing 5000 very simple pieces.

In such an enterprise, you want to use, if possible, the activity measure of *standard hours produced*. Let us examine this measure further, because it is probably the single most widely used activity measure in budgeting practice. With this measure, you have a time standard for every operation on every item made. It may be simply a cost standard used only by the accounting staff, or it may also be used as a labor standard to measure individual operator performance. In either case, the time standards are applied to every operation actually performed, and the total standard hours' worth of work produced is the activity measure standard hours produced. Notice that standard hours produced is not a measure of time; it is a measure of the amount of work produced.

For example, a given turret lathe operation on a given piece has a standard of one hour per piece. An operator working eight hours has produced ten pieces. He thus has eight actual hours, and he has produced ten standard hours' worth of work, i.e., ten pieces times one standard hour each. For the budget month, those ten standard hours produced plus all the other standard hours' worth of output produced by him and by all the other operators equals total standard hours produced by the shop in the month. Thus, the application of standards provides a common denominator that yields an activity measure independent of the type of work produced.

In other enterprises, absolute measures of activity can be practically used. In a grain terminal, for example, *bushels handled* is an entirely usable activity measure. It doesn't matter whether these are bushels of corn, wheat, milo, or soybean. Grains are handled so much the same that you can ignore differences in type.

2. The activity measure must measure activity changes which result in cost changes. This is a more subtle requirement and one that is usually not a problem. However, you occasionally do meet situations in which an ostensibly applicable measure of variations in activity does not correlate to cost changes.

3. The activity measure should be readily available from current records, without undue additional clerical or recording expense. Thus, in the case of standard hours produced, we commonly have that data available from existing payroll or cost records.

For example, you may want to test *machine hours used* as an activity measure and then find that there is no record kept of machine hours. In that case, you often retreat to another activity measure rather than start a whole new record. Or you will start the record for future testing, but use another measure for the immediate need.

4. The activity measure should have commonality with other costs and cost centers to allow the easiest possible application for other uses, such as estimating and product standard costing.

The ideal situation in practical budgeting is to identify and apply an activity measure that is usable with all the costs involved not only in one department but also in other departments. This is possible surprisingly often. (Standard hours produced is one such measure.) An activity measure of this type can also be used as a base for product standard costing. In less fortunate situations, the conditions demand a variety of activity measures, and thus the budget data is somewhat less easily applied to other uses such as for product standard costing.

## FIXED COSTS

This type of cost has been given many names, such as constant costs, burden, and overhead. In England they have been called *on* costs from "ongoing," though the custom is declining.

A *fixed cost* is one that does not vary, i.e., it does not change with variations in activity. Some costs are truly fixed, such as interest on bonded indebtedness. But many costs that we call fixed are not, in actuality, constant. They will change if the change in activity is great enough. Consider that well-known fixed cost—depreciation. If you start to produce 20, 30, 40 percent more, at some point you will have to add tooling, machinery, and/or plant, and depreciation costs will increase. If your president is managing an ever-growing and profitable organization, his salary will increase. The practical fact is that most fixed costs will remain constant only for a limited range of activity. Above that range they will increase; below that range they will decrease—at least they had better if you want to stay profitable. Thus, over a broad range of activity, the fixed costs will follow a step, or "staircase," pattern in relation to activity.

From the standpoint of actually developing budget allowances, these fixed costs usually cause us no great problems. We normally have a reasonably good idea of the activity range within which our budget will be working in the coming year, and operating managers or the accounting department specifies the money level of the individual fixed costs. As a result, these fixed costs are easily identified and laid into the budget. However, in this context, keep in the back of your mind the above reservation, that fixed costs cannot always be regarded as constant. This is the first of two difficulties management has with fixed costs.

Often management is too prone to accept them blandly as "fixed." The cost concept called "noncontrollable" is at work again! Typically you hear: "We have always had a certain sized administrative staff in this department. It doesn't change. It's a fixed cost." This kind of bland attitude assumes that the cost can't change, when perhaps it can.

Certainly a fixed cost should be reviewed periodically, and critically, to see if it can be reduced. And the larger the cost, the more frequent and critical should be the review.

*A case in point.* Insurance premium cost is an example of a cost that in many instances is not critically reviewed often enough. It is also a cost that can be quite substantial. Insurance is a very esoteric subject. Most operating managers have little or no knowledge of it. Necessarily, they depend on others, who are often outsiders, for providing coverage and thus for determining premium costs. Often the resultant cost is incurred unchanged year after year, and accepted as a fixed cost. It is not reviewed, not subjected to analysis, perhaps not put out for other bids. However, such a cost should not be accepted as fixed. Like any cost, insurance premiums should be studied periodically and dispassionately. In fact, some companies have made very fine cost improvements in this area—buying the same coverage for a lower premium or more coverage for the same premium.

This problem of the bland acceptance of fixed costs is particularly prevalent in good times. When the revenue and the backlog are up, the natural management tendency is to develop a too ready acceptance that a cost is fixed. In practice, the problem goes even beyond that. During such good times it is very easy for management to permit the emphasis to shift, to ease off the careful guard on fixed costs, and to allow them to climb. Sometimes, this is necessary. We do need more overhead as activity increases. But as we all know, the situation can easily grow out of control. Good budget standards help prevent this. But at any stage of activity we should never blandly accept a cost as fixed and immutable.

In practice, the very act of analyzing costs to isolate the fixed costs can discourage their bland acceptance. When these fixed costs are seen in their sheer dollar size, they can cause concern, and thus, spark new interest and attention. Some companies have grouped their fixed costs into subcategories. Having the categories identified then resulted in some groups being given intense and continued scrutiny because they were considered more susceptible to change, up or down, than other fixed costs. Other companies knowing their fixed costs have been led into business planning action on product marketing and capital investment. Such planning action was aimed at better profitability from the use of the existing fixed costs. The action might not have been taken had the fixed costs not been identified. What you can do to control your fixed costs better, or to utilize them more profitably, will depend on your given situation. ("Different strokes for different folks.") In any case, we usually do better when we have the facts.

There is a second, more serious problem that too many managements have with their fixed costs: It is the absolutely primitive and incorrect way in which these fixed costs are allocated to different products or services.

For an example in terms of manufacturing, suppose a company produces four product lines, A, B, C, and D. And everyone in the organization is aware of the fact that because of the way fixed costs have been allocated, D is carried by A, B, and C. In other words, costs that product D should be bearing are not charged to it. Instead, they are borne by A, B, and C.

How common is this situation? Again, I know of no recent survey available. However, at each budget seminar, after describing the A-B-C-D example, I ask, "Do any of you have this situation?" Always, the majority raise their hands. Is it true for your company?

*A case in point.* A very vivid three-sentence example of this absurd situation was provided by one seminar attendee. He said, "We allocate our shipping costs on the basis of sales volume. A major part of our shipping cost is crating. A major part of our sales is in a product line that is not crated."

You always find many reasons being advanced, and usually marketing reasons, for carrying product D. "We need it in the catalog." "We need it to complete the product line." "We need it to be competitive." But it is surprising how these reasons diminish sharply in importance, and how the thinking changes, when the true cost facts are developed, when management spends the time and money needed to allocate its fixed costs as correctly as possible. The analysis never turns out to be a nonproductive effort. You may still carry product D, but the emphasis inevitably shifts, new marketing steps are taken, and more profitable decisions are made. This usually happens when you have the cost facts.

The question of why this situation of poor allocation of fixed costs is frequently encountered is a fascinating one. Often a consultant will be involved in a client's organization on other matters and will hear remarks on a given product line such as, "We tape a $5 bill to every one we ship." This is simply verbalizing the judgment of the other managers in the enterprise who all agree that the costs of the product line are not met by the prices received. Often if the consultant asks why the client does not calculate the real costs of that product, the response is:

"Why rock the boat? Look at that profit and loss statement. We're averaging out beautifully!" This attitude can be categorized under "the dangers of a profit." The position is not good because ultimately it leads to lower profits. There is a lot of work and worry involved in running a business. For that work and worry why settle for 10 percent pretax profit if you can make, say, 11 or 11½ percent, by making better decisions with the correct cost data?

The proper allocation of fixed costs would be an excellent subject for a seminar and a book. Most managers and their cost people are not satisfied with their present allocation procedures. However, discussing the subject in general terms is difficult because it is an individualistic problem. The specific allocation methods depend upon the product or service lines, the process, and the organization. The problem is made more difficult by the harsh fact that when you are all done you still have good-sized chunks of the overhead that you still have no really satisfactory way to allocate to specific products. However, that is no reason why you should not properly allocate the fixed costs that are identifiable to products. When we do not, we commit such mindless inanities as that demonstrated in the example on crating and shipping cost.

What can be done is really not that difficult and expensive. It requires more talent and effort than is presently being provided, but usually not much more. We are not talking about a major investment, but the results can cause major changes in management thinking.

The principles of fixed cost allocation can be easily stated. It just takes intelligence, energy, and management support to apply them. They are the following:

1. The organization's costs have to be identified objectively so that you know which of your individual cost accounts can properly be called "fixed."

2. Each of these fixed cost accounts must then be separately analyzed. This means that each has to be probed and investigated until you know which condition or conditions caused it to be incurred and then what may cause it to fall or rise. This is the thinking part of the problem. With some fixed costs, the answers are obvious because they are directly assignable to a product, to a stage of the process itself, or to a function within the organization. Others, however, involve much more subtle thinking.

Obvious or not, we can determine, for each fixed cost, what causes it to be incurred and what causes it to change in size or quantity when it does change. Those fixed costs that can be tied directly to a product can then be so charged. Those that are assignable to a stage of the process or to a function within the organization are so charged, but then each one must, in turn, be charged to a product. In effect, this is bilevel allocation. In very complex manufacturing situations this fixed cost allocation by product can involve three or four successive allocations before you reach the products themselves.

As we have said, at the present state of the art, there are sizable portions of the overhead for which you have no really sensible basis on which to assign them to individual product lines. For example, in the case of some administrative costs, an overall allocation on the basis of sales volume by product line may be all that you have to use. However, what you are looking for is the fixed cost which is incurred for one product line but which is being borne by other product lines in whole or in part. Examples are tooling, engineering, or advertising costs for one product line being averaged over all the product lines, or crating costs averaged over all product lines, including those not crated. If you simply correct errors such as these, you will be making excellent progress.

And always in the back of your mind must be an awareness of the need to be realistic. There exists the danger of being too theoretical in the allocations that you develop and want applied. The problem requires a balance between theory and the realistic needs of your situation. Remember that you are not trying to build a brilliant model of theoretical perfection, that may be too expensive to implement and too complicated for anyone to understand. You are trying to correct the inanities that presently exist in your fixed cost allocations. If you can just do this, you are doing fine. To do this effectively, you need *practical* fixed cost applications.

3. Finally, use the facts derived from your analysis. Apply the fixed cost allocations that your analysis shows to be assignable to specific product lines. This action can meet great resistance from other management functions. For example, marketing can be highly resistant to making changes in product costs that might affect existing product prices and marketing patterns. They might fight the facts. This is a harsh thing to say, but many of us have actually encountered the phenomenon.

This whole subject of the proper allocation of fixed costs ties into practical budgeting. If you have effective flexible budgets, you probably have done an objective job of analyzing your costs. And it is more likely that your cost accounting function, and management itself, knows a great deal more about these costs and how they are affected by different product lines and varying activity levels. In turn, knowing this, it is more likely that they have detected and corrected the more glaring errors in their fixed cost allocations. Correction is not a sure bet, but the odds are better. Some companies have above-average-quality flexible budgets and still have serious errors in their fixed cost allocations. The connection between effective budgets and good fixed cost allocation is not always a sure thing. But the odds are better if effective budgets are on site.

## PURE VARIABLE COSTS

The second major category of cost is the *pure variable cost*, sometimes called *prime* costs. To be a *pure* variable, a cost must meet two requirements:

First, the initial amount is incurred only when activity starts, rather than when the facility or organization is established. Thus, there is no fixed increment.

Second, there is a *direct* relationship between the cost and the level of activity. When activity increases, the cost increases; when activity decreases, the cost decreases.

What kinds of activity are involved? In a manufacturing company, it is production and sales activity. In a service organization it is operational and revenue activity.

An example of a pure variable cost that varies with sales activity is commissions. You do not pay commissions until a sale is made, and normally, the larger the sale, the larger the commission.

In manufacturing, an example of a pure variable cost that varies with product activity is the raw material to which value is added to make the final product. In a service organization, such as a fast-food chain, it is the food cost. For a jobber, wholesaler, or retailer, it is the cost of goods sold.

Most commonly by far, these pure variable costs increase a fixed amount per unit of increase in activity. If you visualize a graph of dollars of a given cost against activity, dollars of cost will increase the same amount for each given increase in activity. Thus, there is a *straight-line* relationship between cost and activity.

In a very few cases, this type of cost will increase at an increasing or decreasing rate as activity increases. Thus, on a graph, dollars of cost will have a *curvilinear* relationship to activity, sloping out and up to develop a curved shape on the graph. Catalyst cost at an oil refinery has been said to be an example of such a curvilinear pure variable cost. Again, these are very rare and are usually found only in peculiar manufacturing processes. Such a curvilinear relationship should not be confused with set-up costs spread over larger orders, or material costs falling with larger-size purchases, or freight costs falling with larger shipments. All these may have curvilinear relationships but they are an entirely different matter. Instead, we are concerned here with how a pure variable cost will react to increases in total operational activity.

What about direct labor? Is this cost a pure variable? It is often said that because of skill shortages and restrictive labor contracts, direct labor, in practice, is not a pure variable. That concept has validity in some situations, but it can have expensive results if followed where it should not apply.

For example, suppose one of your production departments is a turret lathe department with thirty employees. If you run out of work for one or two of those workers, you probably are not going to send them home. Turret lathe operators are usually too hard to find. The foreman will find some kind of indirect work for them to do. In fact, a good foreman will have some necessary but postponable indirect work set aside for just such a contingency. However, if the foreman does not charge the employees' day to indirect labor, two costs are distorted. The direct labor not being done is overstated and the indirect labor being done is understated. Obviously, the cost of the worker-day should be charged to indirect labor.

Properly charged, direct labor should almost always be a pure variable cost because in practice, a pure variable tends to receive more management attention and stronger control. (There are situations, however, where this is not practical. In oil refineries and chemical plants, for example, production can go down or up quite large percentages but you cannot go below a certain basic crew size as production falls, nor need you increase the crew as production increases. Another example is a heat-treating department in a metal-working plant. Production activity in such a department can go up or down 30 percent and you may need no more men, nor will you be able to use less men. You just have the trays, baskets, or belts filled more or filled less.)

Other examples of pure variable costs can be scrap costs, packing material, and freight costs. In some operations one or more of those examples may not be pure variables. Instead, they may have fixed increments.

Actually, in practice, these pure variable costs are relatively few in number. Also, they are usually identified quite readily. They are important to practical and effective budgeting because a lot of money is involved in them. But while they may amount to large money values, they usually represent a small fraction of the total cost accounts. Many more individual items of cost, which also amount to a lot of money, fall into the third major cost category, i.e., mixed costs.

A point made earlier is worth repeating here. Many companies have available only the budgets to control such large pure variable costs as direct labor and direct raw material. And, the point was made that budgets must be considered as only the beginning tool to use to control such costs. To support this observation, it was pointed out that budgets usually provide only a monthly or, at best, a weekly control report, namely the performance-to-budget report. In cost areas which involve so much money, we should have more and closer-to-the-point controls than a monthly or weekly report can provide. We need labor standards, labor efficiency reports, and material usage and scrap reports.

In those enterprises where management has only provided itself with the control tool of budgets for these variable costs, it is obviously important that the labor and material budget standards be developed as carefully as possible. They will be the only control standards available. Often in such situations, the budget standards themselves can only be developed from historical cost data because there are no detailed product cost standards available to use to build up budget standards. If there were, management would be foolish not to use them in budgeting. Guidelines and warnings for the use of historical data will be discussed later on.

When a company does have labor cost standards, it is important to use them when building up the budget allowances for labor costs. Where labor standards have been developed and are used to measure individual operating performance, and thus where efficiency or performance reports are available, the job is relatively easy. We know the past average efficiency by cost center, and our labor cost reports provide costs at various activity levels. As a result, the budget standards can be readily calculated.

Some companies have labor standards that are only used for product standard costing, not for individual operator performance measurement. In these cases, we still have available the cost records and labor cost variance information. These two together can be the basis for developing our budget allowances for direct labor. However, some companies who have labor standards for product standard costing do not use that data in their budget development. Admittedly, the best labor standards for budgeting are engineered standards developed and applied to individual operators on specific jobs and used to measure operator efficiency. But even if we have only direct labor standard cost data used for product costing, we should make use of the facts it provides for budgeting. That standard cost data, complete with variances, is usually better than only interpolations and extrapolations from raw historical labor cost data.

So far, we have discussed fixed costs and pure variable costs in terms of operating expenses. When thought of in terms of cost per unit of activity, or per unit of product, these two major types of costs demonstrate a peculiar characteristic: *they reverse roles*. The fixed cost becomes variable, and the pure variable cost becomes fixed. This fact is a truism to most accountants, but it is not always remembered by operating managers.

Consider depreciation costs. They are regarded as fixed. Assume a machine with a depreciation cost of $10,000 per year. If you produce 10,000 units on that machine, the depreciation cost per unit is $1. However, if you produce 100,000 units, the depreciation cost is $0.10, and if you produce 1,000,000 units it is $0.01 per unit. The fixed cost is a variable cost in terms of per-unit cost.

Now consider raw material cost. This, as we have seen, is most commonly and practically accepted as a pure variable cost. If you are producing a unit with a raw material cost of $1, then every unit you produce will cost you $1 for raw material, give or take only a little for scrap variations. The pure variable cost is a fixed cost in terms of per-unit cost.

This seems rather obvious, but it frequently is not seared into the consciousness of many operating managers and estimators, and even a few accountants. As a result, they develop some amazing and unfortunate decisions in such areas as product costing, make-or-buy, and capital investment, among others.

## MIXED COSTS

When classifying costs on the basis of how they react to variations in activity, the third and final major category is mixed costs. *Mixed costs* are those that have an increment of fixed cost and an additional increment that varies directly with activity. Thus, a mixed cost contains both fixed and variable elements. Many more items of cost fall into this third major category than into the category of pure variable costs.

The most amazing and absurd mistakes are made by improperly distinguishing between the pure variable costs and the mixed costs. A consultant can become involved in some quite sophisticated operating situations and see obvious mixed costs being treated as pure variables or even as fixed costs. He or she can observe some very impressive computer installations where the computer is churning away, calculating budget allowances and issuing performance-to-budget reports. It is all very impressive until you get behind the scenery and see what the machine has been told to do. You find it has been programmed to calculate the allowance for an obvious mixed cost at the rate of so many dollars per unit of activity. But, as we have seen, there is only one type of cost, the pure variable, that sensibly can be calculated and applied in this manner. Only guesses, not objective cost analysis and identification, can result in such incorrect cost application.

What is really important is that this faulty cost data, together with similar cost data, is all wrapped together and sent topside where the big decisions are made—the capital investment decisions, the marketing decisions, the pricing decisions, the expansion and contraction decisions. Hopefully, the effect of such errors will not be too great, and perhaps some of the errors will be offset by opposite errors. But you have to wonder that if the cost data had been more objective, might not the decisions have been a little better, and more profitable?

Some companies try to avoid mixed costs altogether. They simply classify each cost as either fixed or variable on the basis of the nature of its major portion. There are two subtypes of such companies.

The first type just makes grand and glorious arbitrary guesses that a given cost is mostly variable, and then identifies and uses it as a pure variable. Other costs, they decide, are mostly fixed, and these they identify and use as fixed costs. This is nonsense that may or may not be costly. In very simple situations with simple product lines, it may perhaps be done safely. However, it is hard to believe that it yields the cost data that management should have when the process is varied or complex, or the product line is varied. Every organization has mixed costs. Most organizations have many mixed costs. In total, these costs usually amount to good-sized chunks of money. If we ignore their "mixed" nature, we will budget them incorrectly, we will apply them poorly to our products, and inevitably, we will make some less profitable decisions.

The second type of company that does not use mixed costs is one that has objectively analyzed its individual costs and then has very deliberately grouped them into fixed and pure variable categories for application purposes. At least these companies are not guessing. It is a deliberate decision made after good cost analysis. However, such practice may or may not be good for product costing. It depends on the local, individual circumstances. With such cost data, it is easy to visualize the possibility of some very poor capital investment and make-or-buy decisions.

In any case, both types of companies shut the door to practical flexible budgets. When a mixed cost is applied as a fixed cost in budgeting, you have to select some "average" activity at which you are going to establish its budget allowance. As soon as you do this, you almost certainly will be too loose in your budget allowance at the lower levels of activity and too tight at the higher levels. And the busier the operation, the tighter and more unrealistic your budget allowance.

When a mixed cost is applied as a pure variable, the reverse is true. With a pure variable cost you have to start your allowances at zero for zero activity and increase it directly with activity. A mixed cost, on the other hand, starts at a higher-than-zero level but increases at a lesser rate. It allows less money as activity increases. Thus, when a mixed cost is applied as a pure variable, you almost certainly will be too tight in your budget allowance at the lower levels of activity, and too loose in your budget allowance at the higher levels of activity. And the busier the operation, the looser your budget allowance.

Thus, costs must be identified and applied properly, if you want effective flexible budgets. Examples of correct application of mixed costs will be given below.

There are three subtypes of mixed costs: linear, step, and curvilinear. The first two types are the ones most used in operating budgeting today. The third type, curvilinear, is rarely used. For clarity of discussion, examples of each type of mixed cost will be used. The examples will be taken from an actual case of flexible budgeting at a port grain terminal.

One of the requisites of the cost analyst is that he or she knows the operation. Cost analysis work may be done by a cost accountant, by a budgeting person, or perhaps by an industrial engineer, but regardless of background, an analyst should know the operation. Therefore, if we are going to be doing cost analysis and identification work in a port grain terminal we all should know what kind of an enterprise it is and how it operates.

A port grain terminal is a service enterprise that elevates grain. It doesn't grind it or mill it; it simply handles it. Such a terminal is a material-handling facility, located where ocean-going vessels can reach it to be loaded.

This port terminal is an official weighing and grading station. As an official weighing station, the terminal or elevator has, on site, a representative of the Federal Department of Agriculture. His or her duty is to keep watch on the technical accuracy of the elevator's scales and the accuracy with which they are used. As an official grading station, the elevator also has on-site representatives of the local board of trade who maintain a continuing check that the specific grain being loaded aboard each particular ship is the required No. 2 grade, which is the grade usually exported. Both these functions serve as the guarantee to foreign buyers that they will receive the amount and quality of grain they paid for.

This particular elevator receives its grain from river barges or from railroad cars. It does not handle trucks as some do. It loads out only onto ocean-going vessels. Typical shipments are corn to Holland, soybeans to Japan, and wheat to India.

A simplified side-view diagram of the terminal is shown in Fig. 3-1. A marine dock is located parallel to the river shore. Outboard of the dock, the ships are moored for loading. Inboard, the barges are tied up for unloading. A very long conveyor belt is used to carry the barge grain into the headhouse where the scales are located, and to carry the grain to be loaded out to the gallery conveyor belt and the ships. Alongside the terminal is the railroad-car dump into which the grain brought in by box or gondola car is emptied.

Grain, as it is unloaded from either barges or railroad cars, is brought into the headhouse and to the scales for weighing and grading. After that, it is taken by conveyor belts to huge concrete silos in which it is stored for anywhere from three hours to six months, awaiting shipment. The grain is kept segregated in these silos by type and grade.

When a ship is to be loaded (a daily event), gates in the funnel-

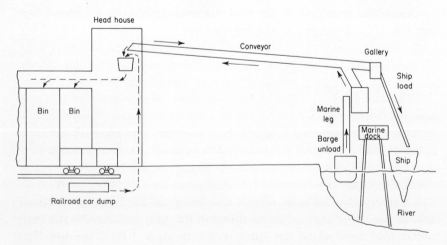

**Figure 3-1** Port grain terminal—side view.

bottoms of these silos are opened and the grain from a number of silos is poured onto a conveyor belt that takes it up to the headhouse for the official weighing and grading. After that it is taken by the big conveyor belt to the gallery belt, by that belt to chutes, and so into the ship's holds.

This terminal elevates grain, and *elevate* means unload and load out. Also, it does not matter what kind of grain you elevate. The cost of unloading or loading 100,000 bushels of soybeans is pretty much the same as unloading or loading 100,000 bushels of corn. However, *bushels elevated* is not a good measure of activity for individual budget months, because in any one month, the elevator will, most likely, unload a different number of bushels than are loaded out. Therefore, our activity measure will be *bushels handled,* which counts a bushel once when money is spent to unload it and once when money is spent to load it out. Thus, if this terminal elevates 120 million bushels in a year, with no change in beginning and ending stock in the silos, it will *handle* 240 million bushels, namely, 120 million bushels unloaded and 120 million bushels loaded out. But if in a given budget month, the terminal handled 10 million bushels, this might represent 6 million bushels in and 4 million bushels out, or vice versa, or any combination totalling 10 million bushels. You could use *equivalent bushels elevated,* calculated by adding bushels unloaded to bushels loaded out and dividing by two. However, in the grain business, operating managers are not accustomed to such terms. They think and speak in terms of "the handle." And in budgeting we want, whenever possible, to use the terms of the operation.

Now we are familiar with the operation. We have a mutually understood enterprise to look at and in its terms we can discuss at least the first two of the three types of mixed costs.

## MIXED LINEAR COSTS

A *mixed linear cost* is a cost that has a fixed increment plus a variable increment that increases in amount, as a linear function, with activity. Thus, its variable segment increases the same amount with each equal increase in activity.

For the port grain terminal let us analyze and identify one specific cost, namely, power. This is the cost of electrical energy purchased from the local utility and needed to run the very large conveyor belt motors and most of all the other equipment, and to illuminate the operation.

**Table 3-1**

| Month | Millions of bushels handled | Cost of power |
|-------|-----------------------------|---------------|
| January | 15 | $3200 |
| February | 10 | 3500 |
| March | 13 | 3600 |
| April | 15 | 4100 |
| May | 18 | 4000 |
| June | 21 | 6500 |
| July | 22 | 6100 |
| August | 23 | 4900 |
| September | 26 | 6800 |
| October | 28 | 6000 |
| November | 30 | 7000 |
| December | 19 | 4300 |

First, let us do a little guessing. If we do not operate the terminal for the month, we should not use any electricity. When we do operate, the more the bushels handled the larger the electric bill. This being the case, we might guess that it is a pure variable cost, namely, one that begins when activity begins and that increases with activity. Now, let's be objective. Let us look at the facts.

For a period of twelve successive months, we have the activity of this terminal, as measured by bushels handled, and we have the cost of power. These facts are shown in Table 3-1.

Clearly, we have two variables, i.e., dollars of cost, and activity, as reflected in millions of bushels handled. The variable of dollars of cost we can call a *dependent variable* because its size depends on the second variable, activity, which we can thus call the *independent variable*.

The relationship between these two variables, for the twelve months, can be pictured by means of a scatter diagram. (See Fig. 3-2)

The scatter diagram is simply a horizontal, or $x$ axis, intersected by a vertical, or $y$ axis. Along the $x$ axis we scale out the activity measure. Along the $y$ axis we scale up the dollars of cost. The scales always start from zero and we use an *arithmetic scale,* which means that on a given scale, equal linear distances always have equal values.

Fig. 3-2 has its $x$ and $y$ axes so scaled. To plot the data given above, we simply plot each individual month given. Thus for January, we go out the $x$ axis to 15 million bushels, then up, parallel to the $y$ axis, to $3200, and we have the first plot. The plot of all twelve months of our data is shown in Fig. 3-2. This provides us with a picture of the relationship between the dependent variable of dollars of cost and the independent variable of activity stated in millions of bushels handled. Examining the picture, it is clear that there is a definite relationship between these two variables. As the terminal handled more millions of bushels, its power costs increased. This is no more than we would expect. But let us measure that relationship. If we draw a line through those plotted points, we can develop a measure of that relationship.

Immediately, we have a problem. You could study those plotted points in Fig. 3-2 and visualize one line. I could study those plotted points and see quite a different line. Someone else, armed with a preliminary guess that it should be a pure variable could well visualize a line starting at the intersection of the $x$ and $y$ axes and draw up through the middle of the plotted points. He would then be calling it a

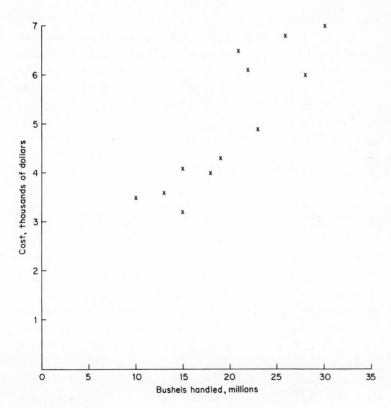

**Figure 3-2** Power cost vs. bushels handled.

pure variable cost. This procedure of arbitrarily drawing a line through points plotted on a scatter diagram is called *eyeballing* a line. It is probably the most widely used approach in the analysis of costs containing variable increments. It is also entirely inadequate for the objective analysis of any important cost. It is still guessing.

The line we want to draw is the *line of mathematical best fit.* The simple arithmetic involved in drawing such a line is covered in the next chapter, that deals with statistical tools used in cost analysis. If we do this arithmetic, we get the line shown in Fig. 3-3 and the first type of mixed cost, a mixed linear cost. Power is a *mixed* cost at this terminal because it has a fixed increment plus a variable increment that increases with activity. It is, even more specifically, a *mixed linear* cost because the variable increment increases with activity as a linear function. In sum, it is a mixed linear cost.

Now, where do we stand? Well, we have destroyed our initial guess that power in this case is a pure variable. By objective analysis of the

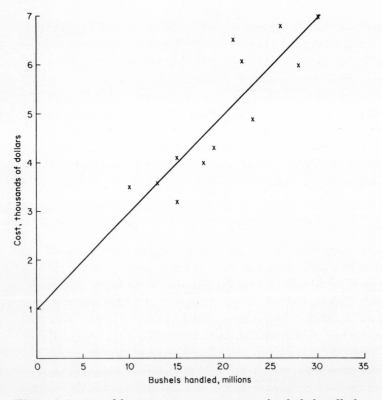

**Figure 3-3**   Mixed linear cost: power cost vs. bushels handled.

facts that we have, we know that it really is a mixed linear cost. We have analyzed. We have identified. Now, we can go one step further. We can formulate such a cost to make it easy to apply. The formula for a line such as that drawn is

$$Y = a + bx$$

Stating this, not in algebraics, but in our terminology, we get: $ cost of power = fixed cost + slope of line × millions of bushels handled.

Inspecting Fig. 3-3, we can read off that the *a* or fixed cost equals $1000. We now can calculate the slope of the line. One way is as follows:

| | |
|---|---|
| Power cost at 10 million bu | $3000 |
| Power cost at 0 bu | $1000 |
| Added cost of 10 million bu | $2000 |
| Added cost of 1 million bu | $ 200 |

The above way is rather pretentiously called "the method of differences for determining the slope of a line." Notice that the values it gives us will depend on the position of the line we draw. In actual practice, this procedure is only used with eyeballed lines. It is not needed when we calculate the line of mathematical best fit. The simple arithmetical procedures discussed in the next chapter for applying the line of mathematical best fit give us the *a* and *b* values that we need. In this case, we see that the slope of the line or the value of *b* is $200 per million bushels handled because we are applying the method of differences to the line of mathematical best fit.

The final formula, ready for use, is

$ cost of power = $1000 + $200 × millions of bushels handled

Now let us apply this in practical flexible budgeting. A month has just ended at this port grain terminal. It happened to be a month in which we handled 20 million bushels. We simply multiply $200 by 20, which equals $4000, add the fixed increment of $1000 and we have calculated the $5000 flexible budget allowance for power at the actual activity for the budget month that just ended. We have analyzed. We have identified. We have formulated. We have applied.

The above procedure for determining the flexible budget allowance for power at this port terminal was the one actually used in the budget installation. It should be noted, however, that in the case of power cost, there is yet another objective way of establishing the budget standard. This second way involves detailed engineering calculations of the kilowatt-hour usages of the various types of equipment involved at the projected activity levels of that equipment. This is the preferred way whenever the equipment involved has great power demands. For example, these detailed calculations are advisable where the process involves such operations as heat treating or electric melting of metals or glass. In most operations, however, power is used for a great variety of motors, lights, battery chargers, instruments, etc. In these situations, the most practical course of action is the one followed in the discussion above.

If you are using the computer to calculate monthly budget allowances, the machine can readily be programmed to solve the $y = a + bx$ formula. Then, the $a$ and $b$ values are given to the computer at the start of the budget year for monthly application. The $x$ value of actual activity is fed to it monthly, after the individual budget period ends.

To the operating manager who has not had the opportunity to see it actually in use, this entire line of approach may seem too elaborate, complex, and even too "theoretical." In actual use, it is relatively simple and very practical. And keep in mind that the only alternate we have is to keep guessing, as so many of us are now doing. It is rather sad to see some of the pseudosophisticated budget installations that exist. They have computerized budget calculations, and each month the computer impressively prints out the budget reports. However, you might discover that power is budgeted with no fixed increment at, say, the rate of $200 per 100 machine hours. As we have discussed, only a pure variable cost can be calculated and allowed on a pure ratio basis such as this. It is obvious nonsense, because power has to be a mixed cost for technical reasons. No one buys power without a demand charge, and if you generate your own power you have the fixed cost of the generating equipment.

If power has to be a mixed cost for technical reasons, there are other costs that usually reveal themselves as mixed when by all theory they should be pure variables. A good example of this is the cost of operating supplies. Just conjecturing on this cost, it would seem obvious that you should have no operating supply costs if the enterprise is not operating. Conversely, the greater the activity, the greater the operating supply cost. It all seems very sensible. The cost should be a pure variable. Yet almost invariably it plots out to be a mixed linear cost. We are faced with a classic conflict between theory and practice, between what should be and what actually is.

Some cost analysts can be quite rigid in their thinking on this point. They feel so strongly that a cost such as operating supplies should be a pure variable that when faced with the actual plotted data they "force fit" a line from zero up through the plotted points. Fig. 3-4 is an example of this situation. The solid line is the line of mathematical best fit to actual plotted data. The dotted line is the forced-fit line that would be fitted, by eye, up from zero and through the plotted points. The latter line is the product of intransigent thinking and is vulnerable on two counts:

1. The forced line up from zero representing a pure variable cost must be steeper in slope than the line of best fit representing a mixed linear cost. Consider the effect in the practical activity range within which the budget will be working and the cost applied. With the forced line, in the lower levels of the activity range, the budget allowance will be too tight. In the higher levels of the activity range, the budget allowance will be too loose. And the higher the activity range, the looser the allowance provided by the forced line.

2. The purpose in force-fitting a line, instead of working with the facts, is to match the line to the cost analyst's theory of what should be the conditions at the very low levels of activity. But these are not the

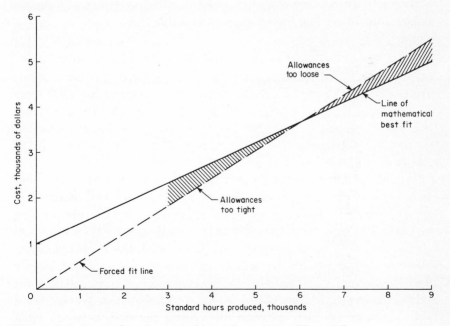

**Figure 3-4**  Line of mathematical best fit vs. line of forced fit.

activity levels with which we are concerned in practice. In fact, if activity ever actually drops down to these low levels, the problem will not be one of cost analysis. It will be a matter of survival! We are seeking to identify cost behavior in the realistic activity range within which our practical budgets will be applied.

## MIXED STEP COSTS

A *mixed step cost* is a cost that increases with activity by increasing in a series of steps, the height increase and depth of which may or may not be constant. Thus, the dollars of such a cost are fixed for a given and limited range of activity. Above that range, the cost increases to a higher level, where it again remains fixed for another given and limited range of activity. The sequence repeats itself over successively higher ranges of activity so that a "staircase" pattern is formed on a graph.

Returning to the grain terminal, we have a second cost to analyze and identify. Whenever you handle millions of bushels of grain you always have dust and chaff and belt spillage. As a result, this terminal has a group of individuals serving as clean-up labor. They handle brooms and sweepers and try to keep the place reasonably clean.

The activity measure is again bushels handled, and the cost is dollars of clean-up labor. The facts are given in Table 3-2.

**Table 3-2**

| Month | Millions of bushels handled | Clean-up labor |
|---|---|---|
| January | 15 | $2700 |
| February | 10 | 2100 |
| March | 13 | 1900 |
| April | 15 | 2400 |
| May | 18 | 2450 |
| June | 21 | 2950 |
| July | 22 | 3100 |
| August | 23 | 2900 |
| September | 26 | 3400 |
| October | 28 | 3600 |
| November | 30 | 3550 |
| December | 19 | 2600 |

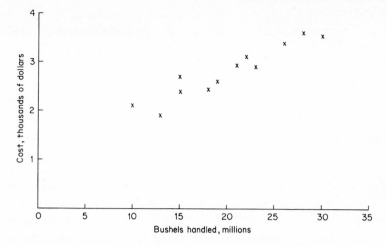

**Figure 3-5**  Clean-up labor vs. bushels handled.

Again, we have two variables, the variable of activity and the variable of cost. They can be plotted and the relationship shown on a scatter diagram such as Fig. 3-5.

Study Fig. 3-5. Compare it with Fig. 3-2. Notice the better correlation between the two variables on Fig. 3-5. Notice how the plotted points are much more closely grouped about an invisible trend line. In fact, on Fig. 3-5, the line almost draws itself.

This happens to be an excellent example of the dangers that face us with any technique. What is a technique? It is a programmed, systematic procedure or approach. And the danger that we human beings face with systematic approaches is that we can fall into the trap of being mechanistic. We are not talking here about cost "mechanics." We are talking about cost analysis, and for analytical work two things are demanded: your good intelligence and your knowledge of the operation. Once again, you cannot do sensible cost analysis from a desk alone—you must know the operation.

Think about this terminal's operation. Place yourself mentally in the chair of the terminal manager. You are in the depths of your slow season and you have a clean-up gang. But in the next months your terminal starts to become busier and begins to handle millions more bushels. You have to add clean-up labor. As you become still busier you have to add even more workers. The result is that you have a classic step cost. See Fig. 3-6.

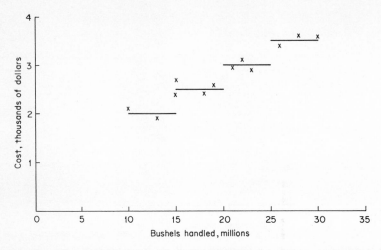

**Figure 3-6** Mixed step cost: clean-up labor vs. bushels handled.

In analyzing any indirect labor cost, the initial question to ask yourself is whether or not your data follows a step pattern. Many of us are convinced such costs should and will do so in well-managed enterprises.

This step pattern should reflect the way much of your indirect labor reacts to activity—your receiving labor, warehouse labor, shipping labor, inspection, even keypunching. If it doesn't, perhaps it could be encouraged to do so by effective budgeting.

Again we have analyzed. We have identified. Can we formulate such a mixed step cost in order to apply it? The answer is that such a cost pattern is not readily formulated. Instead, in practice, you eyeball the line for each of the steps the cost follows over the range of budgeted activity. Theoretically, you could mathematically fit the line for each step to the data you have for successively higher levels of activity. However, this is rarely, if ever, done. Usually you break down the total range of activity into levels, guided by how your data fits. Then, within each activity level, you fit the line to the data by eye.

Notice the inputs of your judgment needed in deciding where to establish the break-off points for successively higher activity levels and where to draw the step lines themselves. This is guessing. You can't call it anything else. Fortunately your guessing is being done within reasonably narrow ranges. As was said earlier, the practical tools of cost analysis and identification that we have are limited. Using them, how-

**Table 3-3**

| Millions of bushels handled | $ Allowed on budget for clean-up labor |
|---|---|
| 10 to less than 15 | 2000 |
| 15 to less than 20 | 2500 |
| 20 to less than 25 | 3000 |
| 25 to less than 30 | 3500 |

ever, is better than permitting indirect labor costs to remain fixed over the entire range of activity, or treating them as linear when in practice they go up in steps.

In applying a mixed step cost a table is drawn up that shows the dollars of budget allowance for successively higher ranges of activity. An application of the cost of clean-up labor at the port grain terminal is shown in Table 3-3.

If the computer is used to calculate monthly budget allowances, it can be programmed to handle such tabular data.

It is not uncommon for a specific indirect labor cost to approach a straight-line pattern against changes in activity, as does this example at the grain terminal. When this happens, there is sometimes a very natural tendency to budget and apply the expense as a mixed linear cost. Mixed linear costs are somewhat easier to apply. A simple formula is used and the tabulation needed by a mixed step cost can be avoided. However, out in the actual operation, that is not the way such a cost reacts to changes in volume. A mixed linear cost assumes and provides quite small incremental changes to dollars of cost as volume changes. That is all that such a line can provide. However, when we deal with indirect labor costs, we are talking "heads." Employees are being added or removed by transfers or by layoffs. The cost is going up, or down, in terms of employees, not in terms of the smaller increments provided by a line.

Also, and more important, the operating manager, particularly the department head, thinks in terms of head counts when thinking of indirect labor. Thus, the step cost, not the linear cost, matches the manager's thinking and practice. In practical budgeting this is a very important advantage for any cost allowance.

For product-costing purposes we might want to calculate a line through the data and apply the variable portion of an indirect labor cost as a product variable cost. In a given set of circumstances such cost

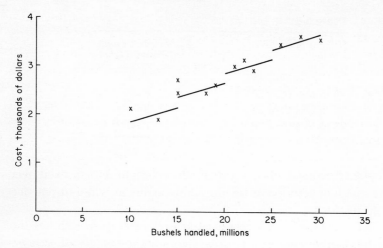

**Figure 3-7** Mixed step cost with tilted steps: clean-up labor vs. bushels handled.

application action may be entirely usable. But, for budgeting purposes, it is not adequate; it does not reflect practice out in the operation. Thus, most often, indirect labor costs should be budgeted as mixed step costs.

In fitting the successive step lines to an indirect labor cost, you occasionally will find the analyst pivoting the individual step lines about their center point. Thus, they will be lowered at the lower end of the activity range and raised at the higher end of the activity range. Fig. 3-7 is an example of doing this in the case of the clean-up labor. This is an artificial refinement, and usually there is not sufficient data to support the action. Certainly, there is not enough data to do so in the example used here.

The arguments usually advanced for tilting the steps upward are that it encourages not replacing absentees at the lower end of the activity range and allows for overtime at the upper end of the activity range. It is a matter of judgment and of what is practical for a given situation. Usually most of us have found the flat steps to be entirely practical. With them, if an operating manager does not replace indirect labor absentees as they occur at the lower end of the activity range, he or she can and will earn favorable budget variances. And not tilting the line upward at the upper end of the activity range encourages keeping a tight rein on overtime costs. Furthermore, the flat step has an additional, perhaps subtle, advantage. Because it is flat at the upper end of the activity range, it can provide a stronger inducement to stay at that cost level even though activity goes beyond the given range. For

example, at the grain terminal (see Fig. 3-6) when the operating manager can keep his clean-up labor cost at $2500 per month, as the
terminal handles 20.5 million bushels, and perhaps 21 million bushels,
he will be developing a greater favorable variance than he would if the
$3000 step were tilted downward. Thus, he has a greater incentive to
avoid adding another clean-up worker as soon as the bushels handled
exceed 20 million. Again, it is a matter of judgment according to the
specific local conditions. We simply want, whenever possible, to avoid
any unnecessary elaborations and refinements. They can sometimes
diminish the effectiveness of our budgets.

## MIXED CURVILINEAR COSTS

A *mixed curvilinear cost* is a cost that increases with activity, above a
fixed increment, at a decreasing or increasing rate, or amount.

If you plot dollars of this cost on the $y$ axis and activity on the $x$ axis,
the cost would plot as a curve, stretching out from a fixed amount, and
upward along a convex or concave path. Figures 3-8 and 3-9 are examples of such cost/activity relationships. Figure 3-8 is a convex path; Fig.
3-9, a concave path.

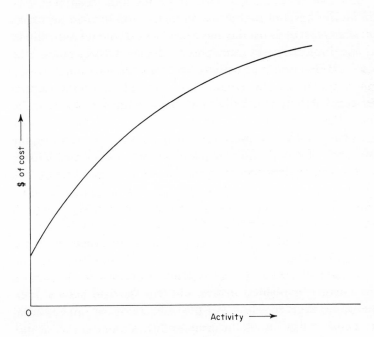

**Figure 3-8**  A convex mixed curvilinear cost.

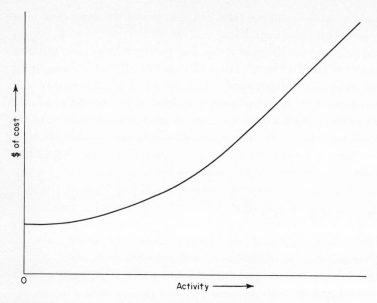

**Figure 3-9** A concave mixed curvilinear cost.

The use of such curves in budgeting and cost analysis implies an extremely high level of accuracy in cost reporting, if the relationship is determined on the basis of past costs. In fact, it requires an accuracy level higher than most of us usually have available. If the relationship is a projected one, unsupported by any past evidence, it assumes a subtle relationship between cost and activity that may or may not be supported by subsequent fact. In such cases, a straight-line relationship between cost and activity is usually more practical to use.

These curvilinear mixed costs can be formulated for purposes of application. The particular formula used will depend, of course, upon the characteristics of the curvilinear pattern that is developed by the data. The curve may be described by formulas such as the following:

$$y = a + bx^n$$

$$\log y = a + bx$$

$$y = a + b \log x$$

Very frequently, where curvilinear relationships are detected in cost analysis, the curve is eyeballed instead of mathematically fitted. This practice should be avoided whenever possible. If you are so sophisticated in your cost analysis work that you are fitting curves, you should develop the line of mathematical best fit.

One very fortunate seminar attendee had a computer terminal on his desk. He had on-line access to the computer which was programmed to fit a straight line and four different types of curves. He would punch in his cost and activity data for a series of months, try the line and then each curve, determine which gave him the best "fit," and then use it. More and more cost analysts will have such facilities in the years ahead.

In actual practice, such curvilinear costs are very, very rare—up to this point in time. Many of us have never identified and applied a cost of this type. This is not to say that we do not have them. Most of us just have not had the data to identify them. However, when you consider this type of mixed cost in the light of your personal experience, you might suspect that some of the costs that you have identified and applied in the past as linear might have been curvilinear had your data been better. The point is that we should not close our minds to such costs because of their rarity to date. As we become better and better in our cost accounting and in our cost analysis, we may probably detect instances of curvilinear cost behavior.

*A case in point.* A very heavily mechanized candy company spent a great deal each year on equipment maintenance labor. Such indirect labor cost was categorized into two accounts: preventive maintenance labor and emergency maintenance labor. The latter account covered the highly trained crews that were continuously on call to fix and adjust machinery. It was and is a big cost. In attempting to budget or predict the cost of this emergency maintenance labor, they first tried *multiple regression analysis.*

In our discussion and examples, we have only applied *simple* regression *(correlation),* which is the detection of the relationship between one dependent variable and one independent variable. In multiple regression, the attempt is made to identify the relationships between more than two variables.

In this case, the company first tried to identify the relationships between the dollar cost of emergency maintenance labor and the two variables of pounds of candy produced and dollars of undepreciated capital investment. A computer was used for the calculation. The first run revealed that pounds of candy produced were not a significant variable because the enterprise was always operating very close to its capacity limits. They ended up with a simple regression (or correlation) of dollar cost of emergency maintenance labor and undepreciated capital investment. They found that dollars of cost increased above a fixed amount as dollars of undepreciated capital investment increased, but in a convex, curvilinear pattern (as in Fig. 3-8). Thus, as more equipment was bought and installed, it caused an increase, but a successively decreasing amount of increase, in breakdown maintenance labor cost.

They budget this cost and apply it on the basis of the formula for the curve that they developed from their analysis.

## USING HISTORICAL DATA

In all the discussion and examples given above, we sought for "objective" cost analysis by identifying how each type of cost reacted, or did not react, to changes in activity. In each case we used historical cost and activity data. Thus, the quality of our cost analysis and our cost identification will depend on the quality of the historical cost data itself. If in a company, we adhere reasonably to the prerequisites of cost analysis listed earlier in this chapter, the data itself should be satisfactory and usable. But we must examine our approach in yet another sense.

We in practicing management are often criticized by the theorists for our use of historical data as the basis for prediction and decision making. In the budgeting context we are frequently told that "we are using the past as a predictive base for the future," and that when we do this "we are in danger of perpetuating the inefficiencies of the past." The harsh fact of practical management life is that usually, historical data is all that we have. It is the only base available. For many of us, the harsher fact is that we do not even have decent historical data to use. And yet we must manage. We must make decisions. Such criticism is no help. It is only destructive, not constructive criticism. We need sensible, practical alternates, and in the area of cost analysis there aren't any. What we can do, in order to be as objective as possible, is to approach the problem as outlined above, by type of cost. All we can hope to do is to minimize our guessing and reduce our area of potential error. Most enterprises have far to go to reach even these goals.

In using historical data, our concern and care should be:

1. That the historical data we use is reasonably accurate in stating the facts. This means we must know the conditions under which it was collected. We must know what the data contains and what it does not contain.

2. That the historical data we use really applies to the operating conditions for which we now want to use it. If the present conditions are quite different from those under which the data developed, the data may not apply. If we recognize and know those changes, we can make intelligent decisions on whether or not the data is still usable.

In the context of budgeting, the criticism that "we are in danger of perpetuating the inefficiencies of the past" can be rebutted on two counts:

First, whenever you read this criticism, or whenever it is directed to you verbally, read on or listen very carefully. What is being offered as a replacement? After all, you are hearing destructive criticism. What is the constructive alternate being offered? To date, the replacement always returns to approaches involving great amounts of subjective human judgment. We might as well continue crudely to call it what it is—guessing. If viable, practical, objective alternates were available, they would be in use, perhaps not by everyone but certainly by enough managers to be well publicized.

Second, it was asserted early on in this book that budgets, when properly installed, save more than they cost to develop and install. If this is true, what will happen in the future to the present costs at the same levels of activity? Won't those future costs be lower than they are at present, or follow a shallower path, or both? In fact, the only way the operating manager can develop a favorable variance is to *beat* his past cost performance.

Consider, for example, the power cost at the port grain terminal (Fig. 3-3). The line drawn is the past "average" line. It represents the terminal manager's past efforts. If he uses it as it stands for his budget allowance, he can generate a favorable variance in power *only* by doing better in his use of power than he has done in the past. His impetus is to do better. His year-end bonus may depend, in part, on his doing better. When he does do better, his power cost line on the graph will be either lower or less steep, or both. If the budget is effective it will not "perpetuate the inefficiencies of the past."

Inflationary pressures do not affect the argument. However, they are an additional factor that bears on the situation. We may have to raise the past line of cost to provide for expected or announced power cost increases. But without effective budgets, the final cost level, including power rate increases, probably would be still higher than it would be with budgets that work.

## PRACTICAL POINTS ON COST ANALYSIS AND DATA PLOTTING

In applying the techniques discussed in this chapter, there are certain practical, well-accepted guidelines that should be mentioned:

1. Avoid, usually, using more than the most recent twelve months of cost and activity data. Some analysts like to examine, say, thirty-six

months of cost/activity relationships, but you have to question how much they know about that two- and three-year-old data. Were the charging procedures unchanged over that long a period? Were the cost account contents consistently maintained? Have operating conditions changed? In many real-life situations we cannot know all that we would like to know about the most recent twelve months of data, much less even older data. In some happy situations, the older data may be usable, but most of us have learned that it is usually wiser to work only with data from the latest year. If a pattern isn't discernible in that data, you have to suspect the usability of a pattern derived upon adding even older data.

2. Be disciplined in your objectivity. Work with the facts you have, and use all of them. Do not be guilty of making subjective decisions that affect the data. Some analysts advocate dropping "out-of-line" data. This is not objectivity; it is guessing.

For a demonstration, refer back to Fig. 3-3. Consider the month of June, in which the terminal handled 21 million bushels, and power costs were $6500. This is certainly an "out-of-line" month. Yet you dare not drop it if you want to call your analysis objective. The only defendable way you could drop that month from your data would be if you studied in depth the reasons why such high power costs had been incurred at that activity level and definitely identified the specific causes as avoidable in the future. If you did all this, you would have a defendable basis for dropping that month of data. If you did not, you could not drop it and still claim objectivity.

3. Apply your ingenuity. Do not be hidebound. You do encounter situations in cost analysis that are out of the ordinary, where you have to think differently. They are not too common, and usually each instance is unique to the given situation. For example, it is not uncommon to have distorted relationships between power costs and activity. The point in time at which the power meters are read may be quite different from the end of the activity period. In certain instances a usable relationship between power cost and activity has been discerned only by plotting February's power bill against January's activity, March's power bill against February's activity, and so forth.

The step of constructing a scatter diagram is an important part of this whole approach to objective cost analysis and identification. We should consider it an integral part of the technique, even though not absolutely essential. (We can, for example, go directly to the arithmetical approach which has already been mentioned and will be discussed in detail in the next chapter. But a scatter diagram is usually advisable for reasons which will be discussed in the next section.)

In real life, this whole approach or technique of scatter diagramming may offer us some problems. For example, the situations given above all show a discernible relationship between cost and activity. But suppose your data does not? Additional steps can and sometimes need to be taken. Here are some practical points that frequently can be applied:

Assume that you have identified an activity measure that by all logic, and in your judgment, meets the requirements of a usable activity measure in your operation. It may even be an activity measure that you have already used for other costs in the same department or operation. Assume also that for twelve successive months you have the data on that activity and the dollars of a given cost. You construct the scatter diagram, and it shows a tremendously wide scatter between cost and activity. There is no discernible correlation. What do you do? You still face the need to identify the cost by type and to estimate some kind of budget allowance. You would like to avoid making a complete guess. Two possible steps, frequently used by many of us, may be helpful under these conditions:

1. Calculate averages for successive two-month periods. Add January and February activity and divide by two. Add January and February cost and divide by two. Do this for the remaining five two-month periods. Plot the six resulting relationships. This reduces the twelve original points of data with which you started to six points, but it may give you a relationship between the two variables that otherwise is not discernible.

2. Try moving averages. The three-month moving average is often used. Add January, February, and March activity, and divide by three. Drop January and add April to February and March, and divide by three. Continue until you have used all twelve months of activity data. Do the same thing for the matching twelve months of cost data. You then have matching activity and cost data for ten successive three-month periods. Plot the ten relationships. This procedure reduces the twelve original points of data with which you started to ten points. Again you are trying to discern some order in the chaotic data you have available.

You must always start your scaling, along the $x$ axis and up the $y$ axis, from zero. Only by doing this will you be able to specify the fixed increment of a mixed cost. Furthermore, you must be consistent in your scaling along either axis. The scales used can be different for each axis, but the one indicated for a given axis must be consistently followed.

The last two basic requirements have been stated earlier, but they are, surprisingly, so often violated that they bear repeating.

## COST ANALYSIS AND DEVELOPMENT OF BUDGET ALLOWANCES

The whole discussion of cost analysis up to this point has been to identify and to apply properly the various kinds of costs. But cost analysis and budgeting are also interrelated in yet another sense. In doing cost analysis for practical budgeting, your efforts usually also result in the development of budget cost allowances, or at least proposed budget cost allowances. Good cost analysis requires in-depth investigation and thinking. When this is combined with the knowledge of the operation developed by the able cost analyst, the most common result is a sound grasp of how much should be spent for a given cost item. This section offers some practical hints on this use of cost analysis to develop budget allowances.

However, before making these points, let us first consider another important aspect of cost analysis, namely, its role in cost improvement. The subject is obviously related to budget cost standards. Frequently, the very act of analyzing a given cost will result in the revelation that money is being wasted and that cost improvements are both possible and needed. A good example can be made in the use of the scatter diagram.

Assume that your activity measure is a proved one. It has been used in a practical way for other costs or in other areas of the operation. Now, for yet another specific cost, you have plotted twelve months of cost and activity data using the proven activity measure. The plot indicates either a very poor correlation, or absolutely no correlation at all, between activity and dollars of cost. What should this indicate to you?

In practice, given an applicable activity measure, it can only indicate two possible conditions:

1. Bad cost reporting

2. An out-of-control situation—money is being thrown out the windows

Theoretically, it could be possible that the cost is well controlled and that the lack of reasonable correlation between cost and activity is simply the result of poor reporting. But don't bet on it. In practice, you can give good odds that money is being wasted. A correlation that should exist does not exist. The cost is *not* being controlled. This, not infrequently, is one of the ways consultants on an operations audit identify for themselves and their clients that costs are "out-of-line," and that improvement action is possible.

How good are *your* cost/activity correlations? They might be profitably checked, particularly in such often neglected areas as indirect labor, administrative and staff personnel, operating supplies, power, fuel, etc.

Now let us consider some practical specifics on the use of our cost analysis work in developing budget allowances.

## Extrapolation of Cost Data

Very often you can use your cost analysis findings to extrapolate budget cost standards for higher levels of activity. Many of us budget under growth conditions. As a result, our budget cost allowances for the coming year must be established for activity levels that are higher than those experienced in the past. Very frequently we can use the data that we have to extrapolate into higher activity levels in order to establish our budget cost allowances for the future.

Refer back to Fig. 3-3, the mixed linear cost of power at the port grain terminal. Our highest activity month was 30 million bushels. Let us assume our next budget year's forecast includes one or more 35 million bushel months. Could you extrapolate that power cost line to 35 million bushels to establish the budget allowances for those expected higher volume months? There is no reason not to do so. The procedure certainly utilizes the best data base that you have available.

What about extrapolating for 60 million bushels? To do this some further investigation and analysis is needed. Will the doubled volume be achieved with the same equipment, but working more shifts? What will be the cost per kilowatt hour at that higher usage? The greater the power usage, the lower the cost per average kilowatt hour. Therefore, at the higher level of power usage, the cost line, while higher, might be at a different slope or on a lower relative slope. The point is that in practice, you frequently can extrapolate your data quite far out. Each cost in each budget situation requires its own questions and analyses but the very acts of data collection and analysis provide a base for extrapolation that is usually incomparably better than your unsupported judgment.

## Variability in Indirect Labor Costs

In analyzing indirect labor cost areas, many of us in budgeting and industrial engineering have come to the conviction that they are best handled as step costs. In any well-controlled operation, that is the way these cost areas are managed and how they should react to activity changes.

However, in practice in many enterprises, it is common to see large areas of indirect labor cost which are allowed to remain fixed despite considerable variations in activity. In these situations if you plot cost against activity, the only cost variations you may detect are the extra overtime costs at high activity levels. Such a lax situation, if it exists in your enterprise, provides an opportunity for cost improvement, using budgets as the tool. It does not matter whether it is a brand new budget installation, a budget revitalization program, or a normal budget maintenance effort; budgets can be applied as an effective cost control tool for indirect labor.

If you are applying flexible budgets, you will be measuring activity. You will be talking to operating managers in terms of variations in activity. Right then and there, when they are recognizing with you the fact that their activity varies over the course of the budget year, is the time to have them set up manning tables. Such tables adjust the indirect labor budget allowances to the actual activity level. Thus, budgets as a cost control tool can initiate action that might not otherwise be taken.

If you are not applying flexible operating budgets, but are only using fixed budgets, you still can use the tool of budgeting for this purpose. We have seen that fixed budgets are a most inadequate cost control tool. But that does not mean that they cannot introduce cost control and cost improvement thinking. With only fixed budgets you can initiate the concept of indirect labor manning tables, so that your operating managers begin to accept the possibility of varying their indirect labor costs as their activity varies.

There are a lot of poor attitudes in the indirect labor area of cost. You hear "Stretch it out"—in slower months; "We need more overtime"—in busy months. These approaches are too frequently encountered and accepted. Budgets can be helpful in overcoming such attitudes. The point is that if your operation has variations of 10, 15, 20 percent in activity over the course of the budget year, and if you have indirect labor cost areas that are not varying, you can use budgets as the wedge to open up some new thinking.

## Tightening the Allowance

In real-life cost analysis and budgeting, it is a common experience, as you analyze specific cost/activity data, to realize that you have before you still another instance of cost slovenliness. There are strong indications in your data that too much has been spent in the past on this item. In terms of the scatter diagram, there is a wide scatter of points, or there are too many out-of-line months on the plot. This is most frequently encountered where budgets have not been used, where only fixed budgets have been applied or where the budgeting job has been poorly done. You study the plotted data and the line drawn and say to yourself, "It's too loose." As a result you drop the line, say, 5 or 10 percent and thus develop a proposed tighter budget allowance.

Guessing rears its ugly head again! Many of us have done this. We will undoubtedly face the need for doing it again in the future. But if we do it, we must show the operating manager whose budget allowances are being developed, both the original line and the new, lower, and tighter-proposed line. The manager has to agree to the new, tighter standard. It will be his budget, his constraint, not the constraint of the budgeting person who is doing or using the cost analysis.

Now in this situation, we come to a rather surprising phenomenon in practical budgeting. You would think that inevitably the operating manager would oppose the tightened allowance and would fight for the original cost line, or more. Not infrequently, just the opposite is encountered. You show the operating manager the plot and the original line and then the proposed tighter and lower line. He or she studies the situation and then says, "Oh, we can do better than that." This reaction can be a real danger to the neophyte budgeting person, who might receive this response and accept the manager's optimistic projection, for which there is no past evidence. The operating manager can innocently set too tight a budget cost allowance and then start off with large unfavorable variances. Such overoptimistic cost goals can wipe out the effectiveness of the budget.

We all have faced, and will face again, situations where we have to tighten up on poor past performances. But as practical people, we must do it carefully. As we have seen, we must even occasionally fend off the overoptimistic operating manager. In practical budgeting, if we err, we should err on the loose side in our allowance tightening. This is a sensible maxim because first, we are reducing the allowance to begin with, and second, the only way the operating manager can develop a favorable variance is to spend still less than the tightened allowance provides. If we do not guard against such overoptimism, the budget might end up in the lower right-hand drawer of the desk, ignored, unused, and ineffective.

## Visualization with the Scatter Diagram

It was proposed earlier that you should always construct a scatter diagram even though it is not a prerequisite for least squares line fitting. The practical fact is that the scatter diagram gives us a *picture* of the relationship between cost and activity. We human beings often see more when we have a visualization of the relationship between two variables than we do when we have only the stark figures to work with. To quote a cliché, a picture is worth a thousand words. It may not be quite a thousand, but every little bit helps in cost analysis.

The scatter diagram offers the following aids:

First, it isolates the out-of-line month, namely, the month in which the incurred costs were higher than past cost/activity relationships would indicate they should have been. Thus, the step has cost improvement implications.

Second, it is a good check on your least squares line calculation. This will be discussed in greater detail in the next chapter.

Finally, it can identify poor operating conditions or practices on the part of specific operating areas, or shifts. Managers occasionally take costly action to meet a given unusual situation or condition. When that situation or condition ends, it does not mean necessarily that the action will be stopped. When it is not stopped, the cost is out-of-line.

It is surprising how often the scatter diagram, and the picture it offers, uncovers a poor operating situation. It can even be embarrassing to all concerned, including the cost analyst, to realize that the facts were there in the cost data all the time, but they simply were never detected. The scatter diagram helps to see the facts.

*A case in point.* A plant made glass bottles. There were five tanks of molten glass, pouring hundreds of tons a day. You can imagine the fuel involved in melting all that silica sand, soda ash, and other inorganic solids to make the glass. Tank operators manually control the fuel flow to the tanks. A plot was made of Btu's of fuel used versus tonnage pulled, *by shift.* (In the industry *tonnage pulled* is the terminology for the quantity poured continuously out of the molten glass tanks.)

The scatter diagram by shift revealed that the second shift had a 10 percent higher fuel cost line than the first and third shift. This was the result simply of sloppy fuel control, equivalent to throwing hundred or thousand dollar bills into the glass tank. It was embarrassing that all this had not been seen in the fuel usage data maintained by shift, but somehow it was not. The scatter diagram exposed the poorer operating practice.

Incidentally, modernized and new glass tanks avoid this danger by sensors and automatic fuel controls. In such plants this particular cost hole will be plugged. There are always many more existing or developing that await discovery.

# STATISTICAL TOOLS
# FOR COST ANALYSIS

No discussion of cost analysis would be complete without an exposition of the statistical tools available for our use. They are simple, yet for many operating managers, they are alarming. This attitude is both unfortunate and unnecessary. Operating managers do not need to know the sometimes involved mathematics that lies behind these statistical approaches. They do not have to derive the formulas. They only have to know where these tools can be used and how to use them. And that is relatively simple.

## FITTING THE LEAST SQUARES LINE

In this day and age, it is embarrassing to see a budgeting person or an industrial engineer, or a cost accountant, blithely eyeball a line through the plotted points of a scatter diagram. He or she does this and has absolutely no assurance that the personal judgment being applied will yield a good description of the cost/activity relationship being analyzed. It is particularly unfortunate because another ten minutes' worth of work can replace the judgment of the fallible human eyeball with the line of mathematical best fit. With a calculator that has one memory (certainly no esoteric piece of equipment today), an analyst can fit such a line in ten minutes, or less with practice. An even better equipped calculator, with a built-in program for linear regression, will reduce the required time still further.

Many management people had statistics courses in college. They learned how to fit such a line to two variables. But once out of school, not needing this skill for a while, they have forgotten it. Even worse, they seem to fear it. They avoid it and simply eyeball the line instead. This very human tendency has to be conquered. No matter how poorly we were taught statistics, or how vaguely we remember what we were taught, the fundamentals are so simple that we should use them when we need them. Certainly, we need them in cost analysis, particularly in the analysis of mixed linear costs.

If you are at a higher management level and subordinates or staff people are doing the actual calculations, you should be knowledgeable enough to ask the right questions. Only with the right questions will you be able to evaluate the quality of the cost data you are given. You should know how the costs were analyzed and identified and whether the lines were fitted by eye or by calculation.

To demonstrate how really simple this line fitting is, consider once again, as an example, the cost of power at the port grain terminal. The cost/activity data is repeated in Table 4-1.

**Table 4-1**

| Month | Millions of bushels handled | Cost of power |
|---|---|---|
| January | 15 | $ 3,200 |
| February | 10 | 3,500 |
| March | 13 | 3,600 |
| April | 15 | 4,100 |
| May | 18 | 4,000 |
| June | 21 | 6,500 |
| July | 22 | 6,100 |
| August | 23 | 4,900 |
| September | 26 | 6,800 |
| October | 28 | 6,000 |
| November | 30 | 7,000 |
| December | 19 | 4,300 |
| Total | 240 | $60,000 |
| Average month | 20 | $ 5,000 |

Because we scaled activity, namely, millions of bushels handled, out along the $x$ axis, we can call the sum of the $x$, or $\Sigma x$, 240 million bushels.

Because we scaled dollars of cost up along the $y$ scale, we can call the sum of the $y$, or $\Sigma y$, $60,000.

The number of occurrences, called $N$, is 12 because we are using twelve months of data. Thus, $N = 12$.

We have already seen in the discussion of mixed linear costs that:

Cost of power = fixed costs + slope of the cost line × bushels handled

To express this algebraically:

$$y = a + bx$$

By algebraic manipulation, which need not concern us here, we can develop formulas to calculate the $a$ and $b$ values. These formulas are:

$$b = \frac{N\Sigma xy - \Sigma x \Sigma y}{N\Sigma x^2 - (\Sigma x)^2}$$

$$a = \frac{\Sigma y - b\Sigma x}{N}$$

There are many formulas available to calculate these $a$ and $b$ values, but those given above are probably the easiest to use.

We already have $N$, $\Sigma x$, and $\Sigma y$. Obviously we need two more values, namely $\Sigma xy$ and $\Sigma x^2$, if we are to use the formulas to calculate the $a$ and $b$ values.

The $\Sigma xy$ is simply the sum of the results of multiplying each month's activity $(x)$ by each month's cost $(y)$.

The $\Sigma x^2$ is simply the sum of the results of multiplying each month's activity $(x)$ by itself, or squaring it.

For later use, though we do not need it for line fitting, we can also calculate $\Sigma y^2$, which is simply the sum of the results of multiplying each month's cost by itself or squaring it.

Our calculations and data are shown in Table 4-2.

Of course, if your calculator has one memory, you do not write down all those individual $xy$, $x^2$, and $y^2$ values. You allow the idiot machine to keep the accumulating total for $xy$ and for $x^2$, which are the cumulative totals you need for use in the formulas. Again, we do not need the $\Sigma y^2$ values for line fitting. However, we will have use for it later when applying another statistical tool so it is a good time to calculate it. Thus, we now have the following data for use in the formulas:

$$N = 12 \qquad \Sigma xy = 1{,}283{,}200$$

$$\Sigma x = 240 \qquad \Sigma x^2 = 5218$$

$$\Sigma y = 60{,}000$$

**Table 4-2**

| Month | Millions of bushels handled (x) | Cost of power (y) | xy | $x^2$ | $y^2$ (000) |
|-------|--------------------------------|-------------------|-----------|-------|-------------|
| J | 15 | $ 3,200 | 48,000 | 225 | 10,240 |
| F | 10 | 3,500 | 35,000 | 100 | 12,250 |
| M | 13 | 3,600 | 46,800 | 169 | 12,960 |
| A | 15 | 4,100 | 61,500 | 225 | 16,810 |
| M | 18 | 4,000 | 72,000 | 324 | 16,000 |
| J | 21 | 6,500 | 136,500 | 441 | 42,250 |
| J | 22 | 6,100 | 134,200 | 484 | 37,210 |
| A | 23 | 4,900 | 112,700 | 529 | 24,010 |
| S | 26 | 6,800 | 176,800 | 676 | 46,240 |
| O | 28 | 6,000 | 168,000 | 784 | 36,000 |
| N | 30 | 7,000 | 210,000 | 900 | 49,000 |
| D | 19 | 4,300 | 81,700 | 361 | 18,490 |
| Total | 240 | $60,000 | 1,283,200 | 5,218 | 321,460 |

First, we need to calculate the value of $b$, and then we can calculate the value of $a$.

To determine the $b$ value, we substitute our data in the formula as follows:

$$b = \frac{N\Sigma xy - \Sigma x\,\Sigma y}{N\Sigma x^2 - (\Sigma x)^2}$$

$$= \frac{12(1,283,200) - 240(60,000)}{12(5,218) - 240(240)}$$

$$= \frac{998400}{5016} = 199$$

The $b$ value is the slope of the line, i.e., how much it goes up the $y$ scale for every increment it goes out along the $x$ scale. Thus, in this case, power costs will increase $199 for every additional million bushels of grain handled. For simplicity's sake, let us round this off to $200 per million bushels handled.

Finally, the $a$ value is found where the line starts on the $y$ axis. It is the fixed increment of this cost. To determine the *a* value, we substitute our data in the formula:

$$a = \frac{\Sigma y - b\Sigma x}{N}$$

$$= \frac{60,000 - 200(240)}{12}$$

$$= \frac{12,000}{12} = \$1000$$

To state it in our terms:

$ of power cost = $1000 + $200 × millions of bushels handled.

This is the formula for the *least squares line* for this cost. The least squares line is the line so positioned in relation to the plotted points that the sum of the *squares* of the distances of the plotted points to the developed line is a *minimum*. Only one possible line can meet that definition. Any other line that you draw will result in a higher total when you add the squares of the distances of the plotted points from the line drawn. For that reason, the least squares line is justly also called the line of mathematical best fit.

M. J. Moroney once said that most things in this life are harder to explain than do. That is certainly true for least squares line fitting. It is really only simple arithmetic that will take you about ten minutes to calculate for twelve months of cost/activity data. Certainly it should be used for any cost of substantial size.

## CASE PROBLEMS IN COST ANALYSIS

There is no substitute for "hands-on" experience, and the only way to feel at ease with a statistical tool is to practice with it. For the reader who may never have used least squares, or who has not used it for years, it can be helpful to try a practice problem.

The enterprise is a job machine shop, one of the most common of all manufacturing operations. The activity measure is standard hours produced, and there are two costs that need analysis and identification. The first is operating supplies, namely, the miscellaneous supplies needed by the shop. The second is set-up labor, which is treated as indirect labor in this shop. This is the skilled labor that sets up the machine tools, produces the first pieces, has them approved by Inspection, and then turns the job over to a less-skilled operator who produces the quantity on the shop order.

The activity/cost data is shown in Table 4-3.

**Table 4-3**

| Month | Standard hours produced (000) | Operating supplies | Set-up labor |
|-------|-------------------------------|--------------------|--------------|
| J | 25 | 1700 | 3800 |
| F | 26 | 1900 | 4300 |
| M | 28 | 2000 | 4600 |
| A | 21 | 1650 | 3800 |
| M | 20 | 1600 | 3700 |
| J | 18 | 1150 | 2900 |
| J | 15 | 1100 | 2600 |
| A | 20 | 1400 | 3400 |
| S | 23 | 1600 | 3700 |
| O | 28 | 1650 | 4300 |
| N | 30 | 1950 | 4700 |
| D | 22 | 1700 | 3500 |

Draw up a scatter diagram for each cost and decide for yourself what kinds they are. How would you apply them in the shop's flexible budget? If one or both of them are mixed linear costs, state the formula developed by using the least squares formulas. Answers are provided at the end of the chapter.

## PRACTICAL POINTS ON LEAST SQUARES

Because so many of us in management have too little opportunity to make and use least squares calculations, a few practical pointers may be helpful:

1. Round off your data, particularly your activity data. If you are going to use your computer for the calculations, this is not necessary. But if you are going to use your desk or portable calculator, rounding off makes the calculation a lot easier. Round off activity to the nearest hundred, or even thousand, if the figures are large enough. Round off

your costs to at least the nearest fifty dollars. Any error that this rounding off introduces will be insignificant. Try one cost of your own first not rounded off and then rounded off, to prove it to yourself.

2. The least squares calculation will always result in some value for *a*, the fixed increment. However, if with a given cost, the *a* value is very small, you can consider the cost a pure variable. For example, if the cost amounts to, say, $2000 to $6000 per month, depending on activity, and the calculated fixed cost, or *a* value, comes to $20, draw the line from zero and apply the cost as a pure variable. In actual practice, the activity and cost data that you have available to analyze is very rarely accurate enough to justify the use of such a small fixed cost increment.

3. At times, the least squares calculation will result in a negative quantity for the *a* value. Things now can become difficult. You are on your own, and each case has to be handled on its own.

For example, sometimes you can still use the formula including the negative *a* value that it has, because the line best fits the data you have and is usable in the forecast range of activity. The only alternative you have is guessing.

Sometimes you can dig deeper into the extreme, out-of-line months and identify instances of cost mischarging. If you can correct the data, it may swing the negative *a* to a positive value.

Sometimes you cannot identify the mischarging in order to correct it. The bad practice is lost in the past. You only know that you have some distorted data because of mischarging. As a last, desperate measure, you might have to discard several of the months of bad data and use only the remaining months. This violates a principle stated earlier, namely, that you should be disciplined in your objectivity and not throw out an out-of-line month unless you have identified the underlying conditions as correctable. But the situation in question is extreme. For example, you have twelve months of data and a least squares line with a negative *a* value, and you question the whole idea of using the line. But you still want to avoid a raw guess. You analyze further and see that two extreme months are among the twelve and if you drop them, you will have a more reasonable line. You perhaps may have to do this, but show the operating manager involved what you have done and double check that the underlying cost mischarging conditions are corrected, so that you will not have to do it in the future.

This procedure is the one most often attempted when the cost analyst has bad, uncorrelated activity/cost data to work with and yet still wants to be as objective as possible, using what data there is. Ideally, it would be better never to resort to this. Instead, we should correct the underlying cost reporting defects and start collecting the correct data for future analysis. Unfortunately, we often need at least some estimates now. Under these harsh circumstances, using the ten months of data in the example above is probably better than just guessing.

Sometimes you can try pairing months, or using quarter-year periods or three- or four-month moving averages. Doing this for power costs at the grain terminal yields the results shown in Table 4-4.

**Table 4-4**

|  | a value | b value |
| --- | --- | --- |
| 12 discrete months in original data | 1000 | 200 |
| 6 successive paired months | 1057 | 197 |
| 4 successive quarter-years | 1221 | 189 |
| 10 three-month moving averages | 1245 | 191 |
| 9 four-month moving averages | 1293 | 191 |

You can have more practice in least squares calculations by checking the accuracy of the above values. You simply have to convert the activity and power cost data to six paired months, four quarter-years, ten three-month moving averages, and nine four-month moving averages. Then apply the least squares formula for $a$ and $b$ to each of the developed sets of data.

Sometimes your activity/cost data and relationships are so chaotic that the data is unusable. In that case your only recourse is to correct the underlying conditions and start the record afresh. Then in six to eight months you will have decent data to analyze.

4. Remember that the average values for $x$ and $y$, which the mathematicians call "bar $x$" ($\bar{x}$) and "bar $y$" ($\bar{y}$), always fall on the least squares line. For example, with the power cost at the port grain terminal $\bar{x}$ equals 20 million bushels handled, and $\bar{y}$ equals $5000 in power cost. If you examine Fig. 3-3 you will see that the intersection of these two axes falls right on the least squares line.

This fact provides us with the best and easiest check of the accuracy of our arithmetical calculations in computing the $a$ and the $b$ values. After they have been calculated, place them in the $y = a + bx$ formula with the value of $\bar{x}$. The $y$ value obtained will be the value of $\bar{y}$. If it is not, you have made an arithmetical error.

5. While it is not necessary to make a scatter diagram in calculating the least squares line, it is always helpful and advisable to plot the data on a scatter diagram. Then when you have calculated your $b$ and then

your $a$ value, draw the least squares line through the plotted data. The line helps to visualize the relationship between cost and activity and highlights out-of-line months. It is also another good check on the accuracy of your calculations. Drawing the least squares line through your plotted points is easily done. Your calculated $a$ value, plotted on the $y$ axis at zero value for $x$, is your first point and the start of your line. A second point is the $\bar{x}/\bar{y}$ intersection. Finally, calculate a third point, preferably at a higher-than-average activity ($\bar{x}$) level. These three points should fall right along a straight line. If they do not, you have an error in your calculations. In cost analysis work, when you deal preferably with only twelve months of data, this procedure is a very convenient check on your calculations. It also provides a very handy and clear presentation in reviewing your work with operating management.

In practical budgeting this entire process of scatter diagraming and least squares line fitting can have an excellent psychological effect on operating management. For example, you are analyzing the identifying costs and developing proposed budget cost allowances for a given department. When you lay your diagrams before the department head or foremen, you are offering evidence that you have dug into the matter, that the budget proposal is not based upon your individual judgment but upon the facts you have been able to assemble. You may not talk in terms of "sigma $xy$" of "sigma $x$ squared," unless the department head shows a particular interest, but you do demonstrate how you have developed the proposed allowances based on facts and sound arithmetical practice. Most of us have found that invariably the operating manager readily understands what you have done. Of even greater importance, he or she appreciates both the depth of your analysis and your explanation of your work.

The procedure is also effective at times when you have to deal with an operating manager who pushes hard for the maximum possible budget cost allowance. This is the opposite of the overoptimistic operating manager who wants an unrealistically tight allowance. This manager wants an allowance that is unrealistically loose. When you face the manager who wants more money than the facts indicate should be allowed, the scatter diagram presentation can be a real help in fighting off such demands.

## HIGH-LOW METHOD OF LINE FITTING

Another method of formulating a mixed linear cost that is frequently and unfortunately mentioned is the so-called high-low method. Under this method, you use only two months of your activity/cost data, namely, the busiest month and the slowest month. For both activity and cost, you then deduct the latter from the former, divide the cost difference by the activity difference and thus calculate the so-called slope of the cost. Finally, you apply the slope to either the busiest or the slowest month, or to both, as an arithmetical check, and calculate the fixed increment of the cost.

To demonstrate this method in the case of the power costs at the port grain terminal:

High—November     30 million bu—$7000 power cost
Low—February      10 million bu—$3500
Differences       20 million bu—$3500
Thus: $3500/20 = $175 per million bushels

Nov: $7000 − (30 × $175) = $7000 − $5250
                         = $1750 calculated fixed cost
Feb: $3500 − (10 × $175) = $3500 − $1750
                         = $1750 calculated fixed cost

The formula developed in this case by this method would be:

$ of power cost = $1750 + $175 × millions of bushels handled.

Contrast this with the formula developed by the least squares calculation:

$ of power cost = $1000 + $200 × millions of bushels handled.

Thus in this case, the high-low method would yield a poor description of the relationship between cost and activity. It would yield a line that allowed too much at low activity and too little at high activity, and the busier the terminal became, the tighter and more unrealistic would be the allowance calculated.

The only thing this method has to recommend it is its simplicity. It is completely inadequate for serious cost analysis and flexible budgeting because it assumes that two months are representative of the entire year. It ignores the other ten months of activity/cost relationship, or 83 percent of the data. In some cases, it can yield allowances quite close to the actual data being used. However, in each case you should determine whether it does or does not come close, by testing the developed formula against the twelve months of data you have. But by the time you have done this, you could have already completed the least squares calculation. In still other cases, the formula it yields can be completely undescriptive of the actual activity/cost relationship involved.

All in all, it is a crude approach, that would best be abandoned by all practitioners. Least squares is a simple enough replacement that does the kind of job we want to do.

## COEFFICIENT OF CORRELATION

It is a harsh and unfortunate fact that many operating managers and budgeting people do not have the activity and cost facts to do the kind of analysis and identification job that has been discussed. Those more fortunate, that do have adequate cost data, are often entirely satisfied to calculate a least squares line and let it go at that. This is human and understandable. After all, they are among the avant-garde in cost analysis and budgeting work. However, we should keep in mind that there are still other statistical tools that are applicable to our area of effort. Under the principle that each passing year should see us doing a better and better job, we should consider the use of these additional tools where they might be helpful in our individual situations.

It is possible to assign a numerical value to the degree of relationship between the two variables, i.e., activity and cost, we use in cost analysis. The statistical device to do this is the *coefficient of correlation*. This tool can be of practical help when you have, say, a choice of two activity measures and you would like objectively to choose between them. The activity measure that you want to use normally is the one that has the higher coefficient of correlation.

A perfect correlation has a coefficient of 1.0. When there is perfect correlation between two variables, the points plotted on graph paper will fall right along a straight-line pattern. Where no correlation exists, the coefficient is zero, or very close to it. The plotted points are scattered in a formless pattern all over the scatter diagram. Thus, the range of the coefficient of correlation can be from zero to one. (There is a negative correlation, but it does not apply to cost analysis for cost identification and budgeting.)

When we have a good correlation between our given activity measure and dollars of cost, we clearly have a basis upon which to predict what the cost should be in the future at these and other levels of activity. The higher the coefficient of correlation, the better the activity measure as a predictive base.

What is a "good" coefficient of correlation? There is no flat answer to that question. The coefficient of correlation is a measuring tool, and its qualitative meaning will depend on the use to which it is being placed.

In practical cost analysis, however, we can apply these statistical guidelines:

$$0— .20 = \text{no, or negligible, relationship}$$
$$.20— .40 = \text{low degree of relationship}$$
$$.40— .60 = \text{moderate degree of relationship}$$
$$.60— .80 = \text{marked degree of relationship}$$
$$.80—1.00 = \text{high relationship}$$

One further interpretative point should be made. We have seen that the coefficient of correlation is a quantitative measure of the relationship between two variables. We must not assume that it is necessarily a *causal* relationship. There are such things as nonsensical or spurious correlations. For example, there has been over a .90 correlation between the average salary of ministers and the per capita consumption of alcohol in the United States. This high correlation does not necessarily mean that these two variables are causally related. However, in practical cost analysis work, a causal relationship between the activity measure and cost is rarely a problem to identify.

The calculation of the coefficient of correlation in cost analysis is a simple arithmetic procedure using a rather frightening formula. It is really quite easy, using your calculator. The coefficient of correlation is designated as $r$ and

$$r = \frac{N\,(\Sigma xy) - (\Sigma x)\,(\Sigma y)}{\sqrt{N\,(\Sigma x^2) - (\Sigma x)^2}\,\sqrt{N\,(\Sigma y^2) - (\Sigma y)^2}}$$

Refer back in this chapter to the section in which the least squares line was calculated for power costs at the port grain terminal. In that section, the following data was developed:

$$N = 12 \qquad \Sigma xy = 1{,}283{,}200$$
$$\Sigma x = 240 \qquad \Sigma x^2 = 5218$$
$$\Sigma y = 60{,}000 \qquad \Sigma y^2 = 321{,}460{,}000$$

Substituting these figures in the formula, we have:

$$r = \frac{12\,(1{,}283{,}200) - (240)\,(60{,}000)}{\sqrt{12\,(5218) - (240)\,(240)}\,\sqrt{12\,(321{,}460{,}000) - (60{,}000)\,(60{,}000)}}$$

$$= \frac{998{,}400}{(70.82)\,(16{,}047.43)} = \frac{998{,}400}{1{,}136{,}479}$$

$$= .879$$

Thus, we have a quantitative measure that there is a high degree of relationship or association between our activity data and our power cost data. The calculation might strike you as belaboring the obvious. In this case, it is. But you might have occasions in the future where you must choose between two or more activity measures. In that situation, the calculation of the coefficient of correlation for the respective activity measures can be a real help in choosing which to use as a predictive or budgeting base.

## CASE PROBLEMS IN COEFFICIENT OF CORRELATION

Refer back to Table 4-3, which shows the activity/cost data for the job machine shop. To see how simple calculating the coefficient of correlation really is, try finding it for the operating supply cost and the activity measure, using the formula given above. Do the same for set-up labor cost. You might even want to do this for the clean-up labor cost at the port grain terminal. (See Chapter 3.) To check your calculations, answers are provided below.

## ANSWERS TO CASE PROBLEMS

### Answers, Least Squares Line Fitting

*Operating supplies, job machine shop.* This is a mixed linear cost, the calculation of which is:

$$\Sigma x = 276, \quad \Sigma y = 19{,}400 \quad \Sigma xy = 458{,}650, \quad \Sigma x^2 = 6572 \quad N = 12$$

$$b = \frac{N\,(\Sigma xy) - \Sigma x \Sigma y}{N\,(\Sigma x^2) - (\Sigma x)^2} \qquad\qquad a = \frac{\Sigma y - b\Sigma x}{N}$$

$$b = \frac{12(458{,}650) - 276(19{,}400)}{12(6572) - 276(276)} \qquad\qquad a = \frac{19{,}400 - 55.58(276)}{12}$$

$b$ = \$55.58 per 1000 std. hrs. produced $\qquad$ $a$ = \$338.32 fixed cost

Rounding these figures out, the formula for determining the budget allowance for operating supplies is:

\$ operating supplies = \$340 + \$55.60 per 1000 std. hrs. produced

Notice how easy it would have been to eyeball a line up from zero through the plotted points and thus call the cost a pure variable. The procedure would be easy, but it is not correct.

*Set-up labor, job machine shop.* Set-up labor is probably best applied as a step cost and tabulated as follows:

> From 15 to 20,000 std. hrs. produced     allow $2700
> Over 20 to 25,000 std. hrs. produced     allow $3600
> Over 25 to 30,000 std. hrs. produced     allow $4500

The plot shows a very good relationship between cost and activity. It could readily be described with the formula for a mixed linear cost:

Set-up labor cost = $674 + $134.82 per 1000 std. hrs. produced

However, the operating manager thinks in terms of adding or dropping set-up people as activity rises and falls. Thus, a mixed step cost, rather than a mixed linear cost, best fits the realities of shop operation and practical budgeting.

## Answers, Coefficient of Correlation

*Operating supplies, job machine shop.* For this case of activity/cost relationship the data for the formula is as follows:

$$N = 12 \qquad \Sigma xy = 458{,}650$$

$$\Sigma x = 276 \qquad \Sigma x^2 = 6572$$

$$\Sigma y = 19{,}400 \qquad \Sigma y^2 = 32{,}250{,}000$$

$$r = \frac{N\,(\Sigma xy) - (\Sigma x)\,(\Sigma y)}{\sqrt{N\,(\Sigma x^2) - (\Sigma x)^2}\,\sqrt{N\,(\Sigma y^2) - (\Sigma y)^2}}$$

$$= \frac{12(458{,}650) - (276)\,(19{,}400)}{\sqrt{12(6572) - (276)\,(276)}\,\sqrt{12(32{,}250{,}000) - (19{,}400)\,(19{,}400)}}$$

$$= \frac{149{,}400}{(51.85)\,(3261.90)} = \frac{149{,}400}{169{,}130} = .883$$

*Set-up labor, job machine shop.* For this case of activity/cost relationship the data for the formula is as follows:

$$N = 12 \qquad \Sigma xy = 1{,}072{,}100$$

$$\Sigma x = 276 \qquad \Sigma x^2 = 6572$$

$$\Sigma y = 45{,}300 \qquad \Sigma y^2 = 175{,}470{,}000$$

$$r = \frac{12(1,072,100) - (276)(45,300)}{\sqrt{12(6572) - (276)(276)} \sqrt{12(175,470,000) - (45,300)(45,300)}}$$

$$= \frac{362,400}{(51.85)(7317.79)} = \frac{362,400}{379,427} = .955$$

*Clean-up labor, port grain terminal.* Data for the formula is as follows:

$$N = 12 \qquad \Sigma xy = 708,250$$
$$\Sigma x = 240 \qquad \Sigma x^2 = 5218$$
$$\Sigma y = 33,650 \qquad \Sigma y^2 = 97,677,500$$

$$r = \frac{12(708,250) - (240)(33,650)}{\sqrt{12(5218) - (240)(240)} \sqrt{12(97,677,500) - (33,650)(33,650)}}$$

$$= \frac{423,000}{(70.82)(6309.32)} = \frac{423,000}{446,826} = .947$$

# BUDGETING'S POSITION
# IN THE ORGANIZATION

We pay dearly for poor organization. Unfortunately, the high cost of a poor organizational structure often cannot be measured because it is not recognized or admitted. Good budgeting and thus, effective cost control are most likely to be achieved when the enterprise is well organized and when the budgeting function is properly positioned in the management hierarchy. In this chapter, therefore, we will consider where Budgeting is best placed in the organization and how it should relate to operating management.

A good organization employs a working system of "checks and balances." No one function should dominate—not marketing, not engineering, not operations, not finance. This approach does not diminish the position or awesome responsibility of the chief executive officer, who is ultimately answerable for profit or loss. There can be only one captain—and that individual is also subject to checks. However, the CEO is wise to listen with equal intensity to the views of *every* function, and, what can be even more difficult, to induce all the functions to express their views and ideas under the existing personality dynamics and political structure.

In most operations of any substantial size, the task of budgeting is recognized as a separate function and is assigned to a budgeting staff. In their work, the budgeting staff has to deal with and relate to the various levels of operating management, from the department heads to the president. In small organizations, budgeting may be one of several jobs handled by one person or by a group performing other functions. However, no matter who is engaged in budgeting, the same principles apply.

## BUDGETING AS A JOINT EFFORT

A system of checks and balances in budgeting requires that the budget of a given department, plant, or division be established jointly by the operating manager and an independent budgeting staff. In some companies, the budgeting function is either understaffed or is simply a recording or accounting function, and in effect, the operating managers determine the budgets by themselves. This is *self-budgeting*. It is not good budgeting. (Conversely, you should not have an autocratic budgeting function, working unilaterally and imposing their standards and their ideas on the operating manager.) To be effective, good budgeting must be a shared and common effort.

The dangers of self-budgeting are obvious to the experienced manager:

1. The operating manager is usually already too burdened to do the kind of investigatory and analytical job required for good budgets.

2. Many operating managers, particularly at the department level, lack not only the time but the background budget training required. They need help, and this is not to their discredit. None of us can know everything.

3. Operating managers, being human, will tend to budget for the status quo. All human beings are inclined to resist change, and to accept present performance as future goals. Some managers will build in even looser budget allowances than previously used or, at the other extreme, will be overoptimistic in their goals and thus establish too tight and unrealistic budget standards.

Admittedly, operating budgets, particularly when tied into a profit plan, always are reviewed by successively higher levels of management. But this review does not necessarily avoid the last-cited danger. The poor budget standards that may be established under self-budgeting may not be detected. Worse, they might even be condoned—for the same very human reasons.

Realistic, progressive budgets that improve the operation require, therefore, a joint effort between the operating manager and an independent budgeting function. The budgeting people can provide the time required, and the training and experience in the accounting and organizational aspects. In addition, they have the independence, if properly placed in the organization, to advance ideas for better budget standards and cost allowance improvements.

Notice however, the psychological implications of this independence, the demands it places on the budget person, and the dangers that he or she faces. (Incidentally, they are the same ones faced by the practicing industrial engineer.) It can be all too easy for the budget people to develop the attitude that they are the monitors of company funds and that their success will depend on how many past faults and errors they can expose and push to correct. This attitude can only lead to resistance from the operating managers and a negative attitude on their part toward the budget. Admittedly, it is part of the budgeting staff's difficult job to detect cost and operational weaknesses and to prompt correction by better and tighter budget standards. But how they do this and what attitude they adopt are most important. Budgeting's orientation must be that they are a service function and that their responsibility is to help the operating managers detect their own areas of potential improvement, and set their own improvement goals. When possible, a budgeting person should advance ideas to them on how to achieve those goals. The end result of this work must be the operating manager's participation in decisions to change things and to improve the operation. It all demands sensitivity and skill in human relations.

## BUDGETING'S EFFECT ACROSS THE ORGANIZATION

The operating budget has great effects throughout the organization. Some of the effects are quite obvious, and others are much more subtle. How great the effects are will depend on the attention paid to the budget by senior management and on the location of the budgeting function in the organization.

Obviously the profit plan that is evolved from the operating budgets of the individual departments, and the performance to that plan, will have serious effects on the success and even survival of the enterprise. But there are also many more subtle effects. For example, performance-to-budget results often affect and determine capital investment decisions, expansions, and contractions. Most often, the better performers to budget find a readier ear when more investment is asked for. Furthermore, fixed cost allocations and fixed costs budgeted against departments, plants, divisions, or products can be affected by performance to budget. Not infrequently, the good performer and the higher profit producer may be penalized with heavier, and unjustified, allocations.

Finally, the human effects can be great. Managers may be rewarded, promoted, demoted, or let go because of, in part at least, their performance to budget. This, in turn, affects the organization and the political and power structure within that organization.

All this increases the importance of the proper placement of the budgeting function within the organization, as well as the responsibility of the function itself.

## BUDGETING UNDER THE FINANCIAL/ACCOUNTING FUNCTIONS

The financial and accounting functions are obviously interrelated. In some large companies, however, they are structurally separated on the organization chart with a treasurer in charge of finance and a controller in charge of accounting. In other large companies, the controller is directly under the treasurer or a vice president—finance. In some large and many medium-sized companies, the financial vice president or a controller handles both functions. In some medium-sized companies and many smaller companies, the title *Controller* may not even be used. Instead, a chief accountant handles, in part at least, the controllership function.

However, most enterprises today have a controller, and I propose that the budgeting function is best placed under the direction of that position for several reasons. First, one of the responsibilities of the controller is to identify areas of cost improvement. Second, the controller in most organizational structures speaks with an equal voice to the heads of the other major functions, such as marketing, engineering, and operations. This kind of position is significant to a budgeting effort since, as we have seen, budgeting can have great effects within an organization and across organizational lines. Thus, both the responsibility and the placement of the controller within an organization make him the ideal budgeting director. Fortunately, many, if not most, budgeting efforts are already under the controller's direction.

A relatively new development in some larger companies is the position of vice president—planning, reporting directly to the chief executive officer. This position has the function of developing the long-range plans for the enterprise but not necessarily overseeing the controllership function. Occasionally, you hear of the budgeting function being located under this senior management position, with the idea that the year's operating budget is the current expression of the long-range plan. Therefore, why not place the budgeting staff under the vice president—planning? The idea, however, can present some problems. The vice president—planning position has the function of concentrating on long-range planning and is not usually involved in any month-to-month or week-to-week control action, which is an integral part of operating budgeting. Such participation is normally considered a function of the controller. Some unfortunate conflicts could foreseeably arise between the vice president—planning and the controller, under these circumstances. Additional strains and demands on operating managers might also develop if such conflicts occur.

There is one practical difficulty with the budgeting function located under the controller. Historically, the controller's position has, in fact, been primarily accounting oriented. The full scope and implications of the controller position have not been applied, or even recognized, in many cases. Too many controllers are, in effect, chief accountants. And this situation is not good enough to insure an effective operating budget effort. Obviously, the controller of any enterprise has to have a good knowledge of accounting, but in order to oversee the budgeting function, he or she must also have an in-depth understanding of operations. Of equal importance, the people under the controller, particularly those doing the budgeting, must have an in-depth understanding of operations. They must know the realities of operations, the problems of the operating managers, the things that are possible today, and the things that need group action and outside support if they are to be done by a given department. This brings us to the operations/accounting interface.

## THE OPERATIONS/ACCOUNTING CONFLICT

One of the most helpful things an operating manager can have is an accounting function that knows the realities of the operation and has developed an understanding of his problems and needs. With this kind of support, the operating manager will be provided timely facts that help him make better decisions and take more precise action. Even better, he has other minds working with him that contribute additional ideas to his own thinking. As one lucky plant manager said to me at a seminar, "I have the controller with me, and all he wants to know is how can he help me more."

In contrast to this happy situation, I've witnessed over the years what can only be called a "conflict" between operations and the accounting function. I didn't realize how prevalent this situation was until I started conducting public seminars. Many operating managers who attend express their judgment that the accountants they work with:

> are not realistic.
> are too inflexible.
> don't understand the operating manager's problems.
> don't provide the kind of information they really need.
> if they do, it comes too late.
> think the purpose of the business is accounting.

On the other side, accountants will tell you that the operating people:

> don't understand accounting's needs and purposes.
>
> turn in careless and erroneous data on such vital matters as time reporting, piece count, and material usage.
>
> expect the impossible.

It is the classic interfunctional conflict, similar to the one that exists, so often, between marketing and production. But we must overcome it if we are to achieve effective operating budgets, because the accounting department provides much of the budgeting data, issues the performance-to-budget reports, and when Budgeting is under the direction of the controller, it is responsible for the budget itself.

Why does the conflict ever exist? If we can answer that, we have the beginning of a solution. Like so many human relations problems, the answers are to be found on both sides. Some of the causes, I believe, are:

1. Intransigence or just plain stubbornness. The operating manager believes his or her job is a big one, but so does the accountant. Each feels it is up to the other guy to adapt, to understand, to serve the other's needs.

2. Ignorance, on both sides. The operating manager doesn't understand the needs of the accounting function, because he or she has not had the training in that function, or because any rudiments the manager once might have learned are now forgotten through disuse. The accountant doesn't know enough about the operation and the working problems of the process, material, labor, etc.

3. Fear, on both sides. The operating manager regards accounting as an arcane subject, full of esoteric terminology. He or she doesn't realize

how easy it is to learn how accounting records are kept and how the data for his or her segment of the operation ties in with the data for the other segments to report the total results of operation. The accountant, on the other hand, can be awed by the complexities of operations, particularly in a manufacturing enterprise. Accounting is a specific field, and the accountant often doesn't appreciate that a great deal more about the operation can be easily learned by getting out into it and asking questions. In fact, the accounting person will be pleasantly astonished at how willing the great majority of the operating people will be to answer any questions. They will be pleased by this interest.

4. The top management orientation of accounting. The accounting function deals directly with top management. Its P&L, balance sheet, and other statements and reports are generally aimed upward for senior management use. As a result, it is very easy for the accountant to forget that much of the data for these statements and reports comes from the first line of management, the department heads. Accounting's work is dependent on these operating managers.

Operating managers worth their salt should set out to learn enough about accounting in their company to understand not only what the accounting staff needs but why they need it. Managers should ask questions until they know how their part of the operation and its performance ties in to the rest of the operation and how that tie-in is reported and accounted for.

The accounting function must be ever aware of and sensitive to the fact that it is a *service* function with a large responsibility to serve *all* levels of operating management. Part of that sensitivity is the realization that it is easier for them to learn more about operations than it is for the operating manager to learn more about accounting. As a result, they should take the lead in the cross-familiarization required. They are vitally needed by those operating managers.

One of the first steps that Accounting can take is to conduct a crude "attitude survey." Get out into the operation. Talk to department heads and their bosses. Ask what questions and problems they have. In these conversations, you can get insights into their attitude toward accounting as well as the specifics of their operation. You also might find some ways that you can be of further service to them.

The budgeting function, under the controller, is ideally positioned to demonstrate to the operating managers the service orientation of accounting. Their work in budget follow-up, in budget maintenance and in the use of the budget, requires their involvement with operating managers. In effect, they can represent both budgeting and accounting.

To many operating men, the two are one and the same. The budget function can transmit budget/accounting problems and help work toward solutions. When they initiate this service, they help build up understanding and respect on the part of both the operating managers and accounting for the problems they both have. And this atmosphere will surely contribute to the effectiveness of operating budgets.

Probably the greatest single practical difficulty is lack of time. Many budgeting people and accountants will tell you that they just don't have enough time to visit the operations and to talk to the operating managers. In some cases, the plea is not justified. They could rearrange and reschedule their work and open up at least a little more time, if they gave this matter the priority it deserved for their own and the operation's benefit. In other cases, the plea is justified. The most common error is to understaff the budgeting function, at least in its follow-up aspects. This will be discussed in Chapter 13, on budget follow-up and maintenance.

# SEQUENCE OF THE BUDGETING PROGRAM

Developing and maintaining good operating budgets are big jobs. The larger and more complex the operation, the bigger the job. It takes time, an adequate staff, and thus, money. It is important that management, particularly senior management, realizes what work is involved. This observation grows out of the fact that too many executives at seminars say things such as, "Yes, just last week our foremen were told to start preparing next year's budget." When you think of all the work involved in a budget program, you can only believe that in such situations, the management may not realize what is involved in the budgeting effort. Certainly, it is more than the foremen can do themselves. Therefore, in this chapter, let us review the sequence of the budget program, the work involved, and the necessary working relationship between operating management and the budget function.

## INITIAL REQUIREMENTS FOR BUDGETS

There are certain basics that are needed, on site and working, before good budgeting is possible. Some of these are rather obvious and present no problem to most enterprises. Others need more recognition and achievement. These basics include the following:

1. You need a clear-cut operating organization and well-defined cost centers or departments that match the actual organization as it really works. Simply, you need to know *who* is responsible for making *what* budget.

If subcenters are used in large departments, they, too, must match the organization, even though they may still be the responsibility of the lead foreman or department head. This can be particularly important if specific individuals are in charge of each subcenter and/or wide differences exist in the nature of the operations of the various subcenters.

This basic requirement is no great problem in most organizations. And here operating management owes a debt to the accounting function with its concept of responsibility accounting. Under responsibility accounting, or activity accounting, as it is sometimes called, costs and operating facts are identified and accounted for by segments of the enterprise. The segments used are the various departments of the organization.

However, it is not unusual, particularly in smaller companies, to encounter such situations as the following:

a. A single budget is developed and performance-to-budget reports issued for a very large department managed by a general department head under whom other managers direct parts or subcenters within the department. A gross example of this is the situation where a plant that is one of several within a division has a budget, but no budget is provided for individual departments within the plant. Under these circumstances, the plant manager has no way of knowing what managers under him are responsible for the actual performance to budget. The budget simply is not refined enough for the working organization.

b. Operating managers have no organization chart and express pride in the fact. Their pride is based upon the belief that theirs is a flexible situation, with everyone working together very closely and all sharing a mutual responsibility, i.e., the successful management of the operation. They consider organization charts as indicative of too rigid thinking and as potentially confining to the group. Some of these situations work quite well, but usually misunderstandings and conflicts develop as the enterprise grows. An organization chart in itself need not result in operating rigidity; if it does, the enterprise would probably have the same problems without the organization chart.

To repeat the basic requirement: You have to know what operating manager is responsible for what budget.

2. You need a good chart of accounts. Thus, the cost data must be collected and charged under an accounting system that yields the kind of operating cost data in the detail needed by operating management, i.e., marketing, engineering, manufacturing, or operations in a service company. Many companies have charts of accounts that meet the needs of the financial/accounting functions but that are inadequate for the needs of operating management. This was discussed under the chapter on cost analysis, but it can bear emphasis.

Typical of the kinds of problems you meet in this area are the following:

a. One or more substantial cost items are lumped together into a motley, catchall account. As a result, the identities of these substantial cost items are lost, and no one, especially not the operating manager, has the time to analyze monthly costs in the catchall account and segregate the items. A good example of this can be perishable tooling in a metal-working department. It is not uncommon to see perishable tooling, which can be a costly item over a month's time, dumped into the general account called "Operating Supplies." This might be adequate if perishable tools is a small item. Where it is not small, it deserves its own account.

b. Furthermore, an acute problem, often mentioned at seminars, can exist in large, multidivision companies, when corporate management requires organized, uniform, and prompt accounting data. To achieve this, Corporate issues a chart of accounts for divisional and plant use, but that chart fails to meet also the needs of the individual operating plants and the departments therein. The stories that you hear on this subject can be particularly plaintive on the part of operating managers of what were once single-plant companies. The companies were bought out and each plant is now run as one part of one division of a large corporation. The new owning corporation imposes its chart of accounts and accounting system. Suddenly the local managers are without the cost detail they are used to having and on which they have depended. This situation can be particularly prevalent when the owning company is composed of divisions of widely varying nature. Such unfortunate situations need not occur. There are too many instances of multidivisional companies owning a wide variety of enterprises which maintain their recording flexibility in order to meet the needs of both local operating management and corporate management. They do it by the artful handling of well-defined subaccounts used, or not used, at the discretion and need of local management.

A good chart of accounts represents a successful balance between too little and too much detail. Admittedly, there seems to be no limit to the cost data needs of an aggressive operating manager. He or she always wants more detail and that can mean a heavier accounting workload and greater danger of reporting and accounting error. However, more and more accounting functions have the use of the computer, and as a result, more detail and data can be handled at no, or quite small, additional cost. Also, accounting as a service function has the responsibility of providing the needed data unless the demands are obviously unreasonable.

Again, the basic requirement and principle bears repeating: The chart of accounts must meet the needs not only of the financial/accounting function but also of the operating managers at all levels.

3. You need well-defined and reasonably disciplined cost-charging procedures throughout the organization. This means that for purchased expense items, Purchasing or Accounting or whatever group is involved in applying account numbers to the vendor's invoice must be accurate and consistent in their cost charging. It also means that the stockrooms for material, parts, or supplies must be policing the charge numbers they are given or they are using. You will never realize absolute accuracy in all this but you do need reasonable adherence to this requirement.

Some commonly encountered problems in this area are the following:

a. A fairly expensive operating supply item is used by both the maintenance and the operating departments. To spread the cost, one delivery is charged to Maintenance, the next delivery is charged to General Factory. This might overcharge either department.

b. A person from one department can go to a stockroom, withdraw parts, tools, or supplies, and use another department's charge number.

c. A given expense item is charged to one account one time and to a different account another time. An example might be purchases of high-speed steel drills, with one purchase being charged to Perishable Tooling, and the next to Operating Supplies.

d. An indirect labor person is temporarily transferred to another department for a day or two, but his or her pay is still charged to the home department.

e. Maintenance among the many jobs to which it is charging parts and labor has one that is large and ongoing. Gradually, it becomes a catchall to which they charge the overages from other smaller jobs.

The examples are endless and the point obvious. If you have these or like situations to a serious extent, you are not ready for good operating budgets. For effective budgeting costs must be charged to the correct department and in the correct time period, i.e., at least within the proper budget month.

## SEQUENTIAL STEPS IN BUDGET DEVELOPMENT

Having established the initial and basic requirements, we can examine the sequential steps included in the development of the operating budget. If your enterprise already has effective flexible budgets, some of, if not all, these steps are being done each budget year. However, if you are currently installing flexible budgets or revitalizing weak budgets, many of these sequential actions will have to be taken.

1. The initial step is the development of a sales forecast, which is essential for two reasons: First, if we are to use the operating budget as a profit-planning mechanism, we need to plan our income as well as our costs. Second, we need to know the activity range within which we must be prepared to vary or flex our budget allowances.

Some writers on the subject of budgeting have maintained that a sales forecast is not essential for budgeting. This view can be defended if you limit your thinking to the second reason listed above, i.e., the definition of the expected activity range. You can, by good cost analysis, be prepared to establish budget allowances for a very wide range of activity and forgo any prediction of the expected activity. However, when you include in your operating budgeting its use for profit planning, a prediction of expected revenue is absolutely essential.

Many companies and enterprises have great difficulty with developing a sales forecast. However, it is so important a subject and so integral to profit planning that it deserves its own separate consideration in the next chapter.

2. The predicted product units needed for the forecast sales must be translated into terms of units of operational activity. These units are the measures of physical activity applicable to your particular type of operation. They may be standard hours produced, machine hours, tons, dozen, gross, bushels, or whatever applies.

In this step, one of the basic rules of budgeting again becomes obvious: To budget you need *standards*. To translate the forecast product units into terms of activity measures, you need standards of the number of activity units per unit of product.

In simpler operations, such as the grain terminal, the activity might be expressed in terms of the product itself. Thus, bushels handled is the activity measure used (see Chapter 3). Even here, however, we need standards for budgeting. When we budget labor costs for barge unloading, railroad-car unloading or ship loading, we need to determine the standards of how many bushels per hour the crew should produce on each of these operations.

Many of us have more complex operations to budget. We manufacture a varied line of products, or we perform a varied list of services. In these cases, we need, wherever possible, one activity measure expressed in terms of a common denominator such as hours, i.e., standard hours, machine hours. Obviously we need standards of how many hours per unit of product A or service A, or product B or service B, etc. The nature and source of these standards vary widely between companies. In some companies the only standards available are "guesstimates" off the top of the head of operating management or, at best, based on a minimum of historical data. In other companies engineered standards for measuring operator performance have been established, and a computerized bill of material explosion translates forecast product units to be sold into departmental activity measures.

In some industries, multiple activity measures are used. For example, in glass bottle manufacturing, *cwt pulled* is the activity measure in the tank department where the glass is melted, and *forming machine hours* is the activity measure in the bottle-forming department.

This translation of product or service units into activity terms is the step that provides the measure of flexibility for flexible operating budgets.

3. For each department or cost center, it is necessary to determine which particular activity measure is most applicable. Usually it is possible to select a single activity measure for each department. This is desirable because it makes the budget development and application much more practical and understandable to operating management. Fortunately, it is a relatively rare situation where more than one activity measure must be used in a given department. When this is the case, some analysis and thought should be given to breaking the department up into subcenters, because this multiplicity of needed activity measures can be indicative of too large a department or, at least, one with more than the desired variety of operations contained within it.

As previously stated, the ideal flexible budgeting situation is the one where a single type of activity measure can be used in every operating department within the organization. An example of this happy situation is a metal-working company such as a machine tool plant. There, *standard hours produced* is the activity measure for each and every production department. In other industries, a single activity measure is either not possible or not used because it does not allow as effective an operating budget as the use of several activity measures. The glass bottle plant mentioned above is an example of this latter situation.

4. The next step is to determine what costs must be budgeted for each department. In most situations, this has already been determined by the accounting function, which prescribes the costs charged against the department by the chart of accounts and by the accounting system used.

However, operating management, and the budget staff working with them, should not blindly accept the status quo. It is their responsibility to question existing cost-charging practices and ask for changes if they can prove the need. Such possible changes are particularly important to consider and effect when budgets are being first installed or revitalized.

*A case in point.* The maintenance department of a major airline at a major airport wanted better communications with its dispersed working crews and, therefore, needed walkie-talkies. They tested one installation costing $7000 and found it entirely usable. However, the communications department of the same airline had responsibility for all communications equipment used. They selected the equipment, and the cost was charged to their budget. The communications department insisted on their right to specify the equipment used by the maintenance staff and purchased a $21,000 system. Maintenance happily agreed. After all, the system was not being charged to their budget. The difference in the costs of the two systems was $14,000, and a lot of passengers are needed to make $14,000 in profit. Obviously, if the using department, maintenance, were being charged with the cost, the company would have ended up with the entirely usable $7000 system. Budgets can increase costs if the accounting cost-charging procedure is not correct. In such a case, the budgeting staff should be pushing to have the additional costs incurred by a department charged against that department. The fundamental accounting system should be changed.

A parallel situation is found in many manufacturing and service enterprises. There is no charge-back of maintenance work to the using departments. As a result, the enterprise loses the benefit of the check that such charge-backs provide. If a department is being charged for its maintenance jobs, the department heads tend to be more frugal in what they ask for. Also, the maintenance effort has the department heads watching that time and material are not being wasted and charged to their operation.

5. Next, historical data must be collected on what has been spent in past time periods for each cost account. Where budgets already exist and where cost charging has been reasonably accurate, much of this data is available on the performance-to-budget reports. However, operating conditions change and the budgeting staff working with the operating manager must know enough about the operation to realize where historical data cannot be used, as it stands, to develop the new budget. The money spent in the past might be too much or too little for the new situation.

In practice, however, I have found that in most situations you need this historical cost data for at least a starting point. Certainly where there have been no affecting changes in operations, it is the best base you have to work with to develop the new budget.

At times, it is also necessary to dig deeper into the past data and to segregate it into its component parts. For example, this can be required when (a) operating changes coming in the foreseeable future might require more, or less, money for one of the cost components in the cost account, or (b) a catchall account such as Operating Supplies has several major cost elements contained within its total historical costs and you want to examine past cost levels for each major one individually.

6. Analyze each cost in each department and determine if that cost is to be budgeted as fixed, variable, or mixed. If it is a mixed cost, determine if it should be treated as linear, step, or even, in rare cases, curvilinear. This, of course, is the cost analysis work discussed in Chapter 3.

If flexible budgets are already in use, this step usually requires only a review of the last twelve months to check the relationship between the cost and activity during those periods. In the case of fixed or pure variable costs, this review will determine changes in cost levels that might, as yet, not otherwise have been detected and that should be recognized in the new budget's allowances. In the case of mixed linear costs, this step enables you to check whether the fixed cost portion or the slope of the line has changed. In the case of mixed step costs, it indicates whether the height and depth of the steps, as currently in effect, are still applicable. Finally, for all types of costs, it is a necessary step to insure incorporating operating cost improvements into the new budgets being developed.

If you are developing flexible operating budgets for the first time in the enterprise or revitalizing poor budgets, you have basic determinations to make in this step. You are not simply checking whether or not past budget allowances should be changed in the light of the past twelve months' actual experience. You are building *new* budgets. This step, under these circumstances, is integral to the determination of budget allowances.

7. On the basis of the analysis made, budget allowances for each cost in a given department are determined as follows:

    a. A flat allowance per budget period is made for fixed costs.

    b. Formulas are established for variable and mixed linear costs.

c. Tables of allowances are developed for step mixed costs.

This, of course, is the step toward which all else was leading.

Consider these steps 1 through 7. The sales forecast, step 1, should be developed by Marketing. Theoretically, the other six steps, 2 through 7, should be a joint effort between the operating manager of the department and the budget staff. All too often, this is not possible as a practical reality. The operating manager is just too busy to become deeply engaged in these steps, and therefore has to look to the budgeting staff to do the data collection and analysis work involved.

While doing the cost analysis work, the budget person inevitably develops personal ideas as to what the budget cost allowances should be for each given cost in a department. He (or she) should do this. However, these are only his ideas, his proposal. It is the operating manager's budget that he is helping to develop. Therefore, he must have that manager involved in establishing the budget allowances from the facts revealed by the cost analysis.

Presenting a fully developed budget proposal, complete with cost allowances, to the operating manager can be a real danger to the budgeting effort. Exposed for the first time to the budget as proposed, the manager can readily develop the conviction that it is being given as an accomplished fact. It may be called a "proposed" budget, but the manager can readily believe that it is really the finished budget because of too little time, and perhaps training, to analyze and question it in detail. This is an all too human reaction.

The action to avoid all this has to be taken by the budget person, particularly as he takes step 7. He can perform the preceding five steps to a great extent unilaterally, but he has to have the operating manager involved in the development of the proposed budget allowances. The best way for him to do this is to make the analysis required, then take the report, including any graphs, and discuss everything in detail with the department head. Afterward, both the budget person and the manager should develop the budget allowances. Even better, as the analysis is being made, the budget person should visit the department head and present an informal progress report. He should also ask questions as to operating conditions in the recent months and foreseeable future. He should solicit the operating manager's ideas on any questionable points. He should expose his analysis work as it develops.

The problems, the steps to take, the psychology involved all vary greatly, of course, with the local situation. Where effective budgets have been in use in the recent years, there is no difficulty in obtaining the operating manager's time and attention. Where there have been no budgets, or poor budgets, the budget person may have to persuade, even harass, the operating manager to engage in the effort. He can encounter anything from indifference to overaggressiveness. But he has to take the responsibility and the lead in getting the operating manager involved.

The range of actual practice is tremendous on this vital step 7. In companies in which the budgeting staff is purely a data-collecting function, the operating managers determine their own allowances. In effect, there is self-budgeting. At the other extreme, in some companies, the budgeting function under the financial function, despite what may be said, has the final say on the budget allowances. This is budgeting by fiat.

When you encounter one of these extremes in actual situations, you can sometimes also hear horrified disavowals that it even exists. It is only when you search behind the facade and see how things are actually working that you identify it as a fact. In these cases, you usually find serious budget problems such as unrealistic budget cost standards or indifference on the part of the budgeting staff or operating managers. Which particular series of weaknesses you find will depend on where the power lies.

Good budgeting, of course, is not the result of power plays, which are all unnecessary and too costly. Good allowances are the result of a mutual effort by operating management and the budgeting function. It is an easy thing to talk about, but a successful joint effort can be difficult to achieve. It takes a great deal of understanding and effort, particularly on the part of the budget people. But it is a necessary requirement for effective budgets.

8. The next step is the profit-planning step. Activity has been forecast by month. Cost allowances have been budgeted for all the departments at the forecast activity. By taking the difference between forecast monthly income and budgeted costs, profit is projected for each month and then for the year in total, thus establishing the profit plan.

Notice that the effect of this sequence, as specified here, is to calculate the planned profit *after* the forecast and the budgeted cost allowances have been developed. The projected profit is not calculated by applying a desired profit percentage or return on investment to the forecast sales income and then assuming that the difference, i.e., sales minus profit, is available for budgeted cost allowances. This is a nice and pleasant method but it can be seriously unrealistic. Unfortunately, it often represents the basic orientation of senior management.

Although senior management is responsible for seeing that realized profit yields an acceptable return on investment, they must recognize that budgeted cost allowances should represent the factual needs of operational life and, therefore, cannot be realistically altered to any great extent. If their total, when deducted from forecast sales income, does not yield the desired profit level, then senior management must take additional action. Sales or the product mix must be improved, or cost reduction programs must be initiated. These are serious and longer-range programs that take careful planning and direction to effect.

There are some amazing "games" played in this profit-planning step. In fact, the matter of "budget games" is so important to good operating budgeting that it deserves its own individual consideration, and will, therefore, be the subject of Chapter 15.

9. A statement of budget policy and procedures should be written and distributed to all levels of operating management. This statement should present for the record such matters as:

a. Senior management's policy on the enterprise's need for and use of the budget

b. How they will follow up on the budgets and how they want lower levels of management to follow up on them

c. How they want operating management and the budgeting function to interrelate in budget development and maintenance

d. The budgeting procedures that will be followed in such areas as budget performance reports, changes to budget allowances, and extra-budgetary allowances

Such a written statement of budget policy and procedures covering the above matters, and any other considered necessary, can be an important aid towards good budgeting. This step is not necessarily the last in the sequence. Much of the statement should be developed during the initial planning for the budget. It is a step that should be taken, whether a budget is being installed for the first time, whether a serious revitalization program is underway, or whether budgets are in successful use right now.

Communications between human beings is always difficult. When the organization is large, the problems can be horrific. Innocent misunderstandings can occur so readily that the best thing to do is to put the budget policy in writing. The statements should be simple and clear.

They should not read like a lawyer-written contract. They are for the understanding, guidance, and memory of operating managers and budget people. Once again, the responsibility usually falls upon the budgeting function, who writes them for senior management's approval.

## BUDGET MAINTENANCE AND FOLLOW-UP

To complete the specification of the budget sequence, it is necessary to discuss the steps involved in the budget maintenance and follow-up. As budget periods pass, there obviously must be periodic reports of the actual performances to budget by the various sections or departments within the organization. The most common practice is to issue monthly performance-to-budget reports. Many cost items, such as indirect labor, tooling, maintenance, power, and operating supplies, are most practically controlled and reported on in monthly terms.

Weekly budget performance reports are not uncommon, but usually the cost items reported on at these weekly intervals are the very large costs such as labor and material. In fact, if the only cost control tool available for these large cost items is the operating budget, weekly reports of budget performance should be used for these items. Better cost controls than budgets over these large items are such techniques as engineered labor standards and labor efficiency reports, material usage and scrap reports. But many enterprises do not have these to use. As a result, they must utilize the budget as the control mechanism. If they must, weekly budget performance reports are desirable. In such instances, a complete budget performance report is usually also issued once a month covering all the budgeted costs in the department.

There should also be periodic follow-up sessions between the individual operating managers and the budget people. Such follow-up sessions are necessary to:

1. Identify changes in operating conditions that might require budget changes

2. Investigate possible needs for one-time extra-budgeting allowances

3. Answer questions and reinforce training in the operating budget

4. Detect progressive operating action usable elsewhere in the organization

5. Keep budget personnel current with changing operating conditions

This particular step of follow-up is the area in budgeting in which so many well-started plans begin their decline. As such, it deserves individual consideration later on, in Chapter 13.

# FORECASTING AND BUDGETING

Sales forecasting is so integral to profit planning, and so many companies have problems in this area that we should consider together:

Why a forecast is needed
Who has the responsibility for the forecast
The problems frequently encountered
The techniques available
The timing of the forecast's revision

## THE NEED FOR A SALES FORECAST

We have already seen in the discussion of the sequence of a budget program that a sales forecast is one of the requirements for a *complete* operating budget. Our cost analysis, when properly done, may enable us to be prepared to vary or flex our costs as activity changes over a fairly wide range. For that use, we can circumvent a missing or bad sales forecast. But for profit planning, which is one-half of the operating budget, a usable sales forecast is an absolute essential. It provides one of the key increments of the profit plan, i.e., sales income. It is the base upon which we calculate our projected costs and thus, our planned profit.

However, profit planning is only one of many important reasons why a realistic and usable sales forecast is needed. One of the major needs is that of the production planning and control function in its development of a sensible master production schedule. A manufacturing operation is a relatively inflexible unit. (This can apply also to many service enterprises.) You do not lightly and easily change your capacity up or down a great amount. It takes planning, time, training, and money. If the operation is treated as a yo-yo, going up or down to every vagrancy of sales demand, you inevitably spend more and make less profit than you should. In too many manufacturing companies a great deal of money is unnecessarily spent and wasted in repeated attempts to adjust capacity to short-term fluctuation in market demand. The cost is particularly high on the upswings. Open-shop orders increase, work-in-process turnover decreases, broken setups increase, capacity utilization decreases, late orders increase—all because attempts are made to change capacity in an unrealistic, unplanned, and too rapid manner. One, if not the major, function of production or operations is to service Marketing, but the balance between service and efficient operations is too often impaired and profits suffer. And the painful fact is that usually these costs are never measured. Being unmeasured, they are not recognized and they are allowed to recur.

Admittedly, you can usually react more immediately to a sharp decline in demand than you can to a sharp increase. But even in cutbacks, you have operational realities that can often limit, or at least slow down, your flexibility. Your only hope, in either case, is to establish a sensible master production schedule, and that, in turn, requires a usable sales forecast.

Allied to the need for a sales forecast when planning a master schedule is the need for the forecast by inventory planning. Good inventory planning to yield a competitive inventory turnover and a satisfactory return on the inventory investment is a requirement for the service company as well as for the manufacturing operation. In fact, in some service industries, the need is even more imperative. Their very existence can depend on good inventory planning. Too much stock on the shelves and a limited borrowing capacity can put them out of business.

This, in turn, ties in with the needs of the financial function for a usable sales forecast. This need applies to any type of company. If the financial function is to make effective use of company funds, they have to achieve adequate cash flow and capital investment planning. This depends on capacity scheduling, inventory planning, and operating decisions, and these tie right back to a usable sales forecast.

All this is rather obvious, but the needs for a good forecast are frequently not recognized, as we will see when we examine some of the forecasting ploys that are so frequently encountered.

## RESPONSIBILITY FOR FORECASTING

The principle advanced here is that only the marketing function can have the responsibility for sales forecasting. Marketing is the function that has the opportunity and the means to keep current with the latest in market developments and trends. How can such functions as production planning or budgeting or finance be expected to be knowledgeable about all the "random walks" of the market place? In very large companies or "sophisticated" situations, a special forecasting group, under Corporate Planning, may do much of the economic analyses and may apply the forecasting techniques used. But in this observer's judgment, in all cases the ultimate responsibility for the task and for its results must be assigned to the marketing function.

Next, the forecast, as issued and authorized by Marketing, must be stated in terms not only of money but also of product units and types or models. Where a manufacturing enterprise has different product lines and different models or types within product lines, the sales forecast should be stated in those terms. Only by stating their forecast in this way can Marketing fully meet its responsibility for the underlying data upon which the master production schedule will be laid down.

It is not unusual to see executive (top) management accepting a sales forecast from Marketing that is stated only in money terms, by, say, product lines. But for each product line, there is no breakdown of what particular model or types will be sold. As a result, the production planning and control function must then do the forecasting in terms of its final and needed detail. In effect, Production Planning and Control is taking the responsibility for the forecast as it is finally scheduled in terms of models. This is not good enough. Production Planning does not have enough familiarity with the market. When they have to do this forecasting, they must rely only on past sales data. They may help Marketing with data collection and recent trend projections but they cannot be expected to bear the ultimate responsibility for the sales forecast. Only Marketing can have that responsibility.

Clearly, it is up to executive management to recognize this basic marketing responsibility for usable sales forecasting. It is at that senior executive management level that the responsibility can be properly assigned. That level of management can see that the task is carried out as well as it can be with the talent available, and under the conditions within the industry and the general economy.

Sales forecasting is a difficult job under even the best of circumstances. Some of our largest companies spend great sums of money for computers, statisticians, and economists to do forecasting. With such resources, a company can do a great job for a number of years and can then be caught flatfooted by a sharp change in the economy or a change in the political climate. For the smaller companies, without the resources to do a sophisticated job, the difficulty is even greater. You just cannot expect always to be right. But you can assign the job to the function where it should best be done, i.e., marketing, and then follow up to see that it is done as well as possible under the given circumstances.

In practice, executive management frequently does not assign and enforce this forecasting responsibility to Marketing and in turn Marketing, very humanly, does not assume it, and this can hurt both marketing and company results. For example, if the enterprise makes to stock, the size and turnover of finished good inventory which depends on Marketing's forecast can have a major impact on sales and profits. Or if the enterprise makes to order, the availability of needed material and production capacity will determine lost sales and future profit levels. Either way, marketing results will be affected by the quality of the forecast used. Therefore, Marketing should welcome the forecasting responsibility.

## FREQUENTLY ENCOUNTERED FORECASTING PLOYS

In the face of the many needs for a sensible sales forecast and the clarity of it being Marketing's responsibility, the unfortunate fact is that, in many companies, it all does not happen as it should.

It is not uncommon for an independent outsider to study a company and its operations and find not one but five extant forecasts in use within the enterprise. These include:

> One by Production Planning for master scheduling
> One developed by the budgetary function
> A very "secret" one within Marketing
> One by the treasurer for cash-flow planning
> One by top management for "long-range strategic planning"

And what is so striking are the differences between these individual forecasts.

Usually, this unfortunate situation results from the fact that the various management functions which need a forecast, for budgeting, production planning, or for other reasons, have had one of the following responses from Marketing:

1. "How should we know?"

2. The "shrewdie" response, in which Marketing provides a forecast but is playing it very safe and intends to beat any forecast they give out.

3. The "red-blooded optimist" response, in which the forecast from Marketing, on the basis of any reasonable extrapolation of the recent past, is obviously overoptimistic. This is probably the most commonly encountered phenomenon.

When these other management functions receive such nothing or nonsense answers, they are forced to make their own forecasts.

All this is, of course, the fault of top or senior management because they have not clearly assigned the forecasting responsibility to the marketing function, where it belongs. Or if they have so assigned it, they have not enforced the assignment and have not held Marketing responsible for the reasonable accuracy of past projections.

I hope this situation does not exist in your company, and in your experience you have not received such responses from Marketing as any of the three listed above. However, when I ask attendees at budget or at production planning and control seminars if they have encountered these responses, over 50 percent say they have.

These observations are not meant to be negative or derisive. Instead, they are meant to specify a too commonly encountered problem. It is only by recognizing our problems that we can do something about them. And this problem has its solution at the highest management levels of the enterprise. But first it must be recognized.

## CHOOSING AN APPLICABLE FORECASTING TECHNIQUE

Market forecasting is in itself a subject for a book, and thus cannot be covered in detail here. However, operating managers and budget people should at least be familiar with the various methods that are employed.

The variety of techniques available can be categorized into subjective (or qualitative) and into quantitative groups. However, this is somewhat misleading, because the maker of a forecast should recognize that any method he uses, no matter how highly quantified, or how sophisticated the mathematics, still involves a great deal of judgment and subjective decision making. For one thing, the basic selection of what mathematical tool to apply is a judgment. But the more programmed the approach, and the more rigorously applied the necessary judgments, the greater the likelihood of improving the forecasts.

Before considering some of these techniques, it is important to consider the basic factors that underlie the selection of the forecasting technique to be used.

Possibly the most important factor is the intended use or uses of the forecast. If the forecast is needed primarily for sensible production planning and budgeting, as is the case in most companies, then a sales-force composite may be entirely adequate. If, however, major decisions on costly research and development programs, or capital investments that will be felt over the next decade of operation, are being contemplated, then a longer-range forecast is needed, and the factors and techniques to be used are more intangible and much more complex.

Management recognition of the need and value of adequate forecasts will determine the resources in time and money available for the forecasting effort. The less recognition there is, the simpler and less expensive the techniques that can be used. Similarly, the degree to which the need for better forecasts can be identified and quantified will also have a great effect on the technique used. Senior management, very properly, tends to conserve corporate assets. They want a projected measurable benefit for the cost incurred in applying a technique which is new to the enterprise. If the past cost effects of no, or poor, forecasts can be measured, then there is greater likelihood of having more time and money approved for using better techniques and making better forecasts. Unfortunately, it can often be most difficult to put a money value on the past effects of no, or poor, forecasts.

Among the most widely used forecasting techniques are the following:

## Sales-Force Composite

This is probably the single most effective forecasting technique for the small or medium-size company. It is a subjective approach that collects from each salesperson or sales representative an estimate of the anticipated sales volume, by product, to be expected from his or her territory or each customer. Ideally, an independent set of estimates, by territory, is collected from sales supervision. Then the two sets of estimates are compared and differences are reconciled.

*Pros:*

1. It requires each salesperson to analyze in a systematic, programmed manner, the environ in which he or she operates. The thinking must be by product and by customer.

2. It utilizes the judgment of the individuals closest to the market.

3. It results in a detailed forecast by product and by geographical area.

4. The routines involve a check because two estimates are being compared.

*Cons:*

1. The danger of overoptimism must be recognized and overcome by holding sales supervision, and even salespeople, responsible for making actual sales equal to their forecast.

2. Conversely, the danger of understating the forecast must be recognized and overcome by stressing the need for realism and the important part that marketing personnel, as management, play in the forecasting function.

3. Such forecasts usually fail to indicate market turning points, either up or down, or basic changes in the marketing environ.

4. Reliability can only be reasonably expected for the short-term, probably less than a year.

5. Basic usability is for existing products, not for new products.

## Market Survey

This is basically a subjective approach. It entails identifying the industries and companies that make up the market for a company's products. Then a sample of these companies are surveyed by personal contact to solicit a response on their buying plans for the coming year. From these sample responses the total industry market potential is developed, to which the company's anticipated share of the market is applied, to arrive at the forecast.

*Pros:*

1. It requires an in-depth study of the present and potential market, which, in itself, is a new and positive step for many companies.

2. In a limited market environ, it can produce a good short-term forecast.

*Cons:*

1. Serious, thought-out responses can be difficult to obtain from the companies sampled, particularly noncustomer companies.

2. The accuracy expected varies inversely with the number of companies involved in the industry and the number of industries that are customers for the company's products.

3. The technique is normally most usable for existing products or direct replacements for existing products, not for new products.

## Expert Consensus ("Delphi Method")

This is another subjective method that utilizes the considered, independent judgments of "experts" from within the company and, if available, from outside the company. Under this technique, a panel of executives are selected who should be most knowledgeable about the future market potential. They are then polled independently to obtain their estimates of future sales, together with their statements of the assumptions that lie behind the forecasts they have made. These may be called preliminary forecasts. An independent coordinator then collects these estimates, summarizing them from high to low and summarizing the underlying assumptions. The summary is then discussed in detail with the executives as a group, with each encouraged to defend or argue against any of the assumptions stated. Individual forecast quantities are not discussed. Second independent and private forecasts are then submitted by each executive, and from these a final forecast is developed. Varied refinements to this basic procedure are commonly used.

*Pros:*
1. It solicits the best thinking and experience available to develop a forecast.

2. By the private development of forecasts on the part of individuals, it tends to avoid the "bandwagon effect" and the exertion of undue influence from higher-placed executives.

3. It allows correction of preliminary forecasts.

4. It exposes all concerned to the thinking of others, i.e., their logic and assumptions.

5. It offers independently developed consensus in areas of great uncertainty, such as new product introduction.

*Cons:*

1. Frequently, such forecasts are not developed in sufficient detail as to product line and geographical area.

2. In practice, this can be a time-consuming process, and obtaining the timely, well-thought-out responses to the repeated forecasts can be difficult.

3. If done without quantitative projections from past data, it is entirely subjective.

## Time Series Projections

This broad category of forecasting techniques includes the quantitative approaches that apply statistical procedures to the job of forecasting. Essentially, these techniques use the past as a predictive base for the future. They include the following:

*Moving averages.* Past sales for individual specified periods are totaled, and the total is divided by the periods included in the total. Then one or more of the earlier periods are dropped, an equal number of later periods are added, and a new moving average is calculated. A series of such moving averages are then used to serve as a base from which the forecast is extrapolated. Under this procedure, equal weight is given to each period included in the moving averages.

*Exponential smoothing.* This refinement of the moving average approach gives a greater weight to the latest periods by applying an *alpha* factor that emphasizes the quantitative inputs of the most recent periods. Within this one technique, there are many variations and refinements that can be applied.

## Trend Projections

This technique takes past sales history and mathematically fits a trend line to the data. The trend line is then extrapolated to develop the needed forecast. The line or curve that best fits the data can be a straight line, a second-degree equation, a logarithmic equation, or another type of curve. Of all the available equations, the equation best fitting the data can be determined by least squares analysis.

All the above time series projection techniques are more effective for relatively short-term forecasting, up to one year, and less effective for longer-term forecasts and for predicting market turning points.

## Causal Methods

These forecasting techniques attempt to express mathematically the causal relationships between relevant economic and social indicators and company sales. They are the most sophisticated of all forecasting techniques. Some of the more widely used methods are:

*Regression models.* Economic and social indexes (such as new construction starts, number of college graduates, age distribution of the population) are selected as having a causal effect on company sales and are tested by correlation (regression) analysis. If a correlation is found, there is a basis for projecting a forecast.

*Econometric models.* This causal technique is closely allied to regression models, but it is statistically more complex. It utilizes a series of regression equations that correlate past company sales to a number of relevant economic and social indicators, which then serve as a predictive base for the needed forecast.

*Leading indicators.* This technique is closely allied to time series projection and seeks to identify one or more economic activity time series that have preceded the movement of company sales. If such a series can be identified, it serves as the basis for the sales forecast.

*Input-output models.* This technique is based upon the economic research of Leontief and utilizes the interindustry flow of goods that affect company sales.

All these causal methods require a major investment in staff and money and to date have been made use of only by the larger corporations who have the financial resources to make such investments. They are aimed at longer-term forecasting and the detection of market turning points.

## TIMING FORECAST UPDATING AND REVISION

Forecasting is the act of predicting, and it is unrealistic to expect to do this perfectly for even the year ahead, much less the five-year period ahead. Conscientious, ongoing updating and revising are, therefore, an integral part of the forecasting process.

The application of such forecast revisions will depend on a number of factors, such as the following:

*The nature of the market.* The more volatile the market in the industry involved, the more frequent the need for prompt forecast revisions. Under such marketing conditions, inertness in the face of fast-moving changes can lead to lost sales opportunities or obversely, the building up of excess inventories.

*The nature of the product and process.* The longer the manufacturing lead time required, the less frequent can be the forecasting changes, and necessarily, the longer the period of forecast commitment. For example, in heavy equipment manufacture with its "feast or famine" cycles, the forecast for making basic machines is a firm commitment that once made cannot economically be revised. In such situations, the timing of forecast revisions usually coincides with the length of the manufacturing cycle.

Other process factors that affect the application of forecast revisions are the labor skills involved and the existing plant load. The lower the level of labor skills needed, the prompter, usually, the possible implementation of forecast revisions. The greater the open capacity of the plant, the prompter, usually, the ability of adjustment to upward forecast revisions.

We have already mentioned the unfortunate fact that some top managements treat their manufacturing facilities as a yo-yo. They expect a flexibility from their production functions that is completely unrealistic. Because of top management's position and authority, the production management function meekly obeys the orders and attempts to do the impossible. Often the result is chaos—sharply rising costs, large increases in work-in-process, increases in late deliveries, and tremendous personal pressures on not only production, but on most of the other management functions including purchasing, engineering, and even marketing because of delivery problems.

The solution to this frequently encountered situation is senior management's understanding of the realities of production and careful use of good forecasts in a well-thought-out plan of operations.

*The uses of the forecast.* The forecast has many uses and each of these determine, in practice, how effectively revisions can be implemented.

For example, under conditions of a sharply changing market, the marketing forecast might be reduced, but the master production schedule may not be revisable because the parts are already started in process. Or if additional needs are forecast, the lead times involved do not permit the immediate increase of production schedules.

In another example, the forecast is an integral part of the company's profit plan, and in practice, the usual method followed is to maintain the profit plan and all its integrated operating department budgets for the year despite changes to the market forecast. The exception to this is, of course, the unfortunate situation where a very firm forecast of a rapidly falling market demands immediate downward revisions in the budgets and the profit plan. Notice, however, that while this may be done in the case of a sharply falling market, it does not normally occur when the sales forecasts are revised upward. In that happy circumstance, the market forecast revisions, most commonly, are not built into the current year's profit plan. That plan remains unchanged. Instead, they are built into the next year's plan.

Obviously, some of these factors are conflicting. For example, a company may be in a quite volatile market yet have a relatively long manufacturing lead time. In such situations, the need for good initial forecasts is apparent. In some industries, these factors blend together very happily—the market is relatively stable, the production lead time is relatively short, the labor skills involved are relatively low. But even in these happy situations, the need for good forecasts and prompt revisions to them should be recognized because with them the most efficient operations and improved profits can be realized.

Regardless of how promptly the forecast changes can be implemented in the operation, it is still Marketing's task to revise the existing forecasts as soon as the need arises. As a very general rule, the market forecast should be thoroughly examined at least every three months. A frequently encountered practice is to hold the forecast firm for the current three months and revise as necessary, on an ongoing basis, the future three quarter-year periods beyond the current quarter-year. However, the profit plan as originally laid down is not changed for the budget year unless a major reduction to the original income forecast is indicated.

# DEVELOPING BUDGET ALLOWANCES

The actual step of developing budget allowances will vary with the kind of cost, the amount of money involved, the nature of the operation, and a host of local conditions. Developing the allowances can be simple or extremely difficult. For example, when operating conditions are stable, the cost analysis itself may develop the allowance. In contrast, where operating conditions are in a state of great change, what is, in effect, a pure estimate has to be developed. Because the actual work involved in establishing cost allowances varies so widely, it is impossible to establish specific steps to be taken. We can, however, consider some common problems and some approaches to those problems. (The discussion of cost analysis in Chapter 3 included examples of establishing budget allowances for power, for operating supplies, and for certain aspects of indirect labor.)

Before discussing some specific cost areas, however, let us first review the role of the budgeting function when it is working with operating managers to establish budget allowances.

## BUDGETING'S ROLE IN DEVELOPING ALLOWANCES

The point has been made that effective budgeting is a *joint* effort between the operating manager and the budget function. There should be neither self-budgeting nor budgeting by fiat. A joint effort gives the budgeting function a substantial share in the development of budget allowances. In effect, the budget person is speaking as an equal to the operating manager when they work together to establish the allowances. The budget staff cannot adopt the policelike attitude that they are the sole guardian of company funds. However, they must accept their responsibility to state what the cost facts indicate. They must also feel free to present their own judgments when too few facts are available to make a purely objective decision. In turn, the operating manager must have an open mind and a willingness to consider the facts and the judgments presented by budgeting personnel.

As previously discussed, the budget person who is working with operating managers to establish budget allowances will encounter a great variety of situations, personalities, abilities, and reactions. He or she has to adopt an approach suited to the needs of each case. Some department heads will depend a great deal on Budgeting's ideas and judgments. In fact, some will be overdependent. They will examine the past cost facts that are presented to them, recognize that the budget person knows a great deal about their costs and accept whatever he or she proposes. In a relatively stable operating situation, these "passive" managers represent no great danger to themselves as far as budgeting is concerned, as long as the budget person is intelligent and honest. However, if operating conditions are changing or if major changes are coming within the near future, these quiescent managers can be dangerous to themselves and to their budget. The budget person may not be made aware of the coming changes, or may be innocently ignorant of them and their possible effects on costs. The nonparticipative manager is not being deceptive; he or she just does not recognize what the possible future effects might be. The experienced budget person, knowing a great deal about the operation, should ideally know of coming developments, and be able to ask the right questions as to their effect on this given department. But the odds on better allowance development are greater if the operating manager is not passive.

Some department heads will be overoptimistic in estimating their cost needs or their cost performance for the coming budget year. This experience was discussed in Chapter 3 under the subject of tightening allowances on the basis of poor correlation between past actual costs and actual activity. There the example was given of a budget person who makes the proposed allowance lower than the past actual average cost and an operating manager who proposes an even tighter allowance. This phenomenon is rather hard to believe, but enough of us have encountered it that it demands mention. The operating manager, like the budget person, cannot be permitted to be overoptimistic, particularly where there is no reason for it, or where there is no thought-out cost improvement program underway to support achieving that low a cost. In such a case of overoptimism, the budget person must "push" for realism on the basis of the past cost facts which have been collected and analyzed.

On the other hand, some department heads will be aggressively determined to make their budget life as safe and easy as they possibly can. They push hard for as big an allowance as they can obtain. They wrangle over every item, no matter how small, and advance every conceivable argument to increase their past allowances on every item. All this is very understandable. It is only human to ask for enough to be safe. According to the "rules" of the budget games that some managements play, this is the only sensible procedure to follow. In rebuttal to such demands, the good budget person submits the past cost facts to the manager and keeps insisting that together they give these the greatest weight. The budget person tries to arrive at a sensible allowance, even one that demands some cost improvement if evidence or strong judgment indicates that such is attainable. If they cannot agree on this, then the budget person and the department head must take the matter up with higher authority. This, of course, should be the step of last resort. In practice, a department head who gets to know the budget person better learns to trust and respect him or her as an equal. When that happens, it is rare that this last step is needed or taken. The budget person needs patience, persuasiveness, as many facts as can be collected, and a good knowledge of the operation. But even after mutual trust and empathy have been established, the budget person still must expect an occasional aggressive attempt from this type of operating manager.

All this is not meant to be a diatribe on operating managers. The majority of managers will not react this way. But some will. The various discussions have been meant to exemplify the varieties of human beings and human experience that are encountered in management and budgeting. Effective budgeting people must have the understanding and intelligence, and patience, to adapt themselves to all the various types of managers with whom they work.

In some budgeting situations, the budget is being set for a new department or for one or more departments in which immediate and big changes are in sight. In these uncertain situations, there may be no past cost facts to guide either the operating manager or the budget person. They both have to become cost estimators. They just have to project as best they mutually can what is most likely to happen and estimate the best cost allowances possible. In the case of honest differences on the cost levels anticipated, the operating manager's judgment should prevail, unless there are obvious grossly high estimates being advanced. The more time they both can spend breaking down the foreseeable situation and examining various alternate courses of operating action, the likelier they are to develop better cost allowances in situations with ever changing conditions.

## DIRECT LABOR ALLOWANCES

We have learned that direct labor in manufacturing is the labor which adds value to the raw material used to make a product. It is a well-understood class of labor cost in that kind of industry. In service industries, it is a labor-cost category that is much less used, often not used at all. However, the concept is applicable: in a service business direct labor is the labor or personnel engaged in performing the service being rendered, e.g., nurses and technicians in a hospital, waitresses and counter-people in a fast-food chain, stockmen in a warehouse.

Before dealing with the development of direct labor budget allowances, it is necessary to specify a few basics about labor performance and thus labor costs:

If you place a trained operator at a machine, a secretary at a typewriter, or a sweeper to a broom, with plenty of work in sight, and that is all you do, you will get 40 to 60 percent productivity. This is a maxim of work-measurement experience. An exception to this is an assembly line where the speed of the mechanized line establishes the pace. An automatic machine may be another exception, assuming prompt stock feeding and alert machine attendance. A few individuals are also an exception to this rule. But considering any operating enterprise as a whole, exceptions to this productivity maxim are very, very rare. I have seen one such enterprise in thirty years of consulting.

If you establish labor standards for work measurement, i.e., measuring individual operator performance, you must do three things: establish the standard, tell the operator what the standard is, and then tell him how he performed to the standard. If you do this, you are using *measured daywork* as your standard, and labor cost control, and you can realistically work toward achieving an 85 percent performance. Notice that if you have standard labor costs for, say, product standard cost purposes, you do not have labor standards for work measurement. You only have labor cost standards, which are not told to the operators. Nor are they told how they did to the standard.

If you establish labor standards and then offer incentive bonuses for above-standard performance, you can reach 125 percent average performance. If you average over that, you have to worry about the accuracy of your standards.

The above three points are generally accepted basics in work measurement practice. Any experienced operating manager is aware of them. And, of course, they force us to the conclusion that to control labor costs, we must have labor standards and work measurement. It would be grand if there were another way, if we knew enough about human motivation and had the practical techniques to motivate the enterprise as an entity to the operating performance the working group is capable of achieving. But until we do, the means to use are labor standards and work measurement where it's practical to apply them.

How you will establish direct labor budget allowances will depend on whether your operation has work measurement, only standard labor costs, or no labor standards at all.

In those enterprises where labor standards have been developed and applied, whether for daywork measurement or for incentive plans, the standards can and should be used to develop the budget allowance for direct costs. Most daywork measurement installations express their standards in terms of standard hours per piece. Most incentive plans use either standard hours or piece work values, i.e., so much money per unit produced. Whether the standards are in terms of standard hours or piece work values, they can be used to develop budget allowances for direct labor.

For example, in the case of a standard hour plan for daywork measurement, the usual procedure for direct labor allowances is to calculate a dollar cost per average standard hour produced and factor it upward by the average efficiency or performance achieved in the past under the plan. Thus, if the average performance under the daywork measurement plan has been 85 percent of standard, the weighted average labor cost is divided by 0.85. This is done by department or cost center because average labor costs and efficiencies can vary sharply between departments. Notice also that you have to be reasonably sure of the weighted average labor cost and past average efficiency. If these are seriously in error, the operating manager can develop unearned favorable variances or undeserved unfavorable variances.

When the enterprise has an incentive plan, the budget function can establish very accurate allowances for direct labor. When they do, the operating manager in charge of a department has good measures of his labor cost performance. For example, he can develop favorable variances by improving his average efficiency or by reducing his average hourly labor cost by the labor grade "mix" he uses. Conversely, he can develop unfavorable variances with a decline in average efficiency or by using a higher-cost labor grade mix. In any case, it is a good and just measure of his efforts.

In using these labor standards to develop the profit plan, the starting base is the sales forecast and its resultant master production schedule. Your standards tell you how many labor hours of cost are needed for each product unit, you know how many units are planned to be made, and the extension of the two facts yields your planned labor cost, after factoring in expected average efficiency.

In other enterprises, labor standards are not in use for work measurement, but standard labor costs are developed by accounting for standard product costing. Here we usually can and should use these standards for developing budget allowances for direct labor. In these cases, the average hourly labor cost must be factored upward by the unfavorable variance percentage recorded by accounting. Or, more rarely, the average hourly labor cost must be factored downward by the favorable variance percentage recorded by accounting. In such enterprises reasonable accuracy is just as necessary when calculating average hourly wage rates as it is when using labor standards that are also being used for work measurement. Finally, the average hourly wage rates and variance percentages usually have to be calculated for each individual department.

Although product standard labor cost data should be used to develop budget allowances for direct labor, it often isn't. In some cases, both the budgeting function and operating management do not have enough faith in the accuracy of the standard labor costs. In such situations you can only wonder at the accuracy of product standard costs and the wisdom of the product prices. In other cases, the accounting standard cost data is not recorded in sufficient detail. For example, labor cost variances may be calculated on only an operation-wide or plant-wide basis, and the actual variance percentage may be known to vary widely between departments. Under those circumstances, the data is not available to develop realistic labor budget allowances by department. In yet other cases, the budgeting function just does not have the staff or the facilities, such as computer time, to assemble and analyze the cost accounting data and make the necessary calculations.

Developing direct labor budget allowances is a more difficult task where no labor standards, or at least, no standard labor cost data, are available. And invariably the budget allowances are more crude or "rough." Where no standards are available, the operating manager and the budget function have to establish, together, their own standards. Usually, the standards are calculated and expressed on a product-unit, or operation-unit, basis, such as man-hours per 1000 bushels, per patient days, or per 100 orders, i.e., standard hours per unit of activity. Such rough budgeting standards generally have to be developed by the budgeting function, sometimes with the assistance of industrial engineering, and then reviewed with the operating manager.

In enterprises in which the only form of labor cost control is the operating budget, control is relatively crude and encompasses too long a period of time to allow really good control. The point should be reiterated here that the operating budget is not a substitute for engineered individual work measurement standards. But if the budget is all you have, then you should invest a good deal of effort and time so that your budget labor standards are a realistic and just predictor of labor costs.

One final point should be made to the operating manager and budget person involved in establishing direct labor budget allowances. Standard costs, including those for direct labor, are invariably developed from historical data if there are no engineered work measurement standards on site. You have to use your own judgment based on recent labor cost experience, or you have to use historical cost records equated to past levels of activity. In either case, historical records of an unmeasured labor cost situation have to be utilized. And we have seen that unmeasured labor is 40 to 60 percent effective. If this is true, there is some room for labor cost improvement. You may not believe this to be true in your own operation. However, it is worth checking your labor cost situation by work sampling.

*Work sampling* is the random sampling of the work performed by a group of employees to determine the proportion of their time spent in doing their jobs to the amount of idle time. By a series of observations taken at random times, you determine not only the proportion of idle time, but the kinds of delays that are reducing productivity. The technique has certain striking advantages:

1. It is easy to use; anyone can take the observations.

2. It is economical, and less time is required to achieve initial results than with work standards.

3. It can be used where the work is varied and nonrepetitive.

4. It is readily understandable by operating management.

5. It has a calculable reliability, so that you can have faith in its findings and can use them with assurance.

Work sampling is a well-proven technique of work measurement that is too little used. It can tell you some surprising things about both your labor's performance and your operating conditions. Most important to budgeting, it can help you establish better labor cost allowances, i.e., allowances that incite some needed labor cost improvement action.

## INDIRECT LABOR

*Indirect labor* is the "support" personnel that does not work directly on the product, or does not directly render the service(s) performed by the enterprise. In a manufacturing operation, they would include such support labor as quality control, material handling, tool crib and toolroom personnel, receiving, and shipping.

The cost of this type of labor usually does not react as closely to changes in activity as does direct labor. In fact, in many cases it does not react at all, except to upward changes in activity when overtime costs increase. It is not unusual to see the same work force kept on in these indirect labor areas when activity drops 20 to 30 percent. In the case of some types of indirect labor, there may be no solution. For example, toolroom labor is laid off as only the last resort. Good tool workers are too hard to find. However, there are often indirect labor areas where greater cost flexibility can and should be achieved.

This cost area can be particularly important to the operating results of the smaller and the medium-size enterprise. It may not usually be a matter of life or death, but it can have a definite effect upon profit, and the funds the company has available for development and growth. Many of us believe that maintaining steady employment is a socially desirable objective. But we must also remember the reality of Sam Gompers' statement that the worst enemy of the working man is an unprofitable company.

The operating manager and the budgeting person should be alert to building in flexibility where possible in indirect labor cost areas. A hardcore staff should be budgeted, and temporary help utilized for the peak periods. Again, this is not possible in all indirect labor areas, but the question has to be asked, "Where can we do it?"

In developing indirect labor budget allowances, it is rare that work measurement standards are available. Very few enterprises utilize them for indirect labor. In most cases, the operating manager and the budget person must agree on the indirect labor force needed. Wherever flexibility is possible in the indirect labor area, you almost invariably have a mixed step cost and you establish manning tables for different levels of activity.

The operating budget is the best single means most of us have for controlling indirect labor costs. As a result, it is a cost area in which the operating budget can be not only a cost control but a means to cost improvement. Because of this, it is important to avoid careless or superficial budgeting, as is so often done in this area. Establishing budget allowances for indirect labor costs warrants care and attention. We do not want just to preserve the status quo. Work sampling should be periodically done at various levels of activity. (This technique has as much applicability in indirect labor cost areas as in unmeasured areas of direct labor, perhaps even more.) The findings of the work sampling can very often yield much more objective and realistic manning tables.

## OVERTIME COSTS

Most of us have found by experience that the only way to control overtime is with eternal vigilance. As soon as you take your eye off it, it starts to edge upwards. One of the tools of vigilance available to us is the operating budget.

Overtime cost allowances can be very difficult to determine. Overtime is affected by so many factors over which we may have no, or little, control: the vagrancies of the market that suddenly impose more "rush" orders, unexpected equipment failures, acts of God such as fires and floods, and power failures. They all can and do occur, and the result is usually more overtime.

One pragmatic point to make is that budget allowances for overtime costs should be estimated separately for each individual department. If a uniform overtime allowance, such as a flat 3 percent of direct labor, is set for every department, the result can be an automatic favorable allowance for some production departments and a completely inadequate allowance for others. For some departments there might be no allowance needed.

*A case in point.* At one electronics plant, the budgeting procedure was to allow a flat 3 percent of direct labor as an overtime allowance for every department. The result was an automatic favorable variance for some production departments and a completely inadequate allowance for others.

Furthermore, in using historical data and trends for this cost item, exercise special care. The data might include overtime costs for some unusual conditions that since then have been corrected. Analyze the data for unusually high months or a series of months and try to identify what happened in those periods to cause the high overtime costs.

Unless the cause can be expected to recur in the next budget year, it is careless budgeting to build those same cost levels into the coming year's budget.

Similarly, in a new budget or budget revitalization situation, both the operating manager and the budget person should look with a critical eye at past overtime costs and consider the use of lower allowances for the new budget. If no budgets or poor budgets have been in use, it is often possible that overtime costs have not been properly controlled.

## DIRECT MATERIAL AND SCRAP

Profit planning is done for the enterprise as an entity, and budgeting material costs and scrap are an integral part of the profit-planning portion of operating budgeting. However, material and scrap costs are frequently not budgeted for each individual operating department. There are exceptions to this, but in many companies, material usage and scrap data is not available by department, and as a result, costs cannot be placed on work-center or departmental budgets. Instead, we must settle for total operationwide costs for these two items when we develop the monthly actual results to the profit plan.

How we can develop the budget allowances for material and scrap for the profit plan will depend on each given situation. In some cases, there are bills of material and we can "explode" them, using the computer, if needed and available, to predict what the planned production should cost to make for material and scrap. In other cases, budgeting has to use Accounting's standard material costs which are most commonly based on past material usages and variances. Usually, these cost standards are for the overall operation and not by operating department. In still other cases, if accurate bills of material are either not available, or nonexistent, special engineering studies for each design to be produced might be needed. Or as a last resort, we might have to use past ratios of material costs and scrap costs to some product, or to some activity measure such as machine hours, direct labor hours, etc.

Too often in these situations, the actual monthly material usage is a "book" figure, and it is not until a physical inventory is taken that we know the true figures for material usage and scrap. This can be particularly dangerous when the physical inventory is taken only once a year, because there might be, and not infrequently is, a good discrepancy between "book" and actual inventory. When that happens we realize that we did not, in fact, make the profit reported as "actual" in the past months. Where this once-a-year determination of the difference between book and actual material cost is great, it is a warning to operating management that corrective action is needed in the area of material cost control. To the budget person, it is a warning that the budget standards for material and scrap are too optimistic.

Certainly, it is a truism that we should, wherever practical, record material usage and scrap, by cost center or department. And where it may not be practical for material usage, it still may be possible for scrap costs. If there is any common error in this budgeting area, it is not to spend enough to record the facts. We know everything in total and for too long a period. We do not have enough detailed information as to where the material and scrap costs actually occur. The problem increases in importance with the percent that material costs are of the cost of sales.

The budgeting function can have a very important role in improvement action in this area. For example, the present material usage and scrap reporting can be reasonably adequate to meet the needs of accounting for profit-and-loss reporting, and the discrepancy between end-of-the-year actual and book material figures may not be great enough to alarm operating management. However, it is possible to improve the reporting routines and detail and thus accumulate material usage by, at least, plant area and scrap reporting by department. In such a case, it is probably the budgeting function alone that will push for the action and changes. Accounting and operating management are satisfied with the existing records. If budgeting is successful in their efforts, and manage at least to obtain scrap reporting by departments, there might be real gains to be made in scrap reduction, once the detailed data is available. And again, the greater the material content and costs, the more rewarding the action.

It can be quite difficult to collect scrap costs by department. In some cases, it is difficult to assign scrap responsibility. But we can be dealing here with one of the major cost areas, involving tens of thousands, and in some cases hundreds of thousands of dollars, a month. Such costs deserve attention and detailing because a small percentage gain can pay for the collection effort many times over. Without that detail reporting, by department wherever possible, you just do not know enough to take improvement action. For example, a certain corrugated box plant reduced its overall loss on material usage from 11 to 6 percent by determining scrap loss by department, i.e., corrugating, printing and slotting, fold and paste. It was a relatively small plant, but every 1 percent of scrap reduction meant, at the time, an additional $22,000 a year directly into profit. This is a memorable illustration of how much can be saved when you have complete scrap records, and use that data to take corrective action.

Yet another problem in budgeting material costs for profit planning is reckoning in the effects of anticipated inflation. We are each on our own on this one. We should, however, try to specify, where we can, the bases for our guesses. One source is the collected explanation and findings of our purchasing function plus their judgments as to what they can see coming. On major materials they can often come quite close for one year ahead. Where applicable, we can make some extrapolations from, say, specific Department of Labor Wholesale Price Indexes.

## MAINTENANCE COSTS

This is one of the great areas of uncontrolled costs. Only a very small minority of enterprises have developed and are applying work measurement standards. In most companies, the effectiveness of this particular cost varies directly with the ability of the maintenance managers.

Probably the most common procedure used in most companies is to have a maintenance department or cost center and to charge to that center all maintenance labor and expensed material costs. If this is the practice in your company, the maintenance manager and the budget person together must estimate the money required in the coming budget year for each cost account involved. Necessarily, they must depend on historical cost data, plus the consideration of foreseeable new maintenance programs or major jobs. The better the cost account detail and the cost reporting, the better the job of developing budget allowances can be done. For example, a few companies separate their maintenance labor into preventive maintenance work and breakdown maintenance work. Preventive maintenance work and its costs are relatively easy to calculate. In such enterprises, the task of developing budget allowances for maintenance labor is done better than in the situation in which you have only one total maintenance labor account.

This common procedure of charging all maintenance costs to the maintenance department can have unfortunate and costly consequences. It provides a minimum of control because, in practice, control is exercised through the maintenance department budget alone—and this may, or may not, be good enough. Also, it violates the budgeting principle that each operating department should be charged with all the costs that it specifically incurs. As a result, the enterprise can end up spending more than it needs to spend.

*A case in point.* A major airline at a major airport owns and uses seven different buildings plus its main passenger terminal. There is a building maintenance department in the airline's organization, and this department maintains the buildings, relocates departments, and re-lays out offices and shops as requested. The building maintenance department has its own budget for labor, material, and supplies. Also, the money spent for relaying out or moving or refurbishing a given department is never charged against that department. Instead the labor, material, and supplies used are charged to the building maintenance department. As a result, you wouldn't believe the moving, layout changes, refurbishing, etc. that go on. In effect, each department head has a checkbook with an unlimited balance. Whatever he spends for this sort of thing doesn't go against *his* budget. At least 25 percent of what is spent, conservatively estimated, is for work that is really not necessary. And that amounts to tens of thousands of dollars each year, and costs the profit on a lot of passenger miles.

Under the concept of organizational checks and balances, maintenance costs are best controlled, in large part at least, by the user, i.e., the heads of the departments which use the maintenance services. Also, their budgets should be charged with the maintenance costs that they incur. To achieve this, an allowance for maintenance work in their department is provided on their monthly budget. Maintenance uses a work-ticket system under which it accumulates the maintenance labor hours and the material used on a job within a given department. When the job is completed, the total actual costs are charged to the department and shown on its monthly performance-to-budget report. Finally, and ideally, the department head "signs off" each job done in his department to indicate his approval of the charges and the quality of the work.

There are problems with such a set of procedures but they are not insurmountable. Many companies follow such routines with good success. And they have achieved better maintenance budgeting and better maintenance cost control.

In this labor cost area, as in the others, the use of work sampling should be considered as a means to cost improvement. The technique can be particularly helpful in detecting cases where expensive maintenance labor is being misused.

*A case in point.* At one major operation, work-sampling studies revealed the practice of sending a minimum of two workers out on each maintenance job. Some jobs had more, but never were there less than two workers. On certain jobs, such as electrical wiring work, this was desirable for safety reasons. But 42 percent of the jobs observed were of the type that did not require two workers. This might appear to you to be an extreme situation, but there are parallel practices in many maintenance situations. For example, a lot of expensive maintenance labor is spent chasing parts and finding material.

Establishing equitable budget allowances for maintenance costs for a given operating department is an effort that is most affected by the conditions in each specific situation. Usually we have to depend on historical cost data. In some situations, it can be difficult to build in flexibility in this cost. In fact, inverse relationships may be seen between activity and cost, because maintenance may be able to do much of their work only in periods of reduced activity. Usually, however, when setting maintenance cost allowances for individual departments, you can tie them to activity measures to some extent because normally, the greater the use of equipment, the greater the cost of maintenance.

One analysis that can be helpful is to calculate maintenance costs per activity measure, for example, maintenance cost per machine hour. Then compare these ratios between different departments. The findings can be particularly revealing on the maintenance costs of certain equipment, particularly if the maintenance department itself does not keep records of the maintenance costs by type of machine. The analysis can reveal the need for more preventive maintenance or a different type of machine. The result can be better budget allowances.

## OTHER COST AREAS

The variety of other costs is great, and each has to be treated individually by operating management and the budgeting function in the light of local conditions. They all have to be included in the development of the profit plan. Unfortunately, in practice, the budgeting function does not engage in the effort to establish budget allowances for many of them. Rather, these allowances are determined by senior operating management and given to the budgeting function to include in the profit plan.

### Selling and Administrative Costs (S&A)

This cost area is typical of the preceding point. The top executive hierarchy, its costs, and its expenses are the concern of the chief executive officer, whose decisions determine the budget. Marketing costs are the concern of the senior marketing executive and the chief executive officer, and together, in effect, they establish this segment of the budget. Their major guideline must be the percent of sales income that is spent in the area and how this figure compares with similar or competitive operations.

One continuing concern for senior management in this area is to avoid budgeting for management functions that are no longer needed. This is, not unfrequently, a problem in very large corporations. The company is always changing. What was once a vital function is no longer needed, or at least not needed at its original size or cost. However, some of these functions can go on for years fully budgeted.

Frequently there are few, if any, variable costs recognized and applied in this area. In effect, it is an area of fixed budgeting. On this point the budgeting function does have something to contribute. If budgeting has a high enough position in the organizational hierarchy, and if a potential exists, budgeting can advance the idea of work sampling and even work standards in such areas as clerical staff, typing pools, mailrooms, keypunching, and sales order administration. Alertness and ingenuity on budgeting's part can increase the flexibility achieved in this area of cost, if they see it as part of their job.

## Telephone Costs

In other cost areas, the budgeting function can have much greater impact in establishing budget allowances and in instigating cost improvement action. For example, as telephone rates go up, the need for better budgeting and closer control becomes more necessary. Leased long distance lines have reduced phone costs in some situations, but as operating conditions and marketing patterns change, what was once a requirement may become a luxury. Another possibility is for Budgeting to examine the need for and suggest the use of service companies that review your phone bill to detect mischarges and phone traffic patterns that can be handled more economically in other ways.

## Freight Costs

Budget allowances for freight are very commonly determined on the basis of historical cost patterns. The attention paid to this cost varies directly with the size of the bill. When it is great enough, the company has its own traffic manager and staff. But many operations do not have such a function. Here again, there are service companies that will examine your freight bills to detect the application of incorrect freight rates by outside carriers.

# BUDGETING FOR RESEARCH AND DEVELOPMENT

In some manufacturing companies, a substantial amount of money is spent in research and development. This cost segment of the operating budget is so unique, so different from the other areas of the budget, that it demands its own consideration. In fact, for a very basic reason, it demands its own special budgeting approach.

## SPECIAL PROBLEMS IN R&D BUDGETING

Among the problems inherent in R&D budgeting are the following:

1. There is no detailed body of practice and experience in R&D budgeting such as that available to us in manufacturing cost budgeting or even in service industry budgeting. As a result, most companies are "cutting and trying" and slowly evolving the procedures that seem best to fit their particular conditions and needs.

2. Because of the many intangibles involved, it is frequently very difficult to predict the money needs of specific developmental programs. You just cannot say with certainty, at the start of the year, in what areas the R&D funds can be most fruitfully spent. As a result, reallocation of money and thus revisions to the R&D budget can be more important and numerous than in the other parts of the operating budget.

3. Points-of-progress measurement for R&D programs may be difficult to state in objective terms. As a result, it can be difficult to measure program performance at specified intervals within the budget year and to evaluate how effectively the programs are utilizing their funds.

4. R&D is a highly technical area. Often, it can be an area rife with esoterics that raise fear and doubts in the minds of managers in other areas such as operations, finance, and accounting, and even in the mind of the chief executive officer. As a result, they may doubt their ability to

participate in the R&D budgeting effort. Also, the R&D manager is placed high in the organization, as he (or she) should be, and may be even higher in the political structure than some of the other management functions. In fact, he may be so highly placed that his judgments remain, in effect, unquestioned. As a result, very real psychological barriers can exist against effective inputs to the R&D budget from the managers of other functions within the enterprise.

5. The organization of the R&D effort is frequently a combination of individual developmental programs and scientific disciplines such as the chemistry lab, metallurgy lab, electronic microscopy, etc. Time and cost reporting of services rendered by specific disciplines for many programs can be difficult to collect.

6. Top management's time and attention is needed for effective allocation and control of R&D funds. Such time is always in short supply.

Because of these inherent problems, you find a wide divergence in budget practice between companies, in the R&D area. For example, in some companies the budgeting for R&D is done by the budgeting function that does the rest of the operating budgeting. In other companies, R&D budgeting is done by a separate group which reports to the executive in charge of R&D. In effect, it is self-budgeting. In still other companies, the budget is administered by a group under R&D management, but the company budget director and the chief executive officer (or a delegate) participate with R&D management in periodic budget reviews.

Some companies do a most primitive job of budgeting their R&D effort. They allocate corporate funds for R&D, and then R&D management simply doles out the funds as needed. Program managers are not told how much is apportioned to their specific programs. In these cases, there is usually a monthly report that shows for the *total* R&D effort the monthly budget allowance by cost account and the actual expenditures. Some companies go one step further and apportion the total R&D allocation out to specific programs. A monthly report of actual expenditures versus budget allowance is then issued to the managers for their individual programs.

*A case in point.* At one multiplant electronics company, a very successful budget revitalization program had just been completed. It had covered all of the areas of the business with the exception of R&D. As of that point in time, budgeting consisted of giving R&D its total allocation of company funds. R&D management then split the total allocation over the cost accounts involved, i.e., professional staff, technical labor, supplies, outside services, etc., and divided the total for each account into twelve equal one-month increments. Finally, a monthly computerized report was issued showing, for R&D in total, the actual monies spent for each account versus the budgeted amount. This sequence can only be called "primitive" R&D budgeting.

When the head of R&D was approached to extend the budget revitalization effort into his area, he resisted vigorously, contending that "R&D is a creative effort, not subject to the constraint of budgeting." His judgment prevailed, and no work was done to improve the R&D budgeting effort despite the fact that the company was spending 4 percent of company sales income on R&D, and that amounted to millions of dollars a year. R&D program managers, on the other hand, were saying such things as, "I have had a request for a $2500 piece of equipment upstairs for three months and can't get a reply. If only they would tell me how much I can spend, I'd know what I can and can't do." Thus, the failure to budget by development program and by scientific discipline weakened management's control and led to uncertainty and discontent among R&D personnel.

A situation such as this will be incomprehensible to some readers because in their companies, the allocated R&D funds are apportioned out to specific programs and scientific disciplines, and there is an ongoing appraisal of how well those programs are using their funds.

## THE FOUR A'S OF R&D BUDGETING

There is one basic and vital difference between operating budgeting in the R&D area and budgeting in the other areas of the enterprise: that difference is our lessened ability to predict. We are doing no great management pioneering if we develop a usable income forecast, then predict our operating costs, and then use these projections to plan and control. Many companies do all this quite well, and do it a little better with each passing year. They may not be "dead on," but their projections are reasonably close to the eventual outcome and are entirely usable. However, in the R&D area, we cannot predict with the same closeness. We are dealing with design, development, advancing the state of the art, and therefore, creativity. This doesn't mean that we cannot predict at all; it means that we cannot expect the same usable range of certainty that we can in the other areas of the operating budget. Because of this, we have to orient our budgeting approach in a different manner.

The orientation might be considered as the following four A's:

*Allocation*   How much of corporate funds should be allocated to R&D?

*Apportion*   How should these allocated funds be apportioned to the various segments of the R&D effort?

*Administration*   How are these apportioned funds actually being spent as the budget year evolves?

*Appraisal*   How effectively are the apportioned funds being utilized? Should there be changes in the apportioning as originally laid down so as to increase the effectiveness of the use of the allocated funds?

Each of these steps is a subject in itself and warrants individual discussion.

## DETERMINING THE R&D ALLOCATION

The decision as to the amount of corporate funds that can be allocated to R&D can be made by only one person. This is the person responsible for the operating results, i.e., the profit or loss of the enterprise. In some companies, this is the chairman of the board; in others, the president; in others, the executive vice president. It is this chief executive officer at whose desk "the buck stops," who has to make the ultimate decision. He (or she) can use many inputs—the desires of the marketing staff, the plans of R&D for areas they believe promising, or the judgment of his planning staff, if he has one. But when all has been said, he has to make the final decision.

Some thinkers on this subject maintain that this is the wrong orientation. They hold that the total allocation for R&D should be the sum of the costs for all that Marketing wants plus the programs that R&D believes promising. They maintain that it is a "bubble up from the bottom" process. The trouble with this alternate view is that there is never enough money to do all that everyone wants. President after president has made this observation. Dr. Max Tishler once commented that there were always more good ideas than a company, university, or even the government could afford to pursue. As said earlier, the CEO uses these inputs, but they have to be given him in a priority order, and the final decision only he can make.

In arriving at the R&D allocation, the CEO has many things to balance out, including his shareholders' dividend expectations, debt-carrying charges, capital investment needs, economic conditions as they can be foreseen, and the R&D expenditures of competitive companies. This last-named input, competitive R&D expenditures, can be highly inflated by what the competition chooses to include in R&D. One chairman I know used to be incensed by the claim of one of his competitors that they spent 14 percent for R&D. "What do they include in R&D, the kitchen sink?" he used to thunder.

In some cases, the CEO and his assistants can also utilize outside data and statistics such as general corporate R&D expenditures and trade or industry statistics. These may all be helpful, but the final decision has to be made in the light of the enterprise's own current and foreseeable condition and capabilities.

Finally, the R&D allocation should be stated in terms of a money commitment for the budget year, not in terms of a percent of corporate sales. When it is done the latter way, a less-than-expected sales performance can cause a lot of budget changes and R&D dislocations. One seminar attendee told me that his company allocated to R&D on the basis of a percentage of sales and that in the first three quarters of the present budget year, they had had three major budget changes in the R&D allocation. The better way is to make the decision to spend $x$ dollars for R&D in the coming budget year.

## APPORTIONING TO SPECIFIC R&D PROGRAMS AND DISCIPLINES

This step takes the total allocation and doles it out to the various R&D areas. The work involved depends on how the R&D effort is structured. Some R&D efforts are structured completely by developmental programs, and the task is to give each of the programs the funds it properly should receive. Other R&D organizations are a combination of programs, or projects, and a number of scientific disciplines servicing those programs. In this situation, the apportioning step must fund both the disciplines and the programs.

In one sense, this step is no great budgeting problem. Personnel costs usually represent 60 to 65 percent of R&D costs. Program managers and directors of the various scientific disciplines involved know the staff they have or want and the cost. Also, they can be expected to be able to make reasonable estimates of their equipment and supply needs and the costs of outside services, if any. Their individual requests for funds are then reviewed by the head of R&D and approved or adjusted either downward or occasionally upward, as he sees the need. Thus 60 to 65 percent of the costs go to manpower, the other items are also provided for, and the budget stands as approved by the head of R&D.

The real problem, of course, is the determination of how much manpower and other cost allowances should be funded for the various developmental programs and for the scientific disciplines. Usually, the head of R&D decides what money is needed for the various disciplines involved. In funding the programs however, it is frequently a joint R&D and Marketing decision. At times, the CEO, himself, may become deeply involved because he has to make some decisions on priorities and on which programs to accent. But the bulk of it is usually an R&D/Marketing decision-making process.

A curious and, in some cases, an important phenomenon can frequently be observed in this particular process. In human affairs, every joint decision-making effort is strongly affected by the relative powers of the parties involved. Most of us, I believe, have found that the marketing function is dynamic. It has great clout in the organization power structure—as it should have. It is commonly staffed by forceful, articulate people who have many strong ideas on what they want. Given these dynamics, you would assume that the lead role in the apportioning of the R&D allocation would be taken by Marketing. In practice, just the opposite is often the case. Frequently, after Marketing has had its few favorite programs funded, they have little to say on how the remaining funds should be used. As a result, R&D makes the decisions on how the major portion of the total allocation will be spent and on what R&D programs it will be used. I have known and been told of some opposite cases, but the events as described happen surprisingly often.

Where this situation exists, it may result in less than optimum use of R&D funds. This is not to denegrate R&D management, but they cannot know all that Marketing knows about the marketplace. They do not always have the exposure to, or as much opportunity to learn of, customer preferences or market trends, or to pick up veiled hints of coming developments. Theoretically, all this should be communicated to R&D management by Marketing and used when program funding is being decided. But frequently this information is not communicated, or at least not clearly enough. As a result, the possible subtleties are not recognized.

This situation can have important effects. Industrial R&D has to be basically a pragmatic effort. The largest corporations can afford 15 to 20 percent unfettered research, but the remaining percentage has to be aimed towards desired specific developments. In the smaller corporations, the entire R&D effort has to be on specific programs and toward quite defined results. The company cannot afford more than this effort. As a result, industrial R&D has to be, by and large, marketing oriented. This means an equal involvement by both Marketing and R&D. You do not have this where, in effect, a majority of the R&D allocation is apportioned by R&D management alone.

## ADMINISTERING THE R&D BUDGET

In this step, you need the reporting of actual costs incurred by the various programs and disciplines so that they can be compared against the funds apportioned or budgeted for each R&D program and discipline.

This should be a relatively easy step because, as we have said, 60 to 65 percent of the costs are personnel, and in the case of programs, specific personnel are frequently assigned full-time to specific programs. As the programs requisition supplies, or purchase equipment or outside services, these costs can be charged against the using program. No great administrative difficulties should be encountered.

Problems frequently do arise, however, when scientific disciplines are servicing a good number of programs, and you need to record time and other cost charges for these services which are incurred by the specific programs. It is not uncommon to encounter a reluctance on the part of R&D personnel in these disciplines to keep adequate records. Or if they have been persuaded to keep the time records, you have to look out for fictionalizing. For budgeting purposes, you need reasonably accurate reporting if you are to have usable actual cost data on the programs' individual budget reports. It usually comes down to doing a "selling" job which may include setting up the most simple, possible reporting procedure for the R&D personnel involved. If budgeting can do this, they evince their interest in reducing the record-keeping load for R&D and have a continuing opportunity to explain why reasonable accuracy in reporting actual costs is needed for the budget reports for each R&D program.

## APPRAISING R&D PROGRESS

This is the step that really distinguishes R&D budgeting from the other areas of operating budgeting. It is the step that provides a solution for our inability to predict. This step involves the periodic and continuing reappraisal of how the individual R&D programs are progressing, so that you know where the apportioned funds are being well used, where funds are not being used as well, and where additional funds might be advantageously applied.

After the funds have been apportioned to specific R&D programs and after the budget year is underway, the individual programs will begin to fall into categories:

The first type of program will be right on stream. It has made the progress that was originally expected and it can continue to use effectively the funds apportioned to it.

The second type of program will, fortunately, be ahead of its planned course of progress. If this can be identified and acted upon, the program might be able to use additional funds effectively. However, the R&D allocation has been fully apportioned, and the practical reality usually is that additional funds are not available.

The third type of program is one which has encountered unforeseen problems. It is not as far along as anticipated for this point in time. Because of this, if it can be identified that the program cannot use effectively some of the funds originally apportioned for it, at least for the time being, then perhaps some funds can be freed for better use in the second type of program. But, of course, no program manager is going to reduce his funds voluntarily.

The fourth type, the saddest of all, is the program that is in real trouble. If its progress could be measured, the question of further continuance would have to be asked. Now, no one is going to kill his or her own project, and if we only have another half year, we can get it off the ground. It isn't until a quarter-million is down the drain that the hard decision is made to abandon the program. Fortunately, these are the rarer type of program. But unfortunately, they also sometimes provide the most spectacular stories.

There is a fifth type, fortunately not too common, initiated when a new competitive development requires a completely new R&D program or the great enlargement and acceleration of one already underway. Such a situation can result in taking action all the way back in the allocation stage, and additional funds might be allocated to R&D, out of necessity. Or the decision might be to halt one or more other programs, or cut them back drastically, to make available the funds needed by the program seeking to meet the competitive development.

If you agree that these situations represent the way things actually happen, then you also agree that you cannot predict for the full budget year how the R&D funds should best be apportioned. And, of course, you should not expect that you could. We are dealing here with a creative effort that sometimes goes well, and sometimes very poorly, at least for a time. At the start of the budget year, you can only hope to apportion funds on the basis of the best collective judgment possible at the time. You then must adjust those first judgments as the budget year evolves.

The point of all this is that the substitute for our basic inability to predict in the R&D area is the establishment of benchmarks of progress for each R&D program and then the continuing reappraisal of actual progress to these benchmarks. If we do not do this, we are fixed in and bound to our original apportionments. As a result, R&D funds will continue on, at their apportioned level, in programs where they cannot be used as effectively as they should be, i.e., types three and four, and additional funds will not be available for programs that could use such funds more effectively, i.e., type two.

Establishing benchmarks of progress, developing effective procedures for continuingly reappraising progress, and then acting upon the findings are all things not easily done, particularly at the start. However, it is possible, and some companies do it quite well. For example, benchmarks of progress mean stating what work will be finished, by what period of time. You frequently encounter resistance from some R&D personnel to the idea of doing this. They may not have had to do this in the past, and they resist doing it now. The arguments might be advanced that their work is too original or too complex to allow them to predict future progress. One rebuttal to this is that it was possible to develop and apply Program and Evaluation and Review Technique (PERT), which requires very definite predictions, to as complex a development program as the Polaris missile. Not too many industrial R&D programs are that complex. This does not argue that a formal PERT program should or can be applied to every R&D program, but it should be possible at least to preset reasonably defined progress points for designated future intervals. When we have these, we can have periodic reviews of progress to insure that our R&D funds are still properly apportioned. If we do not do this, we stay chained to the original apportioning. We are ignoring the lessons of history to date.

No hard and fast rules can be advanced for establishing these progress points. The more basic or "far out" the research (and possibly the longer the program's anticipated duration), the less detailed you usually can make the progress predictions. However, even in such more difficult cases, we should at least be able to say what steps should be accomplished by the end of the first quarter of the budget year, and then by the end of the second quarter, and so on. As the program develops, more specific and detailed statements of expected progress should be possible. In most cases of industrial R&D, the effort does not go as deep into the "unknown," and the companies utilizing progress benchmarks expect and receive specific and quite detailed progress reports from the start of the program, and throughout its duration.

How often the progress review should be made varies with the type of company. A surprising number of companies who orient their R&D budget thinking this way do a monthly review. This might be too frequent for a very complex, long-term program. But certainly, a quarter-year review should be made for every program.

What members of management should do the R&D progress review? Again, there can be no hard and fast rules. Three management areas definitely should be involved—R&D management itself, marketing, and budgeting/finance. A very probable fourth area would be manufacturing management. The managers representing areas other than R&D should be experienced executives, i.e., people with a broad knowledge of the business and its current state, rather than junior executives. The important point is that this "board of review" brings to bear inputs from other functional areas of the enterprise. And these inputs are applied to prestated progress benchmarks. The result is not an advisory panel, but a decision-making body seeking the best use of R&D budgeted funds in the light of events up to this point in the budget year.

# A CASE OF FLEXIBLE BUDGETING

To illustrate many of the techniques and procedures discussed in this book, it can be helpful to review a specific flexible budget development and installation. The case is a relatively simple one, but it will have similarities and parallels to your operation. For example, it illustrates such areas as:

1. the use of the budgeting sequence in the profit-plan development

2. the development and application of mixed costs

3. the adjustments of allowances to variations in activity for flexible budgeting

4. the use of the profit/volume ratio, break-even point, and margin of safety

5. the calculation of profit center variances in profit

The enterprise to be budgeted is the port grain terminal, to which you were already introduced in Chapter 3. We know basically how the operation works, and we have seen how power and clean-up labor costs were analyzed and identified for the terminal. However, now that we are going to develop a profit plan and flexible budgets, certain additional facts are needed.

## MORE ABOUT THE PORT GRAIN TERMINAL

This port grain terminal is one of several either owned or leased by a large grain company, with a continent-wide buying effort and a world-wide marketing effort. This particular terminal happens to be owned, and it handles only grain bought and sold by the company. A traffic department at corporate headquarters arranges for the river barges to be loaded at river stations (terminals) upstream, for the railroad cars to be loaded at country feeding stations (terminals) inland, and schedules both barges and railroad cars to arrive at the port grain terminal. The same traffic department contracts for and schedules the ocean-going freighters to be loaded at the terminal. The terminal manager, named Fred, is responsible for running this port grain terminal.

Thus, the terminal is simply a material-handling facility that unloads the various types and grades of grain from river barges and railroad cars, weighs and grades the grain, and stores it by type and grade. When a vessel is to be loaded with a given type of grain, the terminal mixes that grain from a number of different silos to "make" the No. 2 grade shipped overseas, weighs it, and loads it out onto the vessel. We need not go into the complexities of grading grain. Let it suffice to say that grading is done under very well-defined Department of Agriculture regulations, and the terminal's grading for export is checked by an independent outside agency.

Finally, it is important to note that this terminal is not only a cost center but also a profit center. The terminal manager receives both a yearly profit plan and a combined monthly performance-to-budget report and profit and loss statement. Important to Fred, the manager, is the fact that a good part of his year-end bonus is based upon his profit performance.

This then is the operating situation for which we want to develop a profit plan and flexible budgets. To develop the profit plan, we first need a forecast of terminal volume, or activity, for the budget year.

## FORECAST ACTIVITY

Corporate headquarters and the marketing function have forecast that the terminal will be elevating 120 million bushels of grain in the coming budget year. Remember that this means they will be unloading 120 million bushels from river barges and railway cars and loading out 120 million bushels aboard ocean-going vessels. Thus, 240 million bushels will be handled. The terminal has also either been given or has developed the estimates that the average barge will contain 50,000 bushels, that the average railroad car will contain 2000 bushels, that the average ship will be loaded with 500,000 bushels of grain, and that 75 percent of the incoming grain will arrive on river barges.

Thus, the forecast volume for the terminal can be summarized as:

120 million bu elevated
240 million bu handled
90 million bu from barge unloading
1800 barges to be unloaded
30 million bu from railroad-car unloading
15,000 railway cars to be unloaded
120 million bu to be loaded aboard ships
240 ships to be loaded

The terminal is scheduled to operate five days a week, fifty weeks of the year. It is hoped that there can be a two-week period for vital shutdown maintenance and for vacations.

## INCOME INCREMENTS

Being a profit center, the terminal must receive income. The main source of income is $0.02 per bushel elevated. This is the "credit" given the terminal by the corporation. Actually it is the cost per bushel the corporation would have to pay another terminal in the same port if it did not have its own terminal to elevate its grain. That $0.02 per bushel elevated can be applied as $0.01 per bushel unloaded and $0.01 per bushel loaded out.

Additional income increments are derived from certain charges to the ships and barges handled. These charges are:

*Equipment rental.* The ships use some equipment supplied by the terminal. For example, the high-grade metal chutes, down through which the grain is shunted from the gallery belt into the ships' holds, are supplied by the terminal. For these, and for other equipment, the records show an income of $750 per average ship.

*Electricity.* When a ship ties up to the terminal dock, she usually shuts down her own generators and takes on a power line from the terminal. She is charged for this, naturally, and the average ship will pay $100 for the electricity used.

*Ship wharfage.* Maintaining a dock for ocean vessels is an expensive operation. A given ship is charged according to her gross tonnage and length, but on the average, there is a charge of $900 per ship for wharfage.

*Barge wharfage.* The barges do not use terminal equipment or electricity, but they do tie up to the dock. Therefore, the barge companies are charged $15 per barge for wharfage.

Thus, the terminal's income increments can be summarized as follows:

| | |
|---|---|
| Elevation | $0.02/bu |
| Equipment rental | $750/ship |
| Electricity | $100/ship |
| Wharfage, ship | $900/ship |
| Wharfage, barge | $15/barge |

## COST FACTORS

The cost factors are more numerous and consist of some of each of the three types of cost, i.e., variable, mixed, and fixed.

*Barge-unloading labor.* This is a direct labor cost and is considered a pure variable. Each barge-unloading crew consists of twelve workers, and on the average, their cost is $48 per crew hour. This crew includes the operators needed in the headhouse and in the storage areas as well as those at the barge. One crew is used on each shift. They work an eight-hour shift, and if needed, the terminal can operate three shifts each day by hiring three crews.

*Railroad-car-unloading labor.* This is also a direct labor cost. Each railroad-car-unloading crew consists of six workers, and on the average, the cost is $24 per crew hour.

*Ship-loading labor.* This also is a direct labor cost. A ship-loading crew consists of ten workers and, on the average, the cost is $40 per crew hour.

*Direct labor fringe benefits.* Cost records indicate that this equates to, and can be budgeted as, 25 percent of total direct-labor costs.

*Maintenance labor.* This cost is considered as totally fixed, because in practice, the operation is so busy that the continuing maintenance problem is to find time when the equipment is not being used and can be worked on. The crew consists of twenty-four workers. They will be spread over the shifts worked, as needed, depending on what unloading and loading is done on each shift. Average earnings are $5 per hour. Thus, this cost will be applied at $40 per terminal operating hour if three shifts are worked.

*Repairs and maintenance supplies.* Grain handling is a very abrasive operation. For example, the metal chutes needed at the ship used to develop holes within a week, or at least they did until the terminal learned to coat them on the inside with liquid plastic. Even then, the chutes would only last ten weeks. This supply cost item covers spare motors, belting, switches, and all varieties of expensive maintenance parts and supplies. It is a mixed cost, and the cost analysis reveals that it follows the formula of $3000 per month plus $0.50 per thousand bushels handled.

*Utilities.* This cost includes the electricity, gas, and water costs at the terminal. Each has been analyzed separately and found to be a mixed cost. Their individual fixed and variable increments have been added together for ease of application, and the final formula is $2100 per month plus $0.25 per thousand bushels handled.

*Elevator supplies.* This cost includes all the miscellaneous operating supplies required to run the terminal. It is a mixed cost, and the cost analysis formula is $200 per month plus $0.03 per thousand bushels handled.

*Other fixed costs.* This cost group covers terminal depreciation, taxes, and insurance, and amounts to $48,000 per month.

*Salaried personnel.* Fred, his shift superintendents, and their key salaried foremen cost $20,000 per month.

*Elevator general and administrative.* Any operation handling ocean-going vessels entails a lot of paper work. There is an air-conditioned office building at the terminal with a clerical staff, a conference room, desks for the superintendents, Fred's office, and quarters for the Department of Agriculture and Board of Trade people. All this costs $15,000 per month.

## THE NEED FOR STANDARDS

Up to this point, we have the forecast of terminal volume, and we know all the income increments and the cost factors involved. Can we now develop a profit plan? We cannot. It is possible to develop the income side of the profit plan. But we have no way, as yet, to project the labor costs at the forecast volume. To do that we need standards. And this emphasizes a basic law of budgeting: *To budget you need standards.*

Consider what we know at this point on the cost side. We know how many bushels we have to unload and load out. We know the cost per unloading- and loading-crew hour. But we also need to know how many bushels each crew should handle per hour if we are to budget grain-handling labor costs, and some of the other costs.

The standards are simply stated:

| | |
|---|---|
| Barge unloading | 15,000 bu/crew hour |
| RR-car unloading | 15,000 bu/crew hour |
| Ship loading | 30,000 bu/crew hour |

And the crew hours needed in the year will be:

$$\text{Barge unloading } (90{,}000{,}000/15{,}000) = 6000$$

$$\text{RR-car unloading } (30{,}000{,}000/15{,}000) = 2000$$

$$\text{Ship loading } (120{,}000{,}000/30{,}000) = 4000$$

Thus, to handle the projected volume, the operational and profit plan will have to include around-the-clock operations on barge unloading, two shifts daily on ship loading, and one shift per day on railroad-car unloading.

## THE YEAR'S PROFIT PLAN

We now have all the data we need to lay down the terminal's profit plan for the budget year.

Most managements when they develop the profit plan think only in terms of projected income, costs, and pretax profit. However, let us go further in this case. Because we have flexible budget data, we can also calculate the terminal's profit/volume ratio (marginal contribution ratio), its break-even point, and its margin of safety. To do this, we will keep segregated the fixed and the variable budgeted costs.

The income side of the profit plan is as follows:

| | |
|---|---|
| Elevation (120,000,000 bu × $0.02) | $2,400,000 |
| Equipment rental (240 ships × $750) | 180,000 |
| Electricity (240 ships × $100) | 24,000 |
| Wharfage, ships (240 ships × $900) | 216,000 |
| Wharfage, barges (1800 barges × $15) | 27,000 |
| Total planned income for year | $2,847,000 |

On the cost side, the calculations are shown in Table 10-1. A summary of the profit plan is the following:

| | Year | Average month |
|---|---|---|
| Income | $2,847,000 | $237,250 |
| Costs | 2,106,800 | 175,567 |
| Planned profit | $ 740,200 | $ 61,683 |

The profit/volume ratio, the break-even point, and margin of safety can now be calculated. Fig. 10-1 illustrates these interrelated financial characteristics of the enterprise and its profit plan.

*The profit/volume ratio.* This ratio calculates the portion of each dollar of income after direct or variable costs have been deducted that is

**Table 10-1**

| | Variable | Fixed |
|---|---|---|
| Barge-unloading labor (6000 × $48) | $288,000 | |
| RR-car unloading labor (2000 × $24) | 48,000 | |
| Ship-loading labor (4000 × $40) | 160,000 | |
| Fringe benefits ($496,000 × 25%) | 124,000 | |
| Maintenance labor (24 × 2000 × $5) | | 240,000 |
| Rep. & maint. supp. (240,000 × $0.50) + ($3000 × 12) | 120,000 | 36,000 |
| Utilities (240,000 × $0.25) + ($2100 × 12) | 60,000 | 25,200 |
| Elev. supp. (240,000 × $0.03) + ($200 × 12) | 7,200 | 2,400 |
| Other fixed ($48,000 × 12) | | 576,000 |
| Salaried personnel ($20,000 × 12) | | 240,000 |
| Elevator G&A ($15,000 × 12) | | 180,000 |
| | $807,200 | $1,299,600 |
| Total budgeted costs for year | | $2,106,800 |

available for the absorption of fixed costs and then, once past break-even, for the build-up of profit. Thus, if you sell something for $100 and it costs $60 in variable costs to make, that sale contributes $40 toward your fixed costs. Or if you have already absorbed all of your fixed costs and are past your break-even point, the $40 increases your profit. In that case your P/V ratio is 40/100, or 40 percent. This ratio is also frequently called the *marginal contribution ratio.*

Here at the port grain terminal, using the flexible budget data, the P/V ratio can be calculated as follows:

$$\text{Profit/volume ratio} = (\text{profits} + \text{fixed costs}) \div \text{income}$$
$$= (\$740{,}200 + \$1{,}299{,}600) \div \$2{,}847{,}000$$
$$= 71.65\%$$

This ratio states that, under the terminal's profit plan, every $100 of income should contribute $71.65 toward absorbing the fixed costs, and once past the break-even point, the $71.65 will be an increase in profit.

The use of the P/V ratio is fundamental to modern direct costing. It is certainly true that most manufacturing companies use conventional absorption accounting to cost and price their products or services. But more and more managements are becoming aware of the many advantages of direct costing, and it will find ever-increasing use in the years ahead.

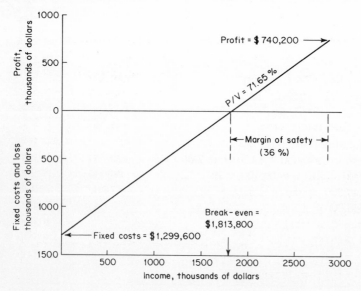

**Figure 10-1** Yearly profit/volume chart—port grain terminal.

Here at the terminal, the data which direct costing provides helps management in such areas as:

1. The calculation of the net effect of capital improvements that increase fixed costs but reduce variable costs, i.e., the effects on profits and on break-even point

2. The evaluation of the effect of cost changes, such as labor rate increases

3. The ongoing visualization of actual performance to the profit plan, by plotting monthly actual profit performance at actual income against the P/V line, as drawn in Fig. 10-1

*The break-even point.* This point is the amount of income above which profits begin, or below which losses begin. It is reached when the fixed costs are totally absorbed by the marginal contribution from the income received to date.

For the terminal, the break-even point for the budget year can be calculated as:

Yearly break-even   = fixed costs ÷ P/V ratio
                           = \$1,299,600 ÷ 0.7165
                           = \$1,813,800
Monthly break-even = \$151,000

In monthly terms at the grain terminal, any month in which income is less than \$151,000 will probably be a losing month.

An amazing number of companies do not know their break-even point. Some managements consider it an academic point, since they are presently well past it, have been, and expect to be in the future. As a result of this attitude, perhaps they are flying a little blind, which is a poor way to pilot a plane. Many, if not most, of the pressures on a business today work to raise the break-even point, and every management should be keeping track of what is happening to theirs. If they do not, they might find their operation alarmingly close to it without realizing what has been happening.

*The margin of safety.* This is the difference between the break-even point and the dollars of income. It is the amount, or percent, that income can be lower than planned before the break-even point will be reached and losses begin.

For the terminal, the margin of safety can be calculated as:

$$\begin{aligned}
\text{Margin of safety \$} &= \text{income} - \text{break-even point} \\
&= \$2,847,000 - \$1,813,800 \\
&= \$1,033,200 \\
\text{Margin of safety \%} &= (\text{income} - \text{break-even point}) \div \text{income} \\
&= (\$2,847,000 - \$1,813,000) \div \$2,847,000 \\
&= 36\%
\end{aligned}$$

The final profit-planning step would be to break this projection of the year's income, costs, and planned profit into monthly segments, with due regard for the expected seasonal pattern. Thus, we would have a profit plan by month, as well as for the total year. Then as the year actually passes, we would compare for each month, the monthly and year-to-date:

Actual income vs. forecast income
Actual costs vs. budgeted costs
Actual profit vs. planned profit

## A MONTH'S FLEXIBLE BUDGET AND PROFIT REPORTING

Flexible budget data was used to develop the year's profit plan. Obviously, the same data can be used to establish the flexible budget for any of the coming actual months in the year.

A 21-working-day month has just ended at the port grain terminal. Let us assume that in the monthly breakdown of the profit plan we had forecast that this just-ended month would be an average month, i.e., one-twelfth of the year. Thus:

| | |
|---|---|
| Forecast income | $237,250 |
| Budgeted costs | 175,567 |
| Planned Profit | $ 61,683 |

As it turned out, this month was not as busy as we had forecast it would be. Instead of handling 20,000,000 bushels of grain, the terminal had only the following actual activity:

| | |
|---|---|
| Barge unloading | 6,000,000 bu (@ average loads) |
| RR-car unloading | 2,100,000 bu (@ average loads) |
| Ship loading | 7,500,000 bu (@ average loads) |
| Total handled | 15,600,000 |

**Table 10-2   Month's income**

|  | Budget | Actual | Variance |
|---|---|---|---|
| Elevation |  |  |  |
| In (8,100,000 × $0.01) | $100,000 | $ 81,000 | $(19,000) |
| Out (7,500,000 × $0.01) | 100,000 | 75,000 | (25,000) |
| Equip. rental (7,500/500 × $750) | 15,000 | 11,250 | ( 3,750) |
| Electricity (7,500/500 × $100) | 2,000 | 1,500 | ( 500) |
| Wharfage, ship (7,500/500 × $900) | 18,000 | 13,500 | ( 4,500) |
| Wharfage, barge (6,000/50 × $15) | 2,250 | 1,800 | ( 450) |
| Total Income | $237,250 | $184,050 | $(53,200) |

Finally, actual costs for the month amounted to $163,600.

Because all the loads were of average size, let us assume for simplicity's sake that each ship and barge paid the expected average charges. Table 10-2 summarizes the income side of the month's performance to the profit plan.

Thus, because actual activity was less than forecast activity, the terminal has a 22 percent unfavorable variance ($53,200/$237,250) in its income for the month.

Under flexible budgeting, for cost control, we want to compare actual costs at the actual activity to budgeted costs at the actual activity. Thus, on the cost side, the performance for the month would be as shown in Table 10-3.

**Table 10-3   Month's performance-to-budget**

|  | Budget | Actual | Variance |
|---|---|---|---|
| Barge unloading (6000/15 × $48) | $ 19,200 | $ 19,000 | $ 200 |
| RR-car unloading (2100/15 × $24) | 3,360 | 4,400 | (1,040) |
| Ship loading (7500/30 × $40) | 10,000 | 9,900 | 100 |
| Fringe benefits ($32560 × 25%) | 8,140 | 8,475 | ( 335) |
| Maintenance labor (21 × 24 × $40) | 20,160 | 20,754 | ( 594) |
| Rep. & maint. supp. ($3000 + $0.50 × 15,600) | 10,800 | 10,371 | 429 |
| Utilities ($2100 + $0.25 × 15,600) | 6,000 | 6,200 | ( 200) |
| Elevator supp. ($200 + $0.03 × 15,600) | 668 | 600 | 68 |
| Other fixed costs | 48,000 | 48,000 |  |
| Salaried personnel | 20,000 | 20,500 | ( 500) |
| Elevator G&A | 15,000 | 15,400 | ( 400) |
| Total Costs | $161,328 | $163,600 | $(2,272) |

**Table 10-4    Month's performance-to-profit plan—for corporate**

|          | Budget    | Actual    | Variance   |
|----------|-----------|-----------|------------|
| Income   | $237,250  | $184,050  | $(53,200)  |
| Costs    | 175,567   | 163,600   | 11,967     |
| Profit   | $ 61,683  | $ 20,450  | $(41,233)  |

Thus, Fred exceeded his budgeted costs by $2272. Notice the justice of the calculation. He has been allowed every nickel of fixed costs. The variable cost allowances, for both pure variable and mixed costs, were calculated for the actual activity he had to handle. As a result, budgeted costs have been compared to actual costs on a like basis, i.e., actual activity.

How then can the month's performance to the profit plan be summarized? Table 10-4 illustrates one way.

This summary shows corporate headquarters that there was a $53,-200, or 22 percent, unfavorable variance in income at the terminal. It shows that profit had an unfavorable variance of $41,233 or 67 percent. However, the favorable expense variance of $11,967 is a completely meaningless figure. It is calculated by subtracting actual costs at actual activity from budgeted costs at budgeted activity. Obviously, this is a comparison of two unlike things. And what is more serious, it would indicate a good operating cost performance, when, as we have seen, Fred had an unfavorable cost variance for the month.

This brings us to a still another problem. Fred's year-end bonus depends, in large part, on his profit performance. Therefore it is important that the budget reporting makes sense and gives justice to Fred. What percent is Fred off the profit plan? Certainly, he should not be assigned the 67 percent unfavorable variance in profit. Much of that is due to a less-than-budgeted income for the month, which is a corporate marketing/traffic responsibility.

The correct calculation is shown in Table 10-5.

**Table 10-5    Month's performance-to-budget—for terminal**

|                           | Budget    | Actual    | Variance   |
|---------------------------|-----------|-----------|------------|
| Income at actual activity | $184,050  | $184,050  |            |
| Costs at actual activity  | 161,328   | 163,600   | (2,272)    |
| Profit                    | $ 22,722  | $ 20,450  | $(2,272)   |

Thus, Fred is charged with a 10 percent ($2,272/$22,722) unfavorable profit increase. He made $20,450 profit, but had he held his costs for the month to the budget allowances, the terminal profit would have been $22,722. In the eventual calculation of his year-end bonus, he should be charged, justly, with a 10 percent unfavorable profit variance for this particular month.

This separation of responsibility for favorable and unfavorable profit variances is required in those companies where operating profit centers have a monthly profit and loss statement but the centers' operating managers have no responsibility for, or authority over, the marketing of

### Table 10-6 Month's performance-to-budget & profit plan

|  | Budget | Actual | Variance |
|---|---|---|---|
| **Performance to budget** |  |  |  |
| Income at actual | $184,050 | $184,050 |  |
| **Costs** |  |  |  |
| Barge unloading | $ 19,200 | $ 19,000 | $ 200 |
| RR-car unloading | 3,360 | 4,400 | ( 1,040) |
| Ship loading | 10,000 | 9,900 | 100 |
| Fringe benefits | 8,140 | 8,475 | ( 335) |
| Maintenance labor | 20,160 | 20,754 | ( 594) |
| Rep. & maint. supplies | 10,800 | 10,371 | 429 |
| Utilities | 6,000 | 6,200 | ( 200) |
| Elevator supplies | 668 | 600 | 68 |
| Other fixed costs | 48,000 | 48,000 |  |
| Salaried personnel | 20,000 | 20,500 | ( 500) |
| Elevator G&A | 15,000 | 15,400 | ( 400) |
| Total costs at actual activity | $161,328 | $163,600 | $( 2,272) |
| Profit at actual activity | 22,722 | 20,450 | ( 2,272) |
| **Performance-to-profit plan** |  |  |  |
| Terminal income | $237,250 | $184,050 | $(53,200) |
| Costs at actual and efficiency variance |  | 163,600 | ( 2,272) |
| Costs at budget and volume variance | 175,567 |  | (38,961) |
| Profit | $ 61,683 | $ 20,450 | $(41,233) |

their product or services. Many companies have this situation, and it inevitably requires the separation of efficiency from volume increments in the profit variance reporting.

The summary report for both corporate and terminal is given in Table 10-6.

# 11

# ADMINISTERING THE OPERATING BUDGET

The operating budget is a complex management mechanism. It encompasses many of the income and cost facts for every management function and for all the departments of the enterprise. Being complex, it is important that budgeting action and performance be properly recorded, and this we might call *budget administration*. Therefore, we will deal in this chapter with the records, forms, and reports that are involved in a good operating budgeting effort.

The recording of budgeting facts and the budgeting reporting procedures used are one of the most individualistic areas of budgeting. You could fill a book with samples of different budget data sheets and performance-to-budget reports. Our interest here is in the purpose of budget administration and the common problems we have with it. A number of sample forms and reports will be provided, but the format and details of such records have to be fitted to each individual situation and local management preferences.

## THE BUDGET DATA SHEETS

One basic principle of good, professional budgeting is the complete recording of how the budget allowances were determined and how the profit plan was developed. An accounting concept, the "audit trail," applies. The budget person, at any time in the budget year, should be able to trace back any individual cost allowance or forecast increment of income. He or she should be able, at any time, to go back and reconstruct the logic which was originally applied and the calculations made to arrive at the budget allowances. The basic mechanism to do this is the budget data sheet.

Two possible formats of budget data sheets are illustrated in Fig. 11-1 and 11-2. The format illustrated in Fig. 11-1 is a general-purpose one that has been used by numerous practitioners in literally hundreds of installations across a wide range of both manufacturing and service industries. Fig. 11-2 illustrates a somewhat more complex and specialized format, complete with graph paper. Again, the format is a matter of local need and personal preference. The goal is to design and use a form that records the facts used by the operating manager and the budget person in the budget decision-making process.

On the budget data sheet, the budgeting person should record the pertinent facts behind the budget allowance as finally developed. Such facts would include:

1. Historical cost records used

2. Any cost formulas to be used, or tables of allowances

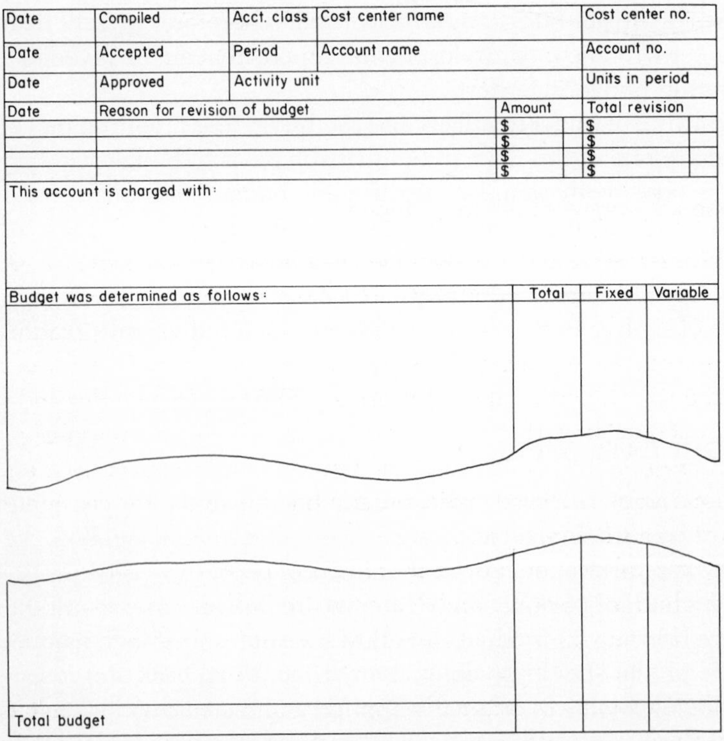

**Figure 11-1**  Basic budget data sheet.

| Year | | | | | |
|------|--|--|--|--|--|
| Date | Compiled by | | Period | | Account |
| Date | Accepted by | | Unit | | Work center |
| Date | Approved by | | Performance | | Department |
| | | | Units/Period | | Plant |
| | | | | | Company |
| | | | | | Remarks |

| Month | Activity | Amount | Activity | Amount | Activity | Amount |
|-------|----------|--------|----------|--------|----------|--------|
| Jan. | | | | | | |
| Feb. | | | | | | |
| Mar. | | | | | | |
| Tot. | | | | | | |
| Apr. | | | | | | |
| May | | | | | | |
| June | | | | | | |
| Tot. | | | | | | |
| July | | | | | | |
| Aug. | | | | | | |
| Sep. | | | | | | |
| Tot. | | | | | | |
| Oct. | | | | | | |
| Nov. | | | | | | |
| Dec. | | | | | | |
| Tot. | | | | | | |

**Figure 11-2**  Budget data sheet with graph.

3. Changes in operating conditions that affected the decision as to the allowance finally developed

4. Any foreseeable conditions that, while not pertinent as yet, might have to be kept in mind for future consideration

One of these budget data sheets should be made out for *every* cost account in every department or cost center. This is a large order and it can be a great deal of work, but it should be done for several reasons:

First, it requires the budgeting function to record the data used and the decisions made in a systematic, programmed manner, by cost center and by cost in each cost center.

Second, it provides an excellent collecting point. To a given sheet can be attached any graphs and least squares calculations that were made, as well as any work papers and analysis sheets that were required and used.

Third, it is a means by which budget revisions and extra-budgetary allowances can be recorded as they occur throughout the budget year.

Fourth, some of these sheets will inevitably be needed by the budget person to answer questions that arise during the budget year. As any experienced budget person knows, six months after you are into the budget year and after you think every conceivable question has been asked, someone will come up with a new one. "What should be charged to this cost account?" "Where should this type of cost item be charged?" "How was this allowance developed?" "Is this current allowance computed correctly?" It is unprofessional to have to search through a lot of unorganized work papers to try to reconstruct the work done and decisions made six or nine months before. Worse, it is most embarrassing not to be able to answer the question at all.

Fifth, in the case of many costs, it is frequently possible to use the existing budget data sheet in the next budget year. In the context of actual operations, the starting date of the new budget year is simply a recording break-off point, and a finance/accounting convention. The operation is still much as it was the day, week, or month before. Admittedly, we do want to revise or realign our budget allowances to reflect inflationary trends or cost improvements or other changed conditions, and the time to do this is at the start of the next budget year. But frequently, this is not the case with every cost. In those instances, the budget data sheet can be carried into the new budget year.

Making up one of these sheets for every budgeted cost is a laborious task, but it is pleasantly surprising how glad you inevitably are that you did the work. You have the answers for those questions.

Notice that on the much-used format illustrated in Fig. 11-1, space is provided to show the fixed, variable, and total allowance. While these may be calculated in terms of the total year, it is also common practice to show them in terms of the average month, or in terms of the *average period* if thirteen accounting and budgeting periods are used. In the case of a fixed cost, this is the monthly or period allowance and it is shown under both the Fixed and the Total column. In the case of a mixed linear cost, the practice is somewhat artificial because you may actually never experience an "average" month during the budget year. However, the monthly calculation shows the fixed segment of the cost under the Fixed column, the variable segment at average activity under the Variable column, and the total of the two segments under the Total column. The formula used for such a cost is always shown on the data sheet. In the case of a mixed step cost, such as, for example, an indirect labor cost, the table of allowances at various levels of activity is always shown on the budget data sheet.

Budget data sheets are usually made up by the budget person after the background data has been collected and after much of the preliminary cost analysis has been completed. Depending upon his or her relations with individual operating managers, the budget person may even complete them to the point of showing on them a proposal for the budget allowance. This can be a convenient way to summarize the data and the analysis. There is nothing wrong with this practice if the communications and relations are good. The only danger is that the individual operating manager might develop the impression that the budget person's proposal is the final allowance and that it is the allowance that definitely is to be used.

Space is properly provided on both formats illustrated for the compiler's or budget person's initials. Additional space is provided in the "accepted" block for the initials of the operating manager in charge of the cost center. In some companies, the operating manager is required to personally initial this block to indicate his agreement with the budget allowance. It is a matter of judgment, but I believe that this can be psychologically poor practice. Certainly, it indicates a rigidity and formality that appears to me to be out of place in what should be a mutual, cooperative effort. What finally is recorded on the budget data sheet is the mutually agreed-upon allowance. One or both parties are dishonest if that record can be justly questioned at a later date. This is a very rare situation when budgeting has been honestly and openly done. Therefore, there should be no real need for personal initialing by the operating manager. The "approved" block may be used by either the operating manager's direct superior or by the head of the budgeting function. In many cases, it is not used at all.

More and more companies are using their computer for the calculation of monthly budget allowances and to print out the performance-to-budget reports. This is a splendid development that usually speeds up the calculation and delivery of the monthly budget reports. However, it does nothing to diminish the need for these budget data sheets. The budget function provides the computer function (EDP) with the data to use in calculating budget allowances and revises these inputs, as needed, during the budget year. However, the budgeting function still retains the basic responsibility for the accuracy of the budget. To meet that responsibility, they need their own records of what the computer was told to use in its calculations. And these records are best kept on some format of budget data sheet.

## THE BUDGET SUMMARY SHEET

For every department or cost center it is good practice for the budgeting function to also make up a budget summary sheet. Such a sheet summarizes the department's budget by listing each cost that will be included in its budget and the money allowance per budget period at average activity. Simply, it is a summary listing of the budget data sheets for the department.

Two typical formats of the budget summary sheet are illustrated in Fig. 11-3 and 11-4. The format illustrated in Fig. 11-3 has been used in many budgeting/product costing installations. Because of this, it has three columns on the right-hand side to develop costing rates per unit. If your budgeted costs are not tied into your product cost calculations, these columns will not be needed. It is a format that can be used in budget administration in any type of enterprise, manufacturing or service, profit or nonprofit. Fig. 11-4 is a type of summary sheet that has been very widely used for individual manufacturing departments for which it is not practical to develop budget allowances for material. As a result, you include on the department's budget only direct labor, indirect labor, and all other expenses excepting material.

The operating manager in charge of the department should always be given a copy of the budget summary sheet. The cost accounts listed on it are the "master" of the listing that will be on his monthly performance-to-budget reports. My preference is also to give each operating manager at the departmental level a copy of each of the budget data sheets for the department. This is not always done, but the minimum the manager should have is the department's budget summary sheet.

| Cost center no. | Cost center name | | Compiled | Date |
|---|---|---|---|---|
| | | | Accepted | Date |
| Units in period | Period | Unit | Approved | Date |

| Accounts | | Class: V,C, etc. | Standard budget | | | Rate/unit | | |
|---|---|---|---|---|---|---|---|---|
| No. | Name | | Total | Variable | Constant | | | Variable |
| | | | | | | | | |
| | | | | | | | | |
| | | | | | | | | |
| | Grand total | | | | | | | |

To determine the current allowance:

V - Variable: Multiply the units produced in current period by variable rate per unit.

C - Constant: Allow the standard budget.

M - Mixed: Calculate the allowance by formula or allow from table on Budget Data Sheet.

S - Special: See instruction on Budget Data Sheet.

**Figure 11-3** Budget summary sheet.

| Cost center no. | Cost center | | | | | For | 19__ |
|---|---|---|---|---|---|---|---|
| Approved        19__ | Period | Unit | | Company | | | |
| by | Prepared by | Units in period | | | | | |

| | | Direct labor | | | | | |
|---|---|---|---|---|---|---|---|

| Acc. no. | Account name | No. of pers. | Budgeted | | Rates | | |
|---|---|---|---|---|---|---|---|
| | | | Units | Dollars | Direct labor | D. lab. & d.exp. | For costing |
| | | | | | | | |
| | | | | | | | |
| | | | | | | | |
| | | | | | | | |

| | Indirect labor & expense | | | | | | |
|---|---|---|---|---|---|---|---|

| Acc. no. | Account name | Acc. class, F,V,C | Fixed portion | Variable portion | Budgeted dollars | Expense rate |
|---|---|---|---|---|---|---|
| | | | | | | |
| | | | | | | |
| | | | | | | |
| | | | | | | |
| | | | | | | |

**Figure 11-4**  Budget for labor and expense.

## THE BUDGET DATA BOOK(S)

Because of the sheer mass of data needed, collected and used, it can become a very real problem to keep it all in an orderly manner. Probably, the most practical single way for most of us to organize our budget data is by the use of a budget data book, or books if the enterprise is large enough.

In these books you place, by department, the budget data sheets and behind each of these all the supporting work sheets and analysis sheets that were used. In front of the budget data sheets for each department you place the budget summary sheet for the department. Each department has its own section of the book with an index tab on a stiff separator page.

Some budget people prefer a separate file folder for each department. It all comes down to a matter of personal preference. But good organization of the budget data is essential for a professional budget installation and follow-up effort.

## THE PERFORMANCE-TO-BUDGET REPORT

Now we consider the reason for all our budgeting work—the feedback for the entire effort. The performance-to-budget report is the management report that reflects the operating manager's efforts to live within and beat his budget's allowances.

The format of this particular report varies widely between companies. We will consider only five variants. The "bare bones" minimum of what should be on this budget report is shown on Fig. 11-5. The report as illustrated shows for a given department, for a given budget month or period:

1. The cost accounts on the department's budget

2. The budget allowance for the month

3. The actual expenditure or charges for the month

4. The difference or variance between the budget allowance and the actual expenditure, listing favorable variances in black and unfavorable variances in red, in brackets, or commonly with an asterisk on computer-produced reports

5. The actual expenditure or charges for the year-to-date

6. The variance year-to-date

7. Totals for the five columns of figures involved

The report as illustrated in Fig. 11-5 has the attributes of being very simple and clean-cut, and that is a virtue in any report. For example, so many of our computer-produced reports lack this attribute. It is so easy to print out another two or three columns of data.

On the other hand, the format and contents of the performance-to-

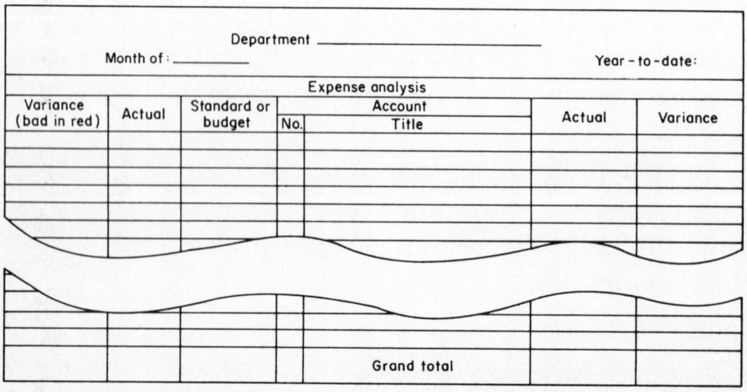

**Figure 11-5** Basic performance-to-budget report.

| Period ending : _____ | | | | | | | |
|---|---|---|---|---|---|---|---|

Dept. name : _____

Dept. no. : _____

Manager : _____

| Activity | |
|---|---|
| Actual | |
| Forecasted average | |
| % activity | |

| Year – to – date | | Cost account | This period | | | | |
|---|---|---|---|---|---|---|---|
| | | | | Budget | | | |
| Variance | Actual | | Actual | Current | Extra– budgetary allowance | Variance | |
| | | | | | | | |
| | | | | | | | |
| | | | | | | | |
| | | | | | | | |
| | | | | | | | |
| | | | | | | | |
| | | | | | | | |
| | | | | | | | |
| | | | | | | | |
| | | | | | | | |
| | | | | | | | |
| | | Total | | | | | |

**Figure 11-6**  Performance-to-budget report including activity data.

budget report must not be so simplified that the operating managers have to do a lot of pencil calculations to extract data that should have been provided on the report.

*A case in point.* One well-known corporation issues to its department heads monthly performance-to-budget reports that list only their cost accounts, and their budget allowances and actual expenditures for each. Each operating manager, upon receipt, then has to deduct actual from budget and calculate his variances for each cost account. The amazing thing about this installation is that the reports are computer-produced. The idiot machine could save a lot of managers a lot of time.

One additional set of facts that could be added to the basic performance-to-budget report of Fig. 11-5 is the current month's actual activity and the activity ratio. An example of this is at the upper right-hand corner on the format illustrated in Fig. 11-6. The three spaces provided show the actual activity, the forecast activity or *average month,* and the percent activity for the current month, which is, of course, the actual activity divided by the forecast average activity. Thus, if the activity measure is, say, standard hours produced, and this current month had an actual activity of 20,000 standard hours produced and the forecast average activity was 18,000 standard hours per month, then the activity section would be filled in as follows:

| | |
|---|---|
| Actual | 20,000 |
| Forecast average | 18,000 |
| % activity | 111% |

This additional activity data shows the operating department manager his activity for the month in concrete terms. Also, it states the activity ratio or percentage that was, in effect, applied to his variable costs and to the variable portion of his mixed costs to develop his budget allowances for this current month.

The format illustrated on Fig. 11-6 also provides an additional column for *extra-budgetary allowance*, so that, should an extra allowance

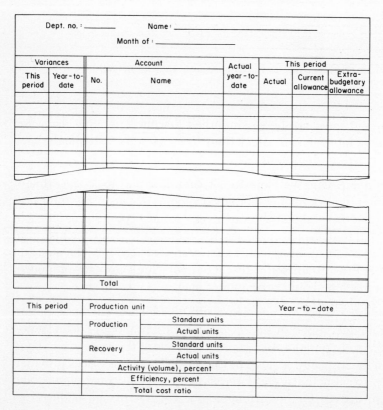

**Figure 11-7** Cost and variance statement.

| Month of: | Dept: | Cost and Variance Statement | | | | Year-to-date: | |
|---|---|---|---|---|---|---|---|
| | | | Expense analysis | | | | |
| Variance (bad in red) | Actual | Standard or budget | No. | Account Title | Standard or budget | Actual | Variance |
| | | | | Material: | | | |
| | | | | | | | |
| | | | | | | | |
| | | | | | | | |
| | | | | | | | |
| | | | | | | | |
| | | | | Total material | | | |
| | | | | Direct labor: | | | |
| | | | | | | | |
| | | | | | | | |
| | | | | Total dir. lab. | | | |
| | | | | Overhead: | | | |
| | | | | | | | |
| | | | | | | | |
| | | | | | | | |
| | | | | | | | |
| | | | | | | | |
| | | | | | | | |
| | | | | Variable o.h. | | | |
| | | | | Total variable | | | |
| | | | | Constant expense | | | |
| | | | | | | | |
| | | | | | | | |
| | | | | | | | |
| | | | | | | | |
| | | | | | | | |
| | | | | | | | |
| | | | | | | | |
| | | | | | | | |
| | | | | | | | |
| | | | | | | | |
| | | | | | | | |
| | | | | | | | |
| | | | | Total constant * | | | |
| | | | | Total overhead | | | |
| | | | | Tot. mfgr. expense | | | |
| | | | | Actual production | | | |
| | | | | Planned production | | | |
| | | | | Ratio of activity | | | |
| Remarks: *Eliminate for Key Man Bonus | | | | | | | |
| This operation is the responsibility of: | | | | | | | |

**Figure 11-8** Cost and variance statement with expense subdivisions.

be warranted and allowed, the amount is kept segregated and shown for the special allowance it actually is.

Another name frequently used for the performance-to-budget report is the *cost and variance statement*. This is the name often used where the budgets are tied into product standard costing and the monthly profit and loss statement. No matter what the name, it is still the report showing the operating manager's performance to budget.

Two formats of a cost and variance statement are illustrated in Fig. 11-7 and 11-8. In Fig. 11-7 the bottom section of the report shows not only the activity or volume ratio (actual units divided by standard units) but also an overall efficiency ratio calculated by dividing actual cost by standard costs. This data facilitates the analysis of variances in terms of both volume and efficiency. The format of the report illustrated in Fig. 11-7 is also different from the other three examples in the way it presents this-month and year-to-date data. Variances in terms of both time periods are kept segregated at the left side of the report. As a result, year-to-date actual costs adjoin the actual costs this-month.

Another example shown on Fig. 11-8 is a very complete and somewhat complex format. It shows budget, actual, and variance for both this-month and year-to-date. It provides room for material, labor, overhead, and what it calls *constant expense*. This company pays a key man bonus based on budget performance, and in effect, is segregating its total overhead for each department into two categories; *variable overhead,* which is considered under the control and the responsibility of the operating department head, and *constant* overhead, which is not included in this responsibility.

The final example of a performance-to-budget report is illustrated on Fig. 11-9. This format has the very attractive feature of presenting variances not only for the current month, but also for the previous three months. Thus, it shows, each month, the performance for the most recent four months, or one-third of the year. Inevitably, for each department, the operating manager, and the budget person involved, want and need to study a series of budget reports for a number of recent months. To do this, they have to carefully range across their desk the individual reports for those months. With this format, the key variance information for three recent months is provided with each new month's budget report. Thus, the information helps them keep an eye on cost trends. When a computer is producing the budget reports, such a format presents no great extra amount of preparation time.

As said earlier, there is an infinite variety of formats. Not illustrated, but frequently encountered, are such features as a *percent variance* column, which is calculated by dividing the dollars of variance by the dollars budgeted. It is a matter of judgment, but I am always wary of the mental deceptions possible with such percentages. A 2 percent unfavorable variance may be much more important than a 35 percent unfavorable variance, if the 2 percent variance is on a very large cost item. I always feel safer thinking and concentrating on the absolute money amount of the variances.

In addition, a *last year* column is often included, which shows the last year's data for the actual cost and sometimes for the variances. Again, it is a matter of preference, but such data has struck me as unneeded, if you have confidence in this year's budget allowances.

| Performance – to – Budget Report |  | Department _____ |  |  |  |  |  |  |
|---|---|---|---|---|---|---|---|---|
| Activity ratio: _____ |  |  |  |  |  |  |  |  |
| Cost account | | Month of : _____ | | | Variance, previous months | | | Variances, |
| No. | Name | Budget | Actual | Variance | 1st | 2d | 3d | year-to-date |
|  |  |  |  |  |  |  |  |  |
|  |  |  |  |  |  |  |  |  |
|  |  |  |  |  |  |  |  |  |
|  |  |  |  |  |  |  |  |  |
|  |  |  |  |  |  |  |  |  |
|  |  |  |  |  |  |  |  |  |
|  |  |  |  |  |  |  |  |  |
|  |  |  |  |  |  |  |  |  |
|  |  |  |  |  |  |  |  |  |
|  |  |  |  |  |  |  |  |  |
|  |  |  |  |  |  |  |  |  |
|  |  |  |  |  |  |  |  |  |
|  |  |  |  |  |  |  |  |  |
|  |  |  |  |  |  |  |  |  |
|  |  |  |  |  |  |  |  |  |
|  |  |  |  |  |  |  |  |  |
|  |  |  |  |  |  |  |  |  |
|  |  |  |  |  |  |  |  |  |
|  |  |  |  |  |  |  |  |  |
| Total |  |  |  |  |  |  |  |  |

**Figure 11-9**  Performance-to-budget report covering previous three-month period.

Certainly, it makes the report appreciably more complex and as a result, it increases the possibility that it might not be attended to as frequently.

The format you use has to be the best balance you can strike between clarity and ease-of-use versus the information the operating managers need to control their operation. The ideal is to make it as simple and clean-cut as possible, such as in Fig. 11-5 or 11-6.

There are two different views as to what should be on a performance-to-budget report. Some managers maintain that only those items of cost that are "controllable" by the department head should be on that manager's report. They believe that since these are the only costs that the manager can do something about, they should be the only ones reported to that manager for control and action. For example, they ask, "What does a manufacturing foreman have to say about his depreciation cost?" It is the production or industrial engineers who decide what equipment will be bought. It is the controller who decides how the equipment will be depreciated. And the foreman can do nothing about the fact that depreciation is, say, $50,000 per month for the equipment on the shop floor. Therefore, why put it on the budget report?

The opposing view maintains that all the costs involved in the operation of the department, and chargeable to it, should be included on that department's and its manager's performance-to-budget report. I, for one, hold strongly to the second view on several counts:

First, department heads should think like owners, which is the way all managers should think. Since we want them to think like "managers," we want them to see what monies are involved in the segment of the business that is under their direction. It is frequently quite impressive, in the case of a given department, to study the performance-to-budget report that shows all the costs assigned to that department. The figures total up to a lot of money in many cases. You realize that the department head is running a good-sized small business. The operating manager in charge who sees that *complete* cost picture is more likely also to be impressed by the money involved in the operation. Simply, he or she is more likely to think and act like a manager. The psychological effect has to be greater after seeing all the costs.

Second, we can miss some important realities when we arbitrarily decide what costs are not controllable, i.e., cannot be affected by a department head. A good example is the cost already cited above, i.e., departmental depreciation costs. True, the manager usually cannot raise or lower that cost. But he or she has a great deal to do with equipment utilization. A manager who sees that the equipment on the department floor costs $50,000 a month to depreciate is more likely to stay concerned with the utilization of that equipment. Thus, when production planning and control changes priorities, or splits runs so that set-up hours increase and machine utilization decreases, the manager is more likely to ask questions and even pound some desks if the answers are not good enough. It is the old "checks and balances" requirement once again, and we need and want those inputs. And we are more likely to get them if the department head sees every month that $50,000 depreciation cost for departmental equipment.

Third, if the performance-to-budget reports are tied into the general books of accounts, and the monthly profit and loss statement is developed from the total of these budgeted reports, then obviously all costs must be included on the performance-to-budget reports. Admittedly, there are accounting methods to circumvent this. It is possible in some operations to lump these departmental fixed costs onto an overall operationwide department such as General Factory and pick up these fixed costs from there for profit and loss purposes. However, ideally, the budgeted costs are also tied into the standard product costing routines. If that is the case, then usually the departmental costs must be complete, particularly if individual department costs are allocated to different products on different bases.

One additional point might be made in this context. If your budgets and their performance-to-budget reports are not tied into the general books, you have in effect "memo budgets." The general experience has been that such memo budgets are somewhat less likely to have continued management attention and support. In contrast, when the budgets are tied into the general books and when the budget reports come out of those general books, the data on the budget reports shows up, in condensed form, on the all-important profit and loss statement. If, for example, the budgets are not well maintained, large variances might develop and be exposed on the profit and loss. To avoid this, the budgets that lay behind the performance-to-budget reports are more likely to receive continuing management support and maintenance monies.

## HELPFUL ADDITIONAL DATA

The performance-to-budget report is a condensation of the results of all the decisions and actions of the department head in the budget period. A lot happens in any given budget period. By the time the operating manager receives the budget report, some of the events can be forgotten. Also costs showing up in this month's budget report might be the result of action taken in previous months. For example, tooling or supplies might have been ordered in February, received in March, and billed in April, so that its costs show up in the April budget report. For all these reasons, it is sometimes helpful for the budgeting function to provide operating managers with additional data accompanying their budget reports.

As a practical matter, such additional data is most commonly possible when the computer is being used to collect the actual cost data. The usual "manual" budgeting system normally does not include the budget staff needed to produce such auxiliary data. However, more and more of us have the computer's data-handling capacity available. When we do, the data can and should be provided, as needs arise. Very often it is the budgeting function, as they engage in the budget follow-up effort, that can best identify these needs. By observing how the operating managers are using their budgets, and by attending to the questions asked by those managers, the budgeting people can usually see what is required.

For example, such costs as supplies and perishable tooling may represent a hundred or more transactions in a budget month. The foreman cannot be expected to remember them all. However, if provided with a computer printout of each charged item, the sum of which totals the actual costs for the month, the foreman has the opportunity to study them in detail and review where the money actually was spent.

Similarly, a computer printout listing the straight time and overtime pay of all the people under the foreman can help demonstrate just where the overtime cost total shown on the monthly budget report was spent.

If you have work measurement, either measured daywork or incentives, the department head is probably receiving weekly, or even daily, printouts of individual employee performances to standard. Monthly summaries of that data are less likely to be received. As a result, the manager, when analyzing actual labor costs, may have to consult four or more past labor efficiency reports to see where the causes of unfavorable labor variances may lie. A monthly summary can save a lot of work and would undoubtedly encourage a more detailed consideration of the facts behind an unfavorable labor variance, if the manager has one.

Prose explanations of the larger variances frequently accompany the performance-to-budget reports as they are sent to higher levels of management. Ideally, these brief explanations should be made by the operating manager who is in charge of the department being reported on, or they should be made by his or her boss. However, in some enterprises, senior management expects these comments from the budgeting people. Even worse, the time involved in issuing the reports may be so short that the budgeting staff has little or no chance to discuss the comments they consider necessary with the operating managers concerned. When this unfortunate set of circumstances exists, a copy of the comments made by Budgeting should be sent directly to the operating managers, with, or following closely behind, the managers' monthly performance-to-budget reports.

# MAINTAINING THE OPERATING BUDGET

Equal in importance to good budget development is good budget maintenance. Too many well-conceived, well-developed, initially well-supported budget programs have been allowed to deteriorate for lack of management emphasis and the needed maintenance funds.

In some enterprises, a not uncommon sequence of budget events falls into the following pattern: The operation has no budgets or very weak and ineffective budgets. Management, recognizing a cost improvement opportunity, decides to install an operating budget or to revitalize the existing weak budgets. They do a reasonably good job and the savings in the first two or three years are quite satisfactory. In fact, the budgets save much more than they cost to install. But in subsequent years, the savings clearly assignable to budgets decrease and management's interest in the budgets decline. And operating costs begin, inexorably, to edge upwards. Eventually, of course, the need for a revitalization program is recognized, and the cycle is repeated.

This phenomenon is much more common where budgets are used only as a cost control technique. However, it is a pity, because increasing costs can go undetected as management attention and budget maintenance weaken. Budgets are not the only management tool that experiences these cycles. Work measurement programs frequently follow a similar pattern.

The subject and problems of budget maintenance have numerous facets including continuing training, budget follow-up, budget revisions, extra-budgetary allowances, and the timing and distribution of performance-to-budget reports. However, in this chapter the attention is to the administrative aspects of budget maintenance. The *budget follow-up* aspect, so critical to good budget maintenance, will be given individual attention in the next chapter.

## THE NEED FOR CONTINUING TRAINING

When a new budget or a budget revitalization program is started, there is usually a great deal of fanfare. Meetings are held; perhaps even the president addresses everyone. Careful and complete explanations are made to all department heads, preferably individually. Ideally, a member of the budgeting staff works with each department head, in a participative effort, to develop the new budgets. And everyone in operating management has the opportunity to ask any question on his or her mind.

After all this has been done, and when the performance-to-budget reports are being issued regularly and everything looks routine, it is a mistake to assume that all the operating department managers completely understand their budgets. Those managers will have questions that had not occurred to them during the budget start-up phase. Even more surprising to the budgeting staff person will be a statement or question from an operating manager that shows a complete misunderstanding of something the budget person vividly remembers explaining to that operating manager. This has to be expected. It is no reflection on the manager's intelligence. Much of it is still strange. He or she needs continuing follow-up training while developing hands-on experience with the budget.

The manager about whom the budgeting staff really has to worry is the one who does not ask questions or make statements about the budgets. The reasons for such silence are many. Some managers are just plain shy. Some are afraid their questions will sound stupid. Others are erroneously convinced of their own complete understanding and do not ask questions to double-check the accuracy of their perceptions. In all these cases, the lines of communications are not yet established and, at first, they usually have to be set up by the budgeting staff. This is a precondition for good budget maintenance.

## FOLLOWING UP WITH OPERATING MANAGERS

Some companies believe that they can handle this required follow-up training in their budgets by monthly budget meetings. Thus, in a manufacturing plant situation, the plant manager holds a monthly budget meeting en masse with all the operating department managers. This procedure, they believe, gives each foreman the opportunity to ask any questions he or she might have.

On several counts this is an inadequate procedure. For one thing, while such meetings may be an excellent forum to highlight and praise favorable variance performances, they certainly are no place to discuss and possibly criticize unfavorable variances. In addition, the practice ignores the psychological realities involved. The average foreman will come to such a meeting, sit as far back in the room as possible, and, at all costs, try to avoid appearing stupid among his or her peers by asking questions. As a result, those questions don't get asked, and the foreman leaves the meeting with the same doubts as before. Frequently a first-line manager will justify remaining silent by deciding that it isn't right to take up others' time with personal questions and problems—but the underlying cause is timidity and fear. Not every foreman will react this way, but enough will to prevent these mass meetings from being an effective technique of continuing education in the operating budget.

These observations do not apply only to operating department managers. Their bosses tend to react in much the same manner. One of the problems in leading a management seminar is to have the group ask enough questions, either to settle any misunderstandings or to confirm the understanding they have of the subject matter being covered.

*A case in point.* I conducted a one-day, in-plant session on cost analysis for the industrial products group of a major conglomerate. Attending were the controllers from the fourteen individual subsidiary companies and the president of the group. The only person that asked questions all day was the president. He asked a lot of questions, some of them on his understanding of the subjects discussed. It became increasingly apparent, as the day developed, that the controllers were afraid that their questions might appear stupid before the boss. Certainly, their silence was not the result of my being perfectly clear on the subjects and techniques discussed.

It is a very human phenomenon, that the budgeting staff has to expect and do their best to overcome, in the given circumstances. In maintaining operating budgets, the best means of continuing training is by personal visits by members of the budgeting staff to the department heads at those managers' desks. There, at the relative privacy of their own desk, they are more likely to ask the questions that they have. The budget person will often find that the questions the managers have may be only half-formed in their minds. In that case, they need help, via judicious questioning, to form the questions they have about their budgets. Obviously, the more informed about the operation and the more psychologically acute the budget person is, the better the help can be.

A rule-of-thumb can be proposed for the frequency of such visits: Once every two months each operating manager should be visited, at his or her desk, by a member of the budgeting staff. Ideally, this should happen monthly, but the minimum should be once every two months. This means that the budget staff has to be of sufficient size that such periodic visits are possible. In some companies such regular visits are routine operating procedure. In other companies departmental operating managers do not see a budgeting person for months at a time.

The budget staff should have their own reasons for wanting to do this. First, it gives them not only a reason but a need for getting out into the operation. It is the means by which they keep current. Second, it gives them the opportunity to identify progressive actions on cost improvement that may be useful in and exportable to other departments and operating areas. This matter will be dealt with in greater depth in Chapter 13, on budget follow-up. Here we are concerned with budget maintenance and that includes continuing training.

Some managers criticize this whole approach, maintaining that it usurps line management's prerogatives and responsibilities. They believe, for example, that in a manufacturing enterprise, it is the plant manager's job to answer the foremen's questions, that the foremen should address all their questions to the plant manager, and that there need be and should be no direct contact between the budget staff and the foremen. This attitude is too rigid, unrealistic, and impractical, and although not widespread, it does exist. A plant manager with any degree of confidence in the budget staff will welcome their help and contact with operating managers. First, he or she will recognize that the budgeting staff needs that contact to keep current and thus, to be more helpful to the managers in the joint development of budget allowances. Second, plant managers, like their foremen, are always heavily burdened and they usually welcome all the help they can get, particularly on such a time-consuming task as continuing training on such a complex matter as budgeting. The properly trained and service-minded budget person is not going to criticize the foremen and sharply question unfavorable variances. They are out in the operation to answer foremen's questions on budgets and possibly to make constructive suggestions on ideas that they have seen work elsewhere and that they believe might work here.

## THE WHEN AND WHY OF BUDGET REVISIONS

Revisions to the budget as originally established at the start of the budget year are needed for two reasons—human error and changes in the operating conditions. Like the establishment of the original budget allowances, budget revisions should be a joint effort by the operating managers involved and the budgeting staff.

No budget is ever originally established perfectly. Things will be missed and errors made. And the larger and more complex the enterprise, the more the likelihood of human error. As the errors are detected during the budget year, they must be corrected. Most corrections are minor. When they are, they can be quickly effected between the budget person and operating manager involved, and the next higher level of management is simply notified of the correction made. If a major error is detected, that markedly affects the basic profit plan, then the correction has to be approved by executive (top) management. Such budget revisions are embarrassing, even cataclysmic, though fortunately rare.

The more common and thus more troublesome budgeting problems are those caused by changes in operating conditions. Such changes often require budget revision, either upward or downward in the sales forecast or the cost allowances. Let us consider first the downward revisions in both sales and costs, then the revisions upward.

## Downward Revision to Sales Forecasts

Ideally, the profit plan can be firmly set for the budget year by means of realistic income projections (sales forecasts) and sensibly calculated cost allowances. Then, as the year unfolds, year-to-date actual income is compared to forecast income, and year-to-date actual costs are compared to budgeted costs. And by deduction, year-to-date actual pretax profit is compared to planned pretax profit. The advantage of a firmly established profit plan, done at the start of the budget year, is that it allows a continuing comparison between what was originally forecast and calculated to what actually happens as the year progresses. The base for comparison is unchanged and variances can be detected and measured against that firm base. As a result, poor projections or poor allowances that might have been made in laying down the profit plan are more readily identified and thus exposed for correction, or at least improvement, in the next budget year.

In contrast, some enterprises favor a "rolling" forecast of sales income. Under such a procedure, the profit plan is under continuing revision and there is no single firm base against which the subsequent actual performance can be compared. Conditions in some industries are so volatile that this can be a necessary procedure, but, there is a subtle danger here. Where the practice is followed, it can become an "excuse" for revising poor forecasts and sloppy allowances that should not have been made in the first place. The very natural tendency, under these circumstances, may be for senior management to overlook the fact that poor projections were made at the start of the budget year, because with rolling forecasts sequential changes are part of the procedure. Thus, the need for changes to the forecast might be blandly accepted instead of questioned as to their need and propriety. This danger is particularly important in the area of the sales forecast. If we have analyzed and identified our costs properly, we are prepared to flex our cost allowances to a reasonably wide range of operational activity. But it is in the sales forecasting area that many of us need improvement. This will come only with increased senior management attention, and anything that might endanger or even reduce that attention should be avoided wherever possible. Rolling forecasts, some of us believe, tend to do this. The use of such changing forecasts is a matter of judgment, but a very important matter. The method has some strong advocates, but perhaps that advocacy should be confined strictly to those situations where it is absolutely necessary. Certainly it should never be accepted as a replacement for realistic income projections at the start of the year, if they can be made, and particularly if they are being made by other enterprises in the industry.

As desirable as a firm yearly profit plan is, and as much as we would like to follow one every year, there are unfortunately hard times when we must revise our income projections downward in the light of a developing economic recession. For example, if sales are off 40 percent year-to-date and there is no hope of recouping the lost sales in the remaining months of the year, then it is unrealistic to abide by the original profit plan. Major revisions to that plan are obviously required. If these revisions are not made, the extent of the necessary cost reduction action might not be as clear, or the action taken might be delayed longer than it should be.

## Downward Revisions to Cost Allowances

Downward revisions to budgeted costs can be required by many types of changes in operating conditions, and each revision has to be evaluated and acted upon on its own individual merits and conditions. For example, if an investment is made in new production equipment that sharply reduces the labor costs in a given department, then the budget allowances for labor in that department should be promptly revised downward, with due regard for the learning curve. It was a capital investment that caused the revision, and the reduced labor allowances, and reduced labor costs, are part of the payback for that investment.

On the other hand, if a department head makes an ingenious change to the operation that results in reduced costs and a very fine favorable variance, it can be poor practice immediately to lower the manager's budget allowances. It is psychologically devastating for an operating manager to make some progressive move, develop a good favorable variance in a given cost, and then have the next month's budget allowance for that cost revised downward to reflect the new, lower cost levels. Very humanly, he or she can feel a dulling of the vigor for future moves to beat the budget.

I, for one, always advocate to clients that they allow favorable variances that are the result of progressive action on the part of a manager to build up for the budget year. It should be understood that every year is a new budget year, and that downward revisions to budget allowances will be made yearly to reflect all improvements in operating conditions. However, within the year, allowances are best not revised downward if favorable variances are the result of the ingenuity and vigor of the operating manager. Unfortunately, even with this policy, you can still have "games" played. A manager who has a good idea near the end of the budget year may spend more time to develop it in order to delay its introduction until the start of the new budget year. But this is not nearly as unfortunate an action as the stifling of improvement action that can result if the cost allowance is reduced immediately upon the reduction of the actual cost.

Normally, downward revisions to cost allowances need not be extended into formal changes to the original profit plan. Instead they are expected to show up as identifiable additions to the favorable variances in actual pretax profit.

## Upward Revisions to Sales Forecasts

Assuming a realistic original sales forecast, there usually should be no need to make upward revisions to sales forecasts, despite the fact that sales may be well above the level originally projected. Under these happy circumstances, if your cost analysis has been properly done, you will be prepared to adjust or flex your cost allowances upward for the higher actual activity. The higher-than-expected income can simply be identified as the cause of the larger-than-ever-expected favorable variance in income.

If, however, such favorable income variances are a recurring phenomenon, senior operating management must be alert to the possibility that "games" are being played. Under the "shrewdie" approach to sales forecasting, the name of the game is to be overconservative in projecting income so that when actual income exceeds the projection, Marketing can point with pride and say, "See, we beat our forecast." This is not realistic forecasting. Recurring favorable income variances, particularly if they are substantial in size, should not be tolerated by top management. They should expect a better original forecasting job from Marketing.

## Upward Revisions to Cost Allowances

Upward revisions to budgeted costs may also be required by many kinds of changed operating conditions. As in the case of downward revisions, each has to be evaluated and acted upon on its own conditions and individual merits.

However, upward revisions are more dangerous to the welfare of the budget. A downward revision to a cost allowance is usually the result of a clearly identifiable and accepted reduction in costs, such as, for example, new equipment on the shop floor that reduces labor costs. In contrast, upward revisions may be sought by operating managers on less identifiable grounds, even on judgmental anticipations of what is expected in the future months of the budget year. Also it is very human to make life as easy as you can, and some operating managers attempt this in the budget area by constantly arguing and pressuring for ever higher allowances. The judgment or pressure that may be involved for higher cost allowances can result in too loose, and thus poor, budgets. Operating to budget and achieving favorable variances should require progressive action and continuing cost improvement. If this is not necessary, and if the budgets can be met by preserving the status quo or, worse, by simply asking for and obtaining higher cost allowances, then the budgets are obviously not effective. Some budget installations have been made futile by too easily obtained upward revisions to cost allowances.

Again, each instance of an increase to a cost allowance has to be evaluated individually. Here are some examples:

If midway through the budget year the time arrives to pay the additional hourly rates agreed to in the labor contract for the second year of a three-year labor agreement, then the labor cost allowances have to be revised upward. This assumes, of course, that operating management is using the labor cost controls provided them and the labor involved, as effectively as is possible under the given conditions.

If the local power company increases its rates, the allowance for power costs may or may not be increased the full amount required by the rate increase. Certainly, it should not be increased if there is opportunity for power use improvements.

Because of the recent sharp increases in power costs, many enterprises, particularly manufacturing companies, have begun seriously to study power usage and to correct poor practice and too costly uses of electrical power. Some of their findings have been stunning. Examples include discovering 600-horsepower air compressors left running twenty-four hours a day, seven days a week, when the operation was on an eighty-hour week; and finding offices and corridors lit for hours beyond their actual use, with footcandle readings way beyond the actual need.

This is poor practice that can be corrected with the proper attention. In addition, there is progressive action that many companies can use effectively, such as power factor correction and computer control of peak demand load.

If, because of inflation, the cost of an important operating supply is expected to increase, the allowance for operating supplies may *not* be increased. Instead the approach may be that it is possible to use that supply item more efficiently or make up that increase by more effective use of other supplies.

Obviously, there can be no flat rules, and each instance requires its own understanding, logic, and decision making.

The problem of whether or not to increase a given cost allowance should be a joint determination between the operating manager and the budgeting person. Their problem is to settle jointly on an allowance that meets the current needs of the operating manager, yet does not allow too much. If they cannot agree, their individual cases may have to go to higher levels of management.

Once again, the budget person faces the danger of starting to think and act as the custodian of company funds. In the area of increasing cost allowances, however, the budget person has a narrow line to walk, and often very judgmental matters to deal with. He or she can only carry out the responsibility to serve both the operating manager and the enterprise as an entity. This means collecting as many facts as possible in the given situation and making what judgments have to be made. The budget person has to attend with an open mind to the judgments of the operating manager involved. Then together they have to decide on increasing the allowance. If that operating manager has learned to respect and trust that budget person, they can usually resolve the problem.

In any case, all such upward revisions to cost allowances must be approved by higher levels of management. Perhaps the best rule is to require the approval of a manager *two* levels above that of the manager involved. Thus, in a manufacturing enterprise, increases to a foreman's given cost allowance would be approved not by the plant superintendent but by the plant manager. This approval from two levels above is, of course, not possible when you deal with matters at the highest management levels. There, the manager's immediate boss usually has to be looked to for the source of approval.

This matter of what management level will approve budget revisions should be dealt with and agreed upon at the start of the budget program. At that time, the agreed-upon procedures, being a part of basic budget policy, should be put in writing and a copy given to all operating managers.

One very important subtlety in the area of budget revisions is the fact that budgets can have an immobilizing effect. They can actually suppress progressive management action. This unfortunate situation is typified by the department head who has a good idea which shows every indication of improving departmental operating conditions or reducing its costs, but which will cost some money to effect initially. Since that start-up money is not allowed in the operating budget, the manager does not think it is possible to make the progressive move. Worse, he or she may not even mention the idea to anyone. Budgets are not handcuffs. They are not a fixed-in-concrete structure. They are a plan, and plans can be changed as new and better opportunities arise. They should never be allowed to delay the start of progressive action. They need not, if the possibility of budget revisions is understood by all the operating managers.

## APPLYING EXTRA-BUDGETARY ALLOWANCES

Budget revisions are changes made during the course of the budget year that will apply to the remainder of that year. In contrast, extra-budgetary allowances are one-time changes to the budget to meet unusual conditions resulting from a single event. Usually they entail additional cost allowances, above the planned level. Very commonly the event requiring these allowances is an emergency or a disaster. In the unfortunate event of a massive power failure, or major equipment breakdown, or fire, or flood, the operating managers can be unjustly penalized if these extra allowances are not made. The unfavorable variances that result from such events might keep them in the "red" for the remainder of the budget year—through no fault of their own. In all fairness in such cases, an extra-budgetary allowance is indicated.

In some operating situations, the need for such allowances may arise for reasons other than disasters and "acts of God." The cause might be, for example, as simple a thing as a marketing/delivery crisis that demands an inordinate amount of overtime beyond the budget allowance for normal operations. Actually in such an instance, the extrabudgetary allowances that are justified are a good measure of the extraordinary costs imposed by the marketing/delivery crisis.

As in the case of budget revisions, there can be no flat rules for extrabudgetary allowances. Each instance must stand on its own, and be decided on its own merits. Some are obvious; others need the wisdom of Solomon to evaluate and quantify. Obviously, they cannot be given out casually or too freely. On the other hand, the department head's budget performance for the year cannot be ruined unjustly. The only guidelines are management's and budgeting's good sense and determination for fair play. And the only guide they have for that is to determine what they would need if they were in the position of the department manager.

It is advantageous to try to put in writing the conditions under which extra-budgetary allowances will be made. This is particularly advisable at the start of a budget revitalization program or at the installation of new budgets. You will not think of all the reasons for such extra allowances, but if you know the operation, you will think of most of them. Having them in writing, as part of the budget policy, can save a lot of disputation later on.

Finally, as with budget revisions, the level of management hierarchy able to authorize such extra-budgetary allowances should be specified in writing. Again, where practical, such approving authority is best located two levels above the manager being affected.

## TIMELINESS OF PERFORMANCE-TO-BUDGET REPORTS

A very important attribute of effective budgeting is the promptness with which the performance-to-budget reports are issued. The later they are, the less useful they are. Operating managers, with their multitude of day-to-day problems, tend to forget the past situations they faced, and the actions they took in the last budget month. Also, psychologically, when faced with data presented too long after the event, they very humanly tend to regard it as history and of much less import than today's situation and problems.

When the performance-to-budget reports are tied into the general books of accounts, as they should be, they are developed from the original and basic accounting records. Thus, their issuance ties very closely to the issuance of the monthly profit and loss statement. That vital statement, of course, has the same demands for promptness. So any step that helps issue the budget reports more promptly, helps improve the timeliness of the P&L and vice versa.

It is an unfortunate fact that too many enterprises reach the twentieth of the following month, or even later, before these budget reports are issued. We should set our goals tighter than that. Budget reports should be issued within ten calendar days after the month's end. The increasing availability and use of the computer should speed up the issuance of the budget reports. Unfortunately, a frequently heard observation is that the advent of the computer has further delayed the performance-to-budget reports. Start-up problems, breakdowns, accidents—all these you can understand and accept. But to have the budget reports consistently delayed because the computer is producing them is intolerable. Such a situation should not be accepted by the senior management and computer managers who are paying for the computer. If they cannot correct it, they should go hat-in-hand in search of other companies in their area who are producing on-time computerized budget reports. From the procedures and practices of others, they will see that it can be done. They may pick up some methods that they can adapt to their own situation. If others can do it, you can do it. It just needs operating management's insistence that the job be done promptly.

## SIZE OF THE BUDGETING STAFF

Obviously, the amount and quality of the budget maintenance work performed is determined by the size of the budget staff. It is a very direct relationship.

One of the questions most frequently asked at budget seminars is how large a budget staff is needed. And, of course, there can be no one answer, nor one way to determine that answer. The appropriate size has to vary directly with the complexity of the operating organization, the complexity of the product, and the complexity of the manufacturing or operating process. If you produce a relatively simple product via a relatively simple process with four manufacturing departments, you obviously need a smaller budget staff than if you produce a very complex product in twenty manufacturing departments.

The minimum staff is needed if the budgets are set unilaterally by a budgeting function under, say, the controller, with minimum or no participation by the levels of operating management. Or a minimum budgeting staff is needed if the operating managers set their own budgets and the budgeting staff only provides accounting and a modicum of administrative services. But both these approaches, I hope we agree, do not result in effective budgets.

The answer to the question of how large your budgeting staff need be for effective budgeting has to lie in the answers of such further questions as:

> Are the budgets effective in that they provide a workable profit plan and encourage continuing cost improvement by operating managers?

> Are the budgets developed under a joint effort between the operating managers and the budget staff?

> Are the budget cost allowances reasonably good, so that variances, plus or minus, are of acceptable size?

> Are the budgets understood by all levels of the operating management?

> Does the first line of management, i.e., the department heads, need continuing training to improve their understanding of their budgets?

> Do the department heads believe they have sufficient access to the budget staff? Do they confer with a member of that staff at least once every two months?

If you cannot, with reasonable confidence, give positive answers to these questions, then the odds are on that you are understaffed in the budgeting function.

Judging subjectively, I would have to conclude that the most common situation is too little staff in the budgeting function. If this were not true, the symptoms of budget weakness would not be so frequently observed. There would not be so much dissatisfaction and criticism of their budgets on the part of so many operating managers.

# 13

# BUDGET FOLLOW-UP

The budgeting job is not completed when performance-to-budget reports are being issued and maintained and when question-answering sessions are being held periodically with individual department heads. The final phase is budget follow-up, in which the budgeting function must have an important role.

Budget follow-up is the action taken to see that the budgets are properly used and that they cause the initiation of improvement steps, if they indicate that such steps are possible. Thus, it is the *control* phase of budgeting and it utilizes the performance-to-budget reports to achieve the results desired from the budgeting investment.

This whole area of budget follow-up can be, and often is, the most difficult of all areas in which the budget person operates. In other phases of budgeting, the budget person is providing more obvious services. For example, when working with the department heads to help develop their cost objectives and budget allowances, the budget person is providing much-needed assistance. Although perhaps questioning some of the desired allowances, he or she is also collecting and providing the data the department heads need, and these time-pressed managers usually welcome this help and participation. But in the follow-up phase the budget person is approaching, in effect, a controlling and directing role and this, if not done well, can be psychologically dangerous. Furthermore, it should be recognized, by all levels and areas of management, that budgets, necessary as they are, can come to be considered a pressure device or bludgeon that, despite initial cost improvements, can cause longer-range problems of anxiety, frustration, and interpersonal conflicts within the various levels of the management hierarchy and between management functions. These dangers are particularly prevalent in the follow-up phase of budgeting.

Therefore, this follow-up phase of the budget task can present great problems to the budget person. The operating manager must accept the part that the budget person plays, and just as the budget person should be sensitive to the manager's problems, the manager should be sensitive to the budget person's problems. If the budget person does the necessary follow-up work well, it offers not a threat but still another service to the operating manager. More than a service, it offers an opportunity.

## DISTRIBUTION OF BUDGET REPORTS

The basic mechanism for budget follow-up is, of course, the performance-to-budget report. At the top management level, it provides the comparison of actual income to forecast income, of actual costs to budgeted costs, and of actual profit to planned profit, all of which can help lead to the detection of problems and to the development of corrective action, if needed. At the lower levels of operating management, the report provides the comparison of actual versus budgeted expenses and the subsequent variances in order to identify possible problem areas and to initiate any needed corrective action on costs.

Obviously, each department head should receive his or her own performance-to-budget report. Other copies should go to his or her immediate superior and to Budgeting.

In large organizations the usual practice is to send successive summaries of these reports to successive higher levels of management. Thus, for example, in a large manufacturing organization, copies of the performance-to-budget reports for each production and service department go to the plant manager. The summary report for that plant, as an entity, together with summary reports for other plants go to the division manager. Summary reports from individual divisions go to corporate management.

There is a danger, however, to such successive summaries. Being summaries, they present the algebraic sum of favorable and unfavorable variances for each item of cost or cost account in all the operating and service departments included. As a result, one or more large unfavorable variances can be greatly diminished, or even completely hidden, because they are overcome by a larger number of small favorable variances. Or some very large favorable variances can be overcome by a larger number of very small unfavorable variances. In either case, the detailed facts are not being made available to the higher levels of management. Admittedly, these higher levels cannot afford to be inundated with too much budget detail. But perhaps the most common error is that they are not told enough, and if any error is to be made, it should be to provide more detail than at first they might think they want. Certainly, in the organization example given above, the division manager should ideally receive the budget reports from each major production and service department of each plant.

It can be a tough balance for top managers between too much and too little budget detail. You have to make your own decisions, but just keep in mind that you cannot afford to see too little. Also, there may be ways to handle, with facility, some of the detail.

*A case in point.* The executive vice president of an eleven-plant electronics company insisted on receiving a copy of the performance-to-budget report for every production department (and there were a lot of departments). He did not reveal the fact, but he had his secretary "tickle" each given department for a specific month of each quarter year. Thus, he reviewed each production department's report once every quarter year. Fortunately, the computer-produced budget reports showed the variance information not only for the current month but for the previous three months.

## MAKING VARIANCE ANALYSIS

Variance analysis is the determination of the reasons for a reported variance, whether favorable or unfavorable. Operating managers are concerned with both types. Unfavorable variances represent actual costs higher than those allowed, and may indicate either the need for budget/accounting correction or for improved operating practice. Favorable variances, if not the result of reporting errors, show progress and may highlight operating improvements that can be applied to other areas of the organization.

Cost-reporting errors, such as wrong cost charging, are commonly detected during variance analysis. Such errors can and must be readily corrected. Variance analysis also reveals errors in determining or applying budget allowances. When an error is found, a budget revision or allowance correction can be made.

The discussion that follows deals primarily with variance analysis under flexible budgeting. If an operation has only fixed budgets, the analysis of variances for some costs is appreciably more complicated. For other costs, it is, in practice, usually impossible. For example, you may be able to analyze the variance in labor costs under fixed budgeting. However, you have not only to segregate the labor efficiency variance (assuming you have labor standards) and labor wage rate variance, you also have to segregate the volume variance. But under fixed budgeting there is, in practice, usually no way that you can analyze the variance in, for example, such costs as power or supplies unless actual activity happens to be equal to budgeted activity for the month. Under fixed budgeting, the only comparison you have is, for example, budgeted power cost to actual power cost. You do not know what power should have cost you at actual activity. You only know what it did cost you at actual activity and what it should have cost you at budgeted activity. With your fixed budgets, you are not prepared to calculate what budgeted power costs should be at actual activity. As a result, you cannot identify the portion of the variance that was due to the difference between budgeted and actual activity and the portion due to operating efficiency or inefficiency.

Some operating managers, and even their superiors, are entirely satisfied to attend to only the performance to the *total* budget for the department. In other words, if the total variance for the department is favorable, or only insignificantly unfavorable, then budget performance is considered satisfactory. This is not good enough. Many managements do this, but the practice results in not getting full use of the budget and all the labor involved in the cost-by-cost analysis of the budget development. In fact, it is a very odd mental attitude. Senior managers in analyzing their profit plan would never consider studying only actual profit versus planned profit. Instead they want to see, monthly, how each product line or division performed in actual versus planned sales, and in actual versus budgeted costs. Yet they will permit their operating managers at lower levels to speak, and think, in terms of *total* variances. Obviously, such practice allows the favorable variances to be lost in the unfavorable variances and the unfavorable variances to be covered up by the favorable ones. This attitude misses profit opportunities, because the right questions do not get asked, i.e., "While we added to profit with the favorable variances, why did we reduce profit with the unfavorable variances?" or "What can we do about those unfavorable variances to reduce them, or to convert them to favorable?" Managers who do not ask these questions fail to remember the truism that every dollar of reduced cost goes into profit and every dollar of increased cost comes out of profit.

The favorable variances of significant size should be examined with the same attention as the unfavorable variances. Such favorable variances can be indications of reporting or budgeting errors. But they might indicate some ingenious and progressive moves that senior management and budgeting should know about in order possibly to apply them elsewhere. Of equal importance, favorable variances should be accented in order to insure the proper recognition of the operating manager who accomplished the cost improvement action.

In analyzing variances, it is usually more helpful for both the operating manager and the budget person to study not only the current month but also the most recent three to four months and year-to-date. In some budget installations this can be an unwieldy thing to do, particularly with the standard 14¾ inch wide computer printout. Probably the best-sized printout for the operating manager's use is the standard 8½ × 11 inch, yet too few computerized budget systems are designed to produce that sized budget report. In any case, with or without the computer, serious budget analysis usually has to consider not only the current month, but also the more recent past months, because only such an examination can detect cost trends. For example, a series of rather small unfavorable variances that have not yet built up to a great year-to-date unfavorable variance on the current budget report may be worth some introspection by both the department head and the budget person. Such a situation probably would not be detected unless the reports for a series of recent months were studied.

In practical budgeting we can only afford the time to analyze significant variances. But what is a "significant" variance? There can be no universal rule in percentage terms or even in absolute dollar terms. What could be insignificant dollars in a very large cost in a very large department could be very significant in a small department or in a smaller company. Certainly, percentage limits can never be accepted as the sole guideline of significance. A 2 percent unfavorable variance in a $50,000 a month cost is very significant in contrast to a 20 percent unfavorable variance in a $1000 a month cost. Both might be worth investigating, but the 2 percent variance involves five times the money. You have to establish your own guidelines for your own individual situation. Probably, for most of us, analysis is best done in terms of absolute variance dollar amounts, by agreement between the individual operating manager and the budget person involved.

As discussed in professional journals, some attempts have been made to apply statistical tools to the determination of significant variances. This approach develops control limits to costs, just like the statistical quality control limits that are placed about measurable tolerances. Thus, in the operating budget application, if favorable or unfavorable variances do not exceed the plus or minus control limits established, they are not considered significant or worth further analysis. The idea has certain attractive aspects. However, it can, unless the control limits are very carefully set, result in the ignoring of substantial dollar variances on large costs, as does the application of flat percentages. Also, it might result in the ignoring of a continuing small unfavorable variance that is within the higher control limit each month. Probably the most serious problem with the approach, up to this point in time, is that most budget staffs do not have the work-hours available to develop and apply the idea to their operation. In the years to come, the increasing use of the computer in budgeting may make the idea more of a possibility for more budget people and installations.

## Analysis of Income or Sales Variance

In actual use and effect the profit plan is a fixed budget, particularly when we consider sales variances. In establishing the profit plan, we lay down, for each month of the budget year, an anticipated sales income. Then as the actual year passes, we compare actual sales to planned sales and calculate the variance for each month. To analyze that sales or income variance we have to split it up into its two components, i.e., volume variance and price variance. Only by knowing these individually can we determine the causes of the variance, and identify any possible needed action.

To demonstrate this with a very simple model, assume that for the month of March, sales income was planned or budgeted for 100,000 units at a $5 selling price per unit, thus predicting $500,000 income. Let us further assume that actual sales in March were $540,000. Therefore:

| | |
|---|---|
| Actual sales income | $540,000 |
| Budgeted sales income | 500,000 |
| Favorable variance | $ 40,000 |

Ostensibly, this is a happy situation, but no smart marketing manager would like to take such a variance at its bare-face value. Things may not be quite as happy as they seem. Suppose for example, that because of inflation the $540,000 of sales income was the result of selling 90,000 units at $6 apiece. Now the favorable income variance breaks down like this:

| | |
|---|---|
| Volume variance (100,000 − 90,000) × $5 | ($50,000) |
| Price variance ($6 − $5) × 90,000 | 90,000 |
| Favorable variance | $ 40,000 |

Thus, sales volume, in terms of units, was 10 percent less than the goal planned. The marketing manager may or may not be able to do anything about it, but he needs to know it.

Such analysis of income variance must be done, whenever possible, by product line or model line, and by sales territory. In some cases, it is even done by salesperson or market outlet. The variance analysis needed depends upon the type of product and the marketing circumstances, but any meaningful analysis of income variance must segregate the volume and price increments.

## Analysis of Cost or Expense Variances

Early in this discussion of variance analysis, the point was made that with fixed budgets, the analysis of variances is appreciably more complicated than it is with flexible budgets, and that for some costs under fixed budgets, analysis is impossible. These points are so basic, and so important, that they deserve more attention and exposition by example.

Assume, in a very simple example, that for the month of March, an activity was budgeted in terms of 100,000 units and that labor for March was budgeted at $300,000. Assume further that actual labor costs were $250,000. Under fixed budgeting the variance would be given as:

| | |
|---|---|
| Actual labor costs (at actual activity) | $250,000 |
| Budgeted labor costs (at budgeted activity) | 300,000 |
| Favorable variance | $ 50,000 |

That $50,000 favorable variance may or may not be true. Suppose for example that March's actual activity was only 80,000 units. If we accept, for the moment, a labor cost per unit of $3, the true situation is as follows:

| | |
|---|---|
| Actual labor costs (at actual activity) | $250,000 |
| Budgeted labor costs (at actual activity) | 240,000 |
| Unfavorable variance | ($ 10,000) |

In actual practice, most companies with *fixed* budgets will not make this type of true variance calculation. In effect, they cannot, because the $3 labor cost per unit, or whatever, is a broad cost-accounting average, used only to develop the labor cost budget for the profit plan and recognized by management as not realistic enough for monthly application in variance analysis. In such situations, the only variance data provided by the budget is the $50,000 favorable variance, and no analysis of the figure is possible. And for those companies with fixed budgets, the problem exists for all the variable and mixed costs involved in the enterprise.

However, some companies with fixed budgets do use their cost-accounting averages to analyze budget variances. When they do, they should segregate both their volume variances and labor rate variances. In such instances, the question should be asked that if the costing rates per activity unit are good enough for just and usable variance analysis, why not employ them for flexible budgets?

When flexible budgets are being used, the work involved in the analysis of variances will depend on the characteristics of each particular cost. Some examples follow:

*Direct material cost variances.* Significant variances should be broken down into material usage variances and material price variances. Such variance analysis obviously demands standards for material usage, usually obtained from Engineering, and standards for material price, usually obtained from Purchasing.

*Direct labor costs.* Ideally, significant variances for direct labor should be broken down into labor efficiency or usage variances and wage rate variances. Usually, the most important portion, by far, is the labor efficiency segment. In fact, many companies with flexible budgets find it practical to consider the direct labor variances on their budget reports as solely efficiency or labor usage variances.

In many companies, labor standards by operation are not available, or the labor cost data is not collected in a way that allows this kind of analytical breakdown. As a result, they have to consider and treat the direct labor variances as all labor efficiency variances.

Probably the great majority of companies do not have the standards, the data, or the procedures installed to analyze, in the detail outlined above, their direct material and direct labor cost variances. As a result, operating management and the budgeting staff must work with "gross" variances. They try as best they can to break down judgmentally the total variances into more informatory segments. However, because of the sheer digging and work involved, they usually do it by special study and only in instances of extreme variances. As a result, you have to wonder in such cases, where the variance analysis is not done in a programmed and continuing manner, if many cost improvement opportunities are not remaining undetected because the variances are not considered "extreme" enough to warrant analytical work. Let me repeat: Big cost items such as direct material and direct labor, involving as they do so much money for most enterprises, deserve the investment and effort required to develop standards, which will make the data needed for variance analysis available on a continuing basis.

In the case of other operating costs, in all their variety, practical limitations of time and data availability usually force us to work with total or gross variances for each cost, i.e., the simple difference between budgeted and actual costs. Usually, in these cost areas, this situation presents us with no great problems. For example, faced with a large unfavorable variance, the department head should have a good idea of the reason, and what must be done to correct it. Or the budget person involved, with a little digging, can determine the cause. However, depending on the circumstances, it may pay to install a better cost record in some areas in order to allow more precise variance analysis. For example, in a multishift operation, if we have only total variance information on a given cost, we may be ignorant of the fact that a correctable large unfavorable variance is being developed by a given shift. Or for another example, in the face of sharply higher power costs, we might find it worthwhile to keep a special watch on the demand costs of the total power bill.

Notice also, that determining *who* does the variance analysis will depend on the specific cost involved. For the "simpler" costs, the department head is best able to explain the reasons for the significant variances. On other costs such as direct material or direct labor, the detailed data for variance breakdown must be provided and the initial analysis done for the operating manager by the budgeting function using accounting data.

## REPORTING ON VARIANCE ANALYSIS

In well-established and fully staffed budget installations, it is not uncommon to have written analyses and explanations of significant variances accompany the budget report to higher levels of management. This writing is most commonly done by the budgeting staff. Ideally, such prose explanations should be reviewed with the operating manager involved and affected before they are sent to the higher management levels. Sometimes, in practice, this review is not possible because of time pressures or the geographical distances involved. In any case, the department head should always be provided with a copy.

In large, complex, or geographically separated organizations, such interpretative expositions can be a real help to the higher operating managers. They do, however, impose an additional burden and responsibility on the budget function. The budget person doing the writing has to have a current knowledge of the operation in order to know the causes for variances commented upon. Any doubts should prompt the budget person to seek the help of the operating manager involved. The danger is in making a mistake on the facts involved, or misinterpreting the underlying causes. Another danger is the development of misunderstandings between the operating manager and the budget person. This last danger is particularly important. These written budget explanations are still another interface between the operating manager and the budget person. If their relations on other budget matters are good, however, such explanatory additions to the budget should present no problems.

## ACTING ON VARIANCE ANALYSIS FINDINGS

We come now to the management part of budget follow-up, i.e., the determination of what can be done about the findings of our variance analysis, so that corrective action can be developed and taken. In the example of an unfavorable variance in direct labor cost, our analysis may have broken the total variance into labor usage or efficiency variance and into wage rate variance. Now we must decide what can be done to reduce that variance or, better, change it in future months to a favorable variance.

In the ideal operating management world, once the operating manager has been given unfavorable cost variance data, he (or she) acts upon it. From his performance-to-budget report and any additional needed variance breakdown, he identifies what must be done to correct the variance and does it. Or if he does not do it on his own, his superior detects the need for action, instructs the department head on what to do, and follows up that it is actually done. But in practice, things do not always work this way. And the fact that they do not means that we must consider a further aspect of Budgeting's involvement in budget follow-up.

It should be noted that the above statements do not necessarily reflect adversely on the abilities, energy, or motivation of the operating manager. Sometimes, unfortunately, you do find inertia, stone-headedness, empire building, and all the other deficiencies to which we humans can be subject. But it is mostly a matter of time and pressure. Most operating managers have so much to do and so many concerns that it is unrealistic to expect that they can always detect and always correct operating problems that may be the underlying causes of unfavorable variances. Also, some of the unfavorable variances may be the result of the action of other department's or management functions, and the department head frequently is not in the hierarchical position to initiate the needed corrective action. For all these reasons both the operating manager and the budget person must recognize and accept the fact that part of the budget staff's function in its follow-up phase involves: (a) participation in detecting and correcting the basic causes of unfavorable variances, and (b) detecting areas where costs can be further improved and budget allowances reduced.

These can be most controversial points. Many budgeting people believe that such a concept results in the budgeting function exceeding its true charter. They see budgeting as responsible only for helping operating managers develop their budget allowances, seeing that budget reports are issued on time, and standing ready to answer any questions that may arise as to the report content. This understanding of the ongoing budget charter is particularly likely to be accepted by budget people with a very heavy accounting background and orientation. In parallel manner, many operating managers hold firmly to the conviction that corrective action on unfavorable variances and the development and introduction of cost improvement action are the tasks solely of operating management. They believe that the broader concept of the budgeting function usurps their own function and responsibilities.

All these responses are very limiting, and in practice they impose unnecessary strictures on the cost improvement performance of the enterprise. Budgeting is a management function, involved in both profit planning and cost control. In its cost control action, however, the budgeting function necessarily has to be involved in detecting areas of potential cost improvement and spurring corrective action on unfavorable budget variances. Certainly, if budget people are doing their job properly, they are getting around to all areas of the operation and are involved with all functions of management. They have, or should have, a good grasp of what can be done. When properly located in the management organization, they have the political position to help one area of operating management make progressive moves in the event the ideas are blocked by another area. For example, it is not uncommon to see the marketing function making costly demands on the production function. As a result, job changes are too numerous, machine utilization too low, and unfavorable labor variances too high. Budgeting support and action may help Production and Marketing achieve a better balance between manufacturing costs and customer delivery performance.

Operating managers at the higher levels can be most helpful if they encourage their department heads in their budget relationships—if they promote more frequent contact and show their people how they can use budget people to obtain more help. But the basic job of making it all work, in practice, lies with the budgeting people. They have to do this budget follow-up job without alienating the operating managers with whom they are working.

Some basic points concerning Budgeting's orientation toward helping managers in this area are worth repeating:

Budgeting is a staff function, with people working out in the operation to advise operating management. It can never direct operating management. It is first and foremost a *service* function. If Budgeting must persist in order to initiate corrective or improvement action, such persistence must be applied as diplomatically and with as much sensitivity to the personalities involved as is possible. Such sensitivity should not lead to inaction, but it must be there. Sometimes heads will have to be gone over, but only as a last resort after every argument has been heard, and all persuasion has failed.

As we have said, good budgeting is a *joint* effort. Department heads do not improve their image with constant accenting and harping on budget inequities and errors, real or imagined. In like manner, budgeting people should not believe that, necessarily, recognition of their work and their advancement will come from how often they expose operating management errors. Rather, their attitude must be that there is enough credit for everyone. And if budgets are effective, there always is.

Included in the sensitivity aspect is the budget person's continuing awareness of the operating manager's possible lack of knowledge and very human reluctance to admit it. The budget person can compound this problem by using technical jargon and worse, by hiding behind technical know-how in the finance and accounting areas. The proper attitude has to be that there are no mysteries in budgeting, that the department heads should know as much as the budget staff does about the budgets, and that a budgeting person will tell a manager as much as possible. In turn, the operating manager has the responsibility for becoming involved, by asking questions, advancing suggestions, and by not fearing, at all, that he or she may appear stupid by asking a lot of questions.

At the same time, the budget person has to keep current with the operation. Only by doing so will it be possible to understand the operating manager's problems. Keeping current means getting out in the operation, including field trips to branch plants or branch operations, and this will provide more opportunities for face-to-face meetings with the department heads with whom the budget person deals.

Implementing this budget follow-up concept where it does not already exist inevitably adds up to a "selling" job. Implementation should not be all one-sided, but very often it starts off pretty much that way. It is not easy to achieve, and it takes time and patience. However, when it is achieved, budget people are doing the whole job and are being of greater service to the enterprise and its operating managers.

## THE TOTAL FOLLOW-UP JOB

In working with operating managers down to the department head level, the budget person learns a lot about the operation. In handling many departments he or she comes to understand the overall process and operation, and the organization and the personalities making up that organization. Finally, the budget person knows how all the cost facts fit together with the sales forecast to develop the profit plan, and thus can perceive the enterprise's immediate future. With this kind of overall understanding, the budget person is well suited to implement the follow-up phase of operating budgeting.

This follow-up work best consists of three types of action:

*Providing data and impetus where needed.* The budgeting function provides operating management with variance breakdowns such as price, usage, and efficiency, as needed and as possible. Then the segmented variances, and all variances, must be studied to develop the necessary corrective action. If the need for action is indicated but is not being taken, it is part of the budgeting staff's function to advance constructive suggestions of what might be done to correct unfavorable variances. They may do this by showing what other departments, or even other companies, have done to improve costs in an account with an unfavorable variance. They may help initiate management action to correct an operating condition that causes the higher costs. They should consider it part of their budgeting responsibility to develop and propose corrective action, particularly if no one else is taking such action.

*Detecting areas of cost improvement.* Any budget staff worth their salt inevitably sees in the operation areas of potential cost improvement. In other words, if something were done better and more smartly, an existing cost and budget allowance could be reduced. This is also part of the budget follow-up phase: the detection, where possible, of a cost improvement opportunity and the development of a constructive improvement action. This last step is the important one. The detection alone is only criticism. The advancement of possible ways to improve a cost is constructive suggestion.

The cost areas and suggested action can be most diverse. For example:

Power can be saved by shutting down alternate lights or shutting down equipment when not needed.

Work sampling can be done in a possibly overstaffed indirect labor area.

A less expensive supply item can be substituted for one being bought.

A procedure, or the forms involved, can be streamlined.

All such cost improvement ideas should be advanced directly to the operating manager or department head responsible for the area affected, never directly to his or her superior. Any supplemental suggestions from the operating manager should be solicited, and very earnestly solicited. The wise budget person keeps an open pair of ears. After working with and getting to know the department heads, he or she often finds that they have excellent ideas they have never advanced. The budget person should encourage and help them to develop, advance, and install these ideas.

All management is the "art of the possible." Therefore, the budget person must choose carefully the areas and costs in which to work and take action. Theoretically, a budget person should spend the most time on the costs involving the most money. But at times, this can be a completely ineffective approach because the necessary action is not possible for many reasons. Higher levels of operating management may be completely obdurate to the change. To effect the change might require a program, the cost of which senior management may not want to incur at this time. Other management functions may be unyielding in their opposition, without necessarily any objective reasons. The possible problems are legion. The point is the budgeting people should not bloody their heads against stone walls that are not about to fall. If they do, both they and the enterprise suffer. Instead they should concentrate, for the time being, on the areas where they can accomplish corrective action. If their ideas in the more costly areas are good, they will gradually build up support, but in the meantime they will accomplish the things that can be done now.

Notice that all this parallels some of the functions of Industrial Engineering. An effective budget person will perform some I.E. functions. But this is not conflicting; it is supplementary. Many enterprises have no I.E. departments, and the budget function can be a good available source for improvement ideas. In many other enterprises, I.E. work is concentrated on major projects or specific work such as labor measurement, parts routing, special studies, etc. As a result, there are always many additional areas where the ideas of others, including the budgeting department, are needed.

Finally, and again, none of this usurps operating management's responsibilities or prerogatives. Very few operating managers have a sinecure. Usually, they are overloaded with work. They do not have the time to see and think of all the improvement opportunities that exist. They need all the service, help, and ideas they can get.

*Identifying need for more staff support.* Finally, budgeting in its follow-up phase has an involvement in the long-range workings and effect of the operating budget itself. This is a somewhat subtle point but it can be very important, with long-lived effects. To explain this, it is necessary to step back and consider what has happened in some budgeting installations.

Senior management, when authorizing funds for a new budget effort or the revitalization of weak budgets, must expect a return on the investment. Also with no budgets, or weak budgets, the profit planning, if it even exists, is probably poorly done, and cost control is ineffective or nonexistent in some areas. For all these reasons, operating budgets when first installed, or when revitalized, should return more than they cost to effect. They will, if properly done. And these operating and cost improvement benefits are produced by operating management, with the help of budget people and others, under the new budgets standards.

However, every effective management must strive for continuing improvement in sales income, cost efficiencies, profit, and return on investment. On the income side, management usually recognizes that to increase sales, certain things have to be changed. As a result, they improve the product line, invest in more advertising, beef up the sales force, start a sales incentive, or take any number of new and different actions.

On the cost side, however, some managements look too singly to the budget as the mechanism to achieve continuing cost improvements. After all, they reason, the budgets produced the needed results in the first years of their installation or revitalization. Why not continue these cost improvements by tightening up the budget allowances and looking to the various levels of operating management to meet the new and tighter cost standards? The difficulty (and danger) with this approach is that there is a practical limit to the improvement that operating management can produce on their own, without added supportive programs. If these programs are not provided, and if the attempt to achieve these tighter cost goals is made simply by tightening budget standards, the result is usually a seriously damaged budget. What happens is that the operating managers, particularly at the department head level, do not have the time or the training in the techniques that may be needed further to improve their costs. As a result, they cannot meet the tighter budget standards and thus, incur large red variances. Since management cannot fire everyone, the budgets simply become ignored. They end up in the bottom right-hand drawer.

This all may appear unrealistic, even simple minded, to you. Hopefully, you have never had the opportunity to observe the phenomenon. But when you examine some actual budget installations that were once quite effective but are now weak, it is not a rarity to find that one of the major causes of their decline was the fact that management used those budgets, unilaterally, as a cost reduction mechanism without providing the supportive programs needed to achieve the desired cost improvement.

The point is that on the cost side, you can expect good initial gains from a new or revitalized budget. However, as you work for continuing gains, you cannot expect them from the budgets alone, by simply reducing the budget allowances. If you do, you will only weaken your budgets.

To avoid this, senior management must authorize supportive cost improvement programs. They might be work measurement programs; better cost accounting systems; additional industrial engineering, methods, or manufacturing engineering support; better capital equipment; value analysis programs; or whatever is needed. And this is also where the budgeting function in its follow-up phase comes in. They should help identify these supportive needs and work with and assist operating management to obtain such support. In some cases, Budgeting will even have to initiate the idea. But this is real budget follow-up.

The last two budget follow-up actions proposed in this section admittedly involve an area of judgment. To some operating managers and budgeting people, this is all standard operating procedure. What else is new? However, to some budget practitioners and operating managers, such action exceeds the function of Budgeting, as they see that function. Or at least, such action is not taken by budgeting people out in the operation, nor would it be welcomed by the operating managers involved. It all comes down to what *you* would want if *you* owned the operation. Would you want your budget people to take such action? Would you want operating managers and budget people to perform budget follow-up and relate to one another in the manner I've described? If you do not, could you be sure that the desired cost improvement action possible in some areas would be taken, or even detected?

# MEASURING BUDGET RESULTS

Very few companies make a serious, ongoing effort to quantify the results of their budgeting effort. The reason for this is that results can be difficult, if not impossible, to measure. Budgets are just one of many things going on, and as a result, the changes and improvement due to the budgets alone frequently cannot be identified, much less measured. As a result, management often has to apply its "experienced judgment" and decide subjectively whether the budgeting function is paying its way. There is nothing necessarily wrong with this. Most senior managers know from experience over the years that without budgets, control over costs begins to weaken, and without profit planning, the overall performance is not as good. (If this were not true, budgets would not be as widely used as they are.)

However, this does not obviate the need to measure budget results where we can do so. Certainly, measurement can and should be done where budgets are either newly installed or revitalized. It is good management to seek the answers to such questions as:

> Have budgets resulted in reduced costs?
> Has the profit plan resulted in a higher profit?
> Is the budgeting effort returning more than it costs?

## A SIMPLE MEASURE FOR NEW OR REVITALIZED BUDGETS

The starting period of a budget program is probably the best time to measure budget results. When you undertake any new budget effort, it is a major project and quite possibly *the* major effort going on at the time. Thus, if any relevant changes occur, it is reasonable to assign them to the budget program.

The measurement is simple and rather easily done, and it should start before, or at least concurrently, with the development of the new budgets. It need not necessarily be all encompassing and include all the operating costs.

An experienced budget person who has learned and knows the operation can detect those cost areas where there is improvement potential, where lack of control or weak budgeting controls have resulted in higher-than-necessary operating costs. It is in these costs that budgets, if effective, should show the greatest improvement. Having picked these more conspicuous costs (usually among the larger dollar costs), the budget person must record at the start what they have been amounting to in the most recent three to six months. If the data is readily available, it is even better to include the entire last operating year. Sometimes this is not possible because record formats have been changed, or it is too difficult to go back a full year, particularly if the chart of accounts is being revised under the new budgeting program. In any case, you want at least a three-month "before" picture of these selected costs. Finally, if you are installing flexible budgets and if one or more of these selected costs are pure variable or mixed costs, as they usually are, record the activity data for the three or six months being used. Remember that it is usually wise to collect all this data at the start. If you wait until later, the task may be more laborious, or even impossible.

Once the new budgets have been in and are being followed-up for six or nine months, add up the dollars these same costs amount to for the *following* three months. If you have installed flexible budgets record the activity data for these same three months. This cost and activity data for the third or fourth quarter of the new budget's first year, you are treating as the "after" picture, i.e., after the new budgets have been in effect for six to nine months.

If flexible budgets have been installed, it is possible and necessary to equate the before and after actual variable and mixed cost data to the same operating activity level. The activity level chosen will be the level of the before period. Equate the actual variable and mixed costs in the after period to the activity level of the before period. Thus, based on the actual after performance, you are estimating what these costs would have actually been at the same activity level as the before period. None of this estimation is necessary if you are fortunate enough to have had the same, or very near the same, activity level in the before and after periods used.

Finally, calculate the difference between the total of the selected costs in the before period and the calculated total amount in the after period. Convert the difference to a yearly basis. If less money has been spent after the budgets were installed and in use for six to nine months, the savings may well and fairly be attributable to the budgets.

This measurement technique is crude in that not all the costs are included, but it has been used successfully to measure overall budget results. And it does have the advantage of simplicity in a difficult measurement area. Even with such an approach you have to be aware of the usual cautions. You have to know the operating conditions in the two periods being compared. For example, if additional mechanization was instituted after the before period and was in effect in the after period and labor costs have been reduced, you cannot assign the labor savings to the new budgets. Perhaps budgets can be credited with part of the cost gain, but who can say what part?

If fixed budgets have been installed, the measurement of budget results is more difficult or even impossible. The only comparison available is the amount spent for like time periods before and after budgets. Any saving may or may not be properly credited to the budgeting effort. For example, less money may have been spent after the budgets, but perhaps it was because the activity level was lower in the after period being used for comparison. Such "savings" cannot be justly assigned to the budgets. Or conversely, more money may have been spent after the budgets, but activity may be higher in the after period. In such a case, the savings, if any, assignable to the new budget cannot be segregated and measured.

## MEASURING CURRENT BUDGET/PROFIT PLAN RESULTS

In a very broad sense there is another measure of ongoing budget results if you consider the profit-planning objectives of the budget. After budgets are installed, or have been revitalized, you can compare profit results after budgets with profit results before budgets for the same month of the year and year-to-date. It is a very gross comparison, but it might enable you to conclude that the new budget and its profit plan helped toward a better operating performance overall. Likewise, in subsequent budget years the same comparison of results, this year versus last year, might indicate continuing budget/profit plan results.

But here again we have to be careful. This year's higher profit might be due to an usually good sales mix, higher-than-planned profit margins, or even a windfall profit margin on a few large orders. In these cases, it was not the budgeting/profit plan effort that really resulted in the higher profit. Conversely, a lower-than-planned profit, or a profit lower than last year's, might still have entailed a good result from your budget, because without the budget, the adverse things that actually occurred in that year might have reduced profit even more.

## BUDGET PROGRESS REPORTING

Perhaps the best and most practical single gauge of budget results available is a subjective one: periodic progress reporting by the budgeting function of the work completed and in progress. This progress reporting can take place, say, four times a year. If the enterprise has a full management-by-objectives program underway, such reporting is being done. But most companies are not applying such a formal approach, and thus few managements receive such reports. As a result, senior management has no method of making an ongoing review of the budgeting function.

There is an interesting parallel here to the industrial engineering and purchasing functions. Most well-run I.E. departments submit a monthly progress report. From polls taken at purchasing seminars, it becomes apparent that about one in four, or at most, one in three, purchasing departments submit monthly or quarterly progress reports. All that do so agree that it is an excellent way to keep management informed of the job they are doing. If such progress reporting is a good practice for these two functions, would it not be good for the budgeting function?

In such a periodic progress report, the budgeting staff would have the opportunity to report on such matters as:

1. The number and nature of any budget refinements accomplished

2. Any new steps completed toward better cost analysis

3. The number of departments, and branch operations visited

4. Accomplishments in working with department heads to effect cost reduction

5. Any supplementary cost information, newly furnished to department heads or higher levels of management

6. The number and nature of budget revisions made

The matters reported on will depend on the circumstances, but the objective is to keep senior management informed of the budget work accomplished and underway. Such a report can, and should be, terse, but informative. As such, it requires introspection and performance by the budgeting staff, and it offers senior management some picture of budget progress.

## THE BUDGET AUDIT

Because it is so difficult to measure ongoing budget results, there is a need for occasional independent evaluations of the budgeting effort and results in a given operation. Thus, someone outside the budget staff should periodically take a dispassionate, overall look at what is being done and the budgets as they are actually working.

Operating management and budget people, very humanly, develop a pattern of relationships and action that works reasonably well, but then tend to follow that pattern too rigorously. It might be too harsh to say that they "fall into a rut," but the human tendency is to avoid change. And effective budgeting is a dynamic effort. It should keep changing.

Also the budgeting staff frequently tends to be too small and, as a result, overloaded. Because of this, they have to take shortcuts and accept certain budget inadequacies out of practical necessity. These they may have evaluated as not critical, and they may have been correct in their evaluation, at the time. But conditions change and what may have been a noncritical deficiency may be approaching serious error. It can be most unfortunate and costly if the bad practice becomes serious before it is detected and corrected. Such detection is one of the objectives of a periodic budget audit.

For all these reasons, an audit of the operating budget should be made once every two or three years by a person, or persons, completely independent of the budget staff. Ideally, they should also be completely independent of the controller's staff if the budgeting function is under the controller. They should report to a (high) senior operating or financial manager. They need this independence to be free of any influence or pressures from either the budgeting or the operating area. Thus, it sometimes pays to use a consultant for such an audit, particularly if there is evidence that the existing budgets are less than well developed or less effective than they should be. Such an independent outsider can bring a breadth of experience that, possibly, is not available from within. A consultant can concentrate on the audit because that is the only task he or she will be assigned. And finally, because the consultant is an outsider paid a fee, his or her findings and recommendations are somewhat more likely to get management attention and action.

It is very important that the person or persons performing the audit be very knowledgeable in the realities of operating management. In fact, they should have a background and experience in *both* operations and accounting/budgeting because operating budgets deal with operating affairs as well as finance and accounting matters. Budgeting is as much a tool of operating management as a mechanism for financial planning. As a result, their audit must be made by people experienced in both areas.

What should be included in such a budget audit? This will depend on the circumstances, but the audit should certainly include:

1. A thorough examination of how correctly the budget allowances were determined to see:

   how thoroughly costs were analyzed, and how accurately they were identified, so that mixed costs were not applied as pure variables, or step costs applied as fixed

   the amount and source of judgmental inputs that were applied in place of past actual data, or as the result of organization and political pressures

   to what degree operating management, down to the department head level, were involved in the development of budget allowances

2. An intensive analysis of recent performance-to-budget reports:

   to identify cost trends

   to detect uncorrected bad allowances, i.e., too loose, or too tight

   to detect if budget maintenance is satisfactory in terms of budget revisions and extra-budgetary allowances

   to see how promptly they have been issued

3. A review of the budget administration, as reflected in:

   the form and completeness of the budget data sheets and budget data books

   the design and content of the performance-to-budget reports

the amount and quality of supportive cost data, if any, supplied to operating management

4. Interviews with a good sample of operating managers, particularly at the department head level, to evaluate:

   their feeling of participation in the development of their budgets

   their understanding of their budget data and budget reports

   their, and their superiors', use of the budget reports—do they try to beat their budgets?

   their belief in the budget's fairness

   their experience with the helpfulness and availability of the budget staff

5. Visits out in the operation with the budgeting staff to determine:

   how the budget staff works and interrelates with the operating managers

   how well they know the operation, and the realities of operating management

   their interest and ability in detecting areas of cost improvement

Thus, the budget audit is an in-depth study of techniques, procedures, human attitudes, and budget effectiveness. Many facets of the budget have to be examined, and this demands an audit plan and even check-off lists for certain aspects, designed especially for the operation being studied. An audit conducted in this way demands altruism on the part of both the budgeting staff and operating management, but they should welcome the audit. Both have a lot to gain. Their ongoing budget problems will be defined for senior management and as a result, they will have a better chance for help and corrective action. Only one good constructive idea that might not otherwise have been developed and used can pay for such a budget audit many times over.

## THE ATTITUDE SURVEY

The budgeting process is fraught with psychological hazards and problems for both the operating managers and the budgeting staff. In some companies, as stated earlier, the existing budget weaknesses stem from the emotional interfaces between operating managers and the budgeting staff. Where these psychological problems are serious enough and where the money involved is great enough, a step beyond the budget audit might be considered. That step is an attitude survey. Such a survey does not replace the budget audit. It is supplemental to the audit in that it goes deeper into the existing psychological effects of the budget.

An attitude survey in the budget area involves in-depth interviews with operating managers and the budgeting staff to evaluate how they perform their jobs, how they react to each other, what convictions they have developed about each other and about the budgets, and what actions they take to communicate or to hide their reactions to the budget and to each other. As such, it can identify deficiencies that might otherwise remain undefined. This, in turn, can indicate steps needed to correct these problems. Also, it can provide both operating managers and budget persons with more insight into their own personal reactions and actions.

An attitude survey is made by industrial psychologists. Many operating managers and budget people have a very jaundiced view of industrial psychology and of psychologists in general. Sometimes that view is justified. But most of us need more insight into how people interreact, and how to do a better job in our interpersonal contacts and relationships. The only way we are going to get this is to open our minds, try different approaches, and learn as best we can, from whom we can. We all like to think of ourselves as effective "practical psychologists." But all of us could do better in human relations, and a competent psychologist can help us learn how.

Such an attitude survey is not necessary or suitable for every operation. Only the company with serious, debilitating budget problems really needs it. At any rate, because of its cost, only the larger operations can afford it. But we learn more and more every year of the importance of human interrelationships on the economics of our operations. Our operating managers and budgeting staff are human beings. If they need help badly enough, it might pay to utilize outside psychological assistance.

# 15

# BUDGET GAMES
# MANAGEMENTS PLAY

The operating budget and the profit plan it develops have long-lived effects on the jobs and investment involved in the operation. If the plans and controls are well developed and effectively implemented, the chances for a more prosperous, even growing, enterprise are enhanced. Obviously, these are serious matters. They require deliberate, well-thought-out management action. They also require continuing management review of past budget decisions and actions to detect any needed corrective action.

Unfortunately, in too many cases management attitudes on the budget are careless and their decisions not well thought out. The result is an unrealistic view of the facts, a continued bland acceptance of obvious errors from lower levels of management, and arbitrary, even emotional, decisions. Too often, managements play what might be called "budget games." How prevalent these budget games are is revealed when you talk to enough operating managers and budget people. At seminar after seminar when the subject is discussed and the questions asked, you have the nods, the knowing smiles, and often the vivid anecdotes of how budget games are played in their companies.

This subject is not discussed simply to be negative and critical. Budgets are too important and expensive, and too valuable in the benefits they can yield, for us not to recognize and define all too common mistakes. Only by doing so, can we begin to consider better, more effective approaches.

## "CUT EVERYTHING 10 PERCENT"

This is a game played by senior management. It normally is initiated after the operating budget has been developed and blended with the sales forecast, and the first draft of the profit plan has been developed. At that point the projected profit may be evaluated as unsatisfactory or not producing enough return on investment. To correct this, the order is issued to "cut everything 10 percent," or 5 percent, or whatever.

The objective of such an order is splendid, but the results can be devastating. The operating budget, as developed, represents the cost allowances needed to produce the products or services at the forecast activity level. If these allowances were developed properly, they are realistic figures. If you arbitrarily reduce the budget allowance 10 percent, either you will not be able to operate at the projected activity or you will not be able to live within the budget. Thus, you will develop unfavorable variances, either in costs or activity. (Such budget cuts can be handled only in a certain few areas. For example, in engineering, it may be possible to reduce costs 10 percent by stopping certain programs, at least for the time being. In such areas with discrete programs, the overall costs can be reduced the required amount by stopping certain efforts, but not others deemed more essential.)

If the operating budget was poorly developed or if "fat" was deliberately built into the budget as first developed and presented, senior management has a new set of problems. Its order to "cut everything 10 percent" will be obeyed and the activity will be handled. However, this leaves senior management with the continuing doubt as to the real worth of the budget allowances even after the 10 percent cut. If operating management were able to reduce their budget allowances 10 percent and still meet the activity as projected, might an even further reduction have been possible? You never know with such proven sloppy budgeting. Any senior management that plays this budget game each year and still has their projected activity actually handled, and the budgets met, should seriously examine their budget program and the job the budget staff is doing (or being allowed to do).

In many cases what happens is that the budgets have been reasonably well established, but when the order to "cut everything 10 percent" is received, it has to be carried out. Then increasing unfavorable variances begin to show up, for which no effective correction action is practical or taken. The result is disregarded, ineffective budgets that end up in the lower right-hand drawer.

Another very important effect of this game is that it initiates defensive action by lower management levels that also makes the budgets less effective, and worse, can even increase the costs of operation. This is discussed in the next section.

One of the mental justifications for this game is the reasoning that if you ask for more, you may not get it all, but you will get more than if you did not ask at all. This is a very enticing argument. It has a natural human appeal. It even works in some business and human affairs. However, in the budget area it causes too many and too strong reactions that in turn, often have serious, long-lived, bad effects upon the budget. There are too many unfortunate experiences, and too many ineffective budgeting situations extant today, because of this game, to support this defense.

As said earlier, the objective of senior management is splendid. Any operation can be improved. For example, there are always unexploited ways to reduce costs or improve volume and increase profit. If the operation's profit objectives are not satisfactory, these ways have to be determined and taken. Often these involve longer-term programs, such as a product redesign, further market development, or a labor measurement program. Operating management, the budgeting function, and other staff functions should identify these needed action areas for senior management so that work can be started. But to try to reduce costs and increase profit by simply and arbitrarily reducing budget allowances that were properly developed does nothing but harm the budgets themselves, and thus undermines any profit or cost control measures the budgets themselves may have achieved.

## JACK UP THE BUDGET REQUEST

This game is played at the middle and department head levels of management. It is the inevitable and natural ploy to the first game, particularly if that game is exercised in successive budget years. Lower levels of management soon learn that they will be expected to reduce their budget allowances as they were initially determined. Therefore they very assiduously build in extra costs, whenever they can, so that they have these available to take out when the order comes to "cut everything 10 percent." Innocent managers who fail to do this may suffer for their sincerity and conscientiousness, because when they obey the order, as they must, their operation suffers or their budget performance looks very bad. Such innocence rarely lasts. They soon learn.

The pity of all this is the amount of time good people have to spend to play the game. It takes time for operating managers to study and determine where to hide extra costs that can be defended to the reviewing or participative budgeting staff. If the game is long-lived, however, they usually do not have to defend the extra costs to their superiors, who are playing a similar game at their own level. In fact, managers at the lower levels may be encouraged and coached on what to do to be prepared for the anticipated cut. In addition, it takes time away from the budgeting staff as they attempt to search out the grosser instances of budget padding.

One seminar attendee told us all about it very vividly. He explained how in managing the multimillion dollar maintenance effort for a large, well-known corporation, he spends an ungodly amount of time planning where he can hide sufficient unneeded budget allowances. Then when the order to cut comes, he has the money to take out of his budget without crippling his maintenance effort. He went on to observe how he wished he could use that time, and how much he needed it, for his basic work of managing maintenance.

Another regrettable result of this game is the higher costs that may be budgeted because of it. The natural tendency of the operating manager is to take all the insurance possible against the anticipated order to cut the budget allowance. The more aggressive and sharper managers may achieve a "padding" in excess of the budget cut as it actually is ordered. The result is a higher-than-needed budget allowance and perhaps an unearned favorable variance. But worse, if the *end-of-the-budget-year* syndrome is in effect (see below), it can mean higher-than-necessary costs for the operation, and lower-than-possible profits.

This game can be most difficult to stop. It develops into an erroneous budget orientation that can be corrected only after senior management demonstrates by their own orders and follow-up actions that they want good, realistic budgets developed and presented at the start of each budget year. They have to convince their lower levels of management that when such budgets are developed, there will not be arbitrary, across-the-board budget cuts if the profit goals are not satisfactory. Instead, all management levels will be engaged in an intense and serious effort to determine and take more appropriate action to improve the profit goals.

## END-OF-THE-BUDGET-YEAR SYNDROME

In this budget game, as the manager of a department (or line or staff function) approaches the end of the budget year, he or she quickly uses or commits any unexpended budget allowances. It is a law of management life in federal, state, and municipal government, and in most nonprofit operations such as universities, hospitals, museums, and associations. In fact the smarter operators start this long before the end of the year, i.e., five or six months ahead, so that it is not too obvious. The reason, of course, for playing this game is the experiences these managers have had in past years in their operation. If they do not spend, or at least commit, the money, the next year's budget allowance will be reduced.

This stratagem is not confined to government and nonprofit enterprises. It can be encountered in profit-making operations, particularly in the larger companies. For example, this observer has seen a $50,000 consulting assignment in marketing for a large chemical company paid for *ahead of* the start of the assignment, so that the funds could be expended before the end of the budget year.

Such action, of course, is the exact opposite of the proper "beat the budget" approach that should be taken by any manager. Certainly, it opposes the attitude a manager would take if he or she owned the operation. In a profit-making enterprise it reflects senior management's continuing acceptance of a budget break-even performance and their failure to recognize and encourage their managers to improve their performance and spend less than the budget allows. In government management, it reflects the operational tone that exists, much of which actively encourages the game. For example, the greater the number of people managed, the higher may be the manager's position and grade.

Management in larger enterprises particularly must guard against the start-up of this game. The larger the organization, the more monolithic the structure and the budget procedures tend to be. It can take a lot of persuasion, demonstration, special awards, and publicity to have the word filter through the organization that a better-than-budget performance will be recognized—that it is one of the bases upon which managers will be evaluated and advanced.

## "DON'T ROCK THE BOAT"

This game is similar to the previous one and is initiated during the course of the budget year. Although the individual department heads usually play it, they sometimes are encouraged by their immediate superiors.

The department head has reasonable allowances and can operate comfortably within the budget. Then he or she has an ingenious idea, but is afraid to act on it and save money, because the budget allowances will just be cut. So why rock the boat?

This inertness usually occurs where there is too little senior management support of the budget program and thus little encouragement or incentive to beat the budget. The likelihood of finding it is increased when, with that lack of support, there exists the situation of overloaded, harassed department heads who earn less than some of the people under them.

This game can be stopped with greater management support of the budgets, particularly from the senior levels, and by recognition of progressive action. Some key-man bonus installations based, in part, on performance to budget have had this very good effect.

## "CORPORATE WANTS IT"

This game can be observed in the division/corporate type of organization and is played by the managements of both Marketing and Production at the divisional level.

For example, divisional management in the marketing area develops an unrealistically high forecast of sales income and thus production activity. When questioned by their fellow managers in the production and the budgeting area, they defend their obvious overoptimism and insist on using their prediction because "corporate wants it."

Or operating management in the production area establishes unrealistically optimistic production or cost goals, and thus an exaggerated profit plan, because they know "corporate wants it."

The amazing aspect of this game is that it is played again in succeeding years. The solution clearly lies with corporate management themselves. They have the responsibility and authority to require realistic projections from divisional management. They may not expect absolute precision in such projections, but they must demand goals that are reasonably approached in the subsequent budget year. And every succeeding year they should expect increasingly closer projections.

## "DO WHAT YOU WANT"

This is an attitude rather than a game. It represents the depths of apathy, in which the department head takes any budget allowance he or she is given, without participative discussion, much less argument, does not pay any heed to the budget, and allows whatever variances to fall where they may.

When you see this situation (and believe me there are cases), you have to wonder why management is spending any money at all on budgets.

The attitude can be encountered in those situations where:

Budgets are imposed by fiat by the financial/accounting function.

There is little or no management follow-up on the budgets.

There is infrequent contact between operating managers and the budget staff.

The manager is past the point of caring, after having suffered too long and too hard from the budgets being used as a pressure device.

The manager has been promoted past his or her level of capability.

The last situation does not reflect on the quality of the budgets and the budgeting effort. The others do. The solutions to apathy lie in all the principles of good budgeting and follow-up.

## "IT'S NOT IN THE BUDGET"

This, too, is a management attitude rather than a game. It is reflected by the department head who does not advance a good idea because it will require some money to be put into effect and cause the manager to exceed his or her budget allowance. The idea is not advanced, therefore, because "it's not in the budget."

This is an innocent error on the manager's part, but it reflects poor instruction in how a budget should work. Budgets cannot run the operation. Managers do that. A budget is not a rigid way of life that can never be changed. It is a mutable planning and control tool used in a changing operation. It is up to the higher levels of management and the budget staff to convince all the department heads that any constructive idea should be advanced. If approved, the money needed can readily be added to the budget allowance.

Ideally, none of these games are played, nor do these attitudes exist in your operation. The odds are reasonable, however, that one or more does occur. Hopefully, they exist only to a degree that does not seriously reduce the effectiveness of your budget effort.

This chapter and these matters do not conclude this book in order to be flippant, negative, or critical. The first step to the solution of any problem is recognition. If you recognize some parallels here to your operation and to your practice of management in the area of budgeting, you may be encouraged to find approaches to change and solutions.

We will never reach budgeting perfection, but at the end of every year, we should be able to say, "Well, we may not be doing the perfect budget job, but we are doing better than we did last year."

# INDEX